Drawing the Line

DRAWING THE LINE

The Father Reimagined in Faulkner, Wright, O'Connor, and Morrison

Doreen Fowler

University of Virginia Press *Charlottesville and London*

University of Virginia Press
© 2013 by the Rector and Visitors of the University of Virginia
All rights reserved
Printed in the United States of America on acid-free paper

First published 2013

9 8 7 6 5 4 3 2 1

Library of Congress Cataloging-in-Publication Data
Fowler, Doreen.
    Drawing the line : The father reimagined in Faulkner, Wright, O'Connor, and
Morrison / Doreen Fowler.
        pages   cm
    Includes bibliographical references and index.
    ISBN 978-0-8139-3399-3 (cloth : acid-free paper) — ISBN 978-0-8139-3400-6
(e-book)
    1. American literature—20th century—History and criticism. 2. Fatherhood
in literature. 3. American literature—Southern States—History and
criticism. 4. Identity (Philosophical concept) in literature. 5. Patriarchy in
literature. I. Title.
    PS228.F38F69 2013
    813'.50935251—dc23
                                                                    2012040070

For Steve and Carina

Contents

Acknowledgments

All books are in some sense collaborative, and, in ways large and small, I owe a debt to more people than I am able to acknowledge here. To begin with, my book builds on the work of previous scholars of race, gender, and community, and my citations document this large scholarly indebtedness. Of the many colleagues who supported the writing of this book, I want to single out for special recognition three extraordinarily generous colleagues, Marta Caminero-Santangelo, Deborah Clarke, and Jean Wyatt, who read early drafts of several sections of the manuscript and offered incisive critical readings that helped me to define my project. Their contributions made this a better book. Other colleagues offered encouragement, helpful suggestions, and stimulating dialogue about the book. These include John Duvall, Richard Moreland, Bob Donahoo, Joseph Urgo, Giselle Anatol, Maryemma Graham, Susan K. Harris, Janet Sharistanian, Charmaine Eddy, Philip Weinstein, Martin Kreiswirth, Don Kartiganer, Jay Watson, Noel Polk, Jean Cash, and Bruce Gentry. I also gratefully acknowledge the College of Liberal Arts and Sciences at the University of Kansas, which funded this project through two sabbaticals. And special thanks go to the University of Kansas's Hall Center for the Humanities. A Hall Center–sponsored Grant Writing Workshop helped me to formulate my early ideas for this book; a Hall Center Research Fellowship supported the writing of the book; and the Friends of the Hall Center helped to fund the publication of this book with a Book Publication Award.

Parts of this book have been previously published. An early draft of chapter 1 on Faulkner's *Intruder in the Dust* appeared in *Modern Fiction Studies* 53.4 (Winter 2007): 788–820. An early version of my chapter on Flannery O'Connor's fiction was published in the *Arizona Quarterly* 67.2 (Summer 2011): 127–54. And a version of my chapter on Morrison's

Beloved appeared in *MELUS* 36.2 (Summer 2011): 13–34. I thank all the editors for their permission to include this material here.

As my dedication suggests, my largest debt is to my husband, Steve, and my daughter, Carina, whose love and support through the years have been unbounded.

Introduction

Uncanny Boundaries

The question I think one ought to ask . . . is: what is to be done
in order that children have a development . . . which permits
them to accede to the various elements of human culture? And
I think that what interferes with that access is the underestimation of the paternal function.

JULIA KRISTEVA, interview

The images of separation and desire are thus joined in the
father, or more accurately, in his ideal.

JESSICA BENJAMIN, *The Bonds of Love*

This book begins with a seemingly simple, but endlessly complex, question: How and when is it permissible for one to say "we" so as to
express solidarity with those of different ethnic, gender, and sexual con-
figurations? As Barbara Christian rightly reminds me, when I say "we," I
pose the threat of speaking for others and co-opting their story ("Race for
Theory" 11–23). The problem of a common subject position is the dilemma
that interpreters of literature face as they explore literature of cultures
not their own. To deal with the problem, it has become standard practice
for scholars to begin by acknowledging that a particular subject position
influences the gendered/racial/sexual politics of their critical intervention. This practice serves the purpose of publicly doing away with the
fiction of objectivity. However, despite this public declaration, the critic
always is aware that her critical practice is boundary transgression—that
is, a crossing of culturally and historically drawn racial, ethnic, gendered,
or other borders—that seems to be transformative. When I read the text
of an African American, a Latina, or an Asian, by a process of transference, I seem to be transformed by it as I identify with a story that is like

my own but also different from it; and when I interpret these cultural texts, I bring to them my cultural experience and thus my intervention becomes something hybrid, a combination of the text and me. Reading across cultural lines is an experience at the boundary, and, by definition, a boundary is a mysterious, dangerous site of transformation, the place where one thing becomes another, where polar oppositions, like high and low, for example, converge and are, paradoxically, distinguished in the site of convergence. It is the project of this book to explore boundary negotiations. And, in taking up this task, I am ever mindful of Michael Awkward's warning: "Boundary transgression—interpretive movements across putatively fixed, biological, cultural, or ideological lines in order to explore, in a word, difference—has come to require extreme theoretical naiveté or unprecedented daring" (4).

My question—what happens when I position myself at the boundary between me and not-me—opens onto the central dilemma of contemporary gender and race politics, the problem of two seemingly mutually exclusive demands: the need to preserve culturally defined differences and the need to overcome polarization. On the one hand, if the critic stays only within the bounds of her own cultural experience, her side of the boundary, she faces the problem of exclusivity. On the other, if she crosses the border, she poses the threat of appropriation. How do we reconcile competing needs for community with people from diverse cultural backgrounds and an opposite need to respect one another's culturally and historically derived differences? For example, feminists call on men to get in touch with the feminine within and encourage women to break out of female gender stereotypes. Does such engagement with the other threaten to efface male and female difference? Does a summons to unity among white and black feminists obscure their racial differences, as Diana Fuss and Elizabeth Abel recently have warned?[1] While theorists of race and gender have sought to undo marginalizing oppositions, they have been stymied because engagement with the other always poses the threat of the culturally dominant subject position appropriating the other.

From the beginning, the feminist project has faced this double bind. For example, Toril Moi describes Hélène Cixous's whole theoretical project as an attempt to "undo . . . patriarchal binary schemes where logocentrism colludes with phallocentrism in an effort to oppress and silence women" (*Sexual/Textual Politics* 105). But at the same time as feminists have repudiated a patriarchal culture's dialectics of domination, they too have been, for the most part, trapped in binaries even as they attempt to deconstruct them. Because the feminist project has been to distinguish a woman's defining difference from a man, feminists have focused on women and excluded men and thus seemed to perpetuate a male female dichotomy. Moi sums up clearly the nature of this feminist dilemma. She argues that while "it still remains *politically* essential for feminists to defend women as women in order to counteract the patriarchal oppression that precisely despises women *as* women," by doing so, feminists "run the risk of . . . taking over the very metaphysical categories set up by patriarchy in order to keep women in their places" (13). It is a measure of the difficulty of the feminist conundrum that the contemporary feminist Julia Kristeva, who has sought to avoid Western culture's exclusionary practice and has creatively explored male-female interrelatedness, has been rejected by some feminists and accused of surrendering the notion of feminine difference.

This same dilemma has been the subject of much debate among theorists of race. From its inception, the project of African American literary critics and theorists has been to seek racial equality by exposing and critiquing the marginalization and oppression of people of color. In pursuing this goal, they have turned to poststructuralist theory to show that racial categories are not biological; rather, they are largely constructed in language. But, while insisting on the artificiality of racial categories, these thinkers also resist the notion of doing away with race difference. Anthony Appiah insists that race difference does exist as a "sociohistorical" construct, and rejects attempts to "minimize race distinctions" as a "denial of difference" (25). Thus, like feminist theory, critical race theory is riddled by a tension between two seemingly mutually exclusive goals, in this case, a desire for racial specificity and a desire for black-white equality. Appiah lays out the terms of this tension and compares it to the feminist dilemma: "We find [this dialectic] in feminism also—on the one hand, a simple claim to equality, a denial of substantial difference; on the other, a claim to a special message, revaluing the feminine Other" (25). Today, the dialogue about race identity politics still seems to center on this conflict. For example, in a recent essay, African American feminist Ann duCille points out that the alternative to a "proprietary relationship to the field" (34) of African American literature seems to be only a takeover by the dominant culture: "To claim privileged access to the lives and literature of African American women through what we hold to be the shared experiences of our black female bodies is to cooperate with . . . the dominant culture's . . . constitution of our always already essentialized identity. Yet to relinquish claim to our experiences of the black body and to . . . affirm its study . . . as a field of inquiry equally open to all, is to collaborate with our objectification. . . . We can be, but someone else gets to tell us what we mean" (25).

Seeking to resolve this double bind, a number of theorists of race and gender have tried to find a way to form heterogeneous communities and to respect one another's culturally defined differences. For example, in a book about coalition building, Magali Michael argues that the "notion of constructing a 'we' does not negate the individual subject; however, it depends on a conception of the subject as involving a continuous interchange and interdependencies between the individual and various communities" (12). Jean Wyatt holds out the hope of a "feminist multicultural community" through "a partial identification with the cultural other that would enable one to perceive things from her point of view while continuing to respect her differences" (*Risking Difference* 9). Abdul JanMohamed articulates a similarly nuanced identification that could enable "openness to the Other" while maintaining "a heightened sense of the concrete sociopolitical-cultural differences between self and other" ("Economy" 93). In essays that largely warn against the dangers of white feminist appropriation of black women's discourse, duCille and Abel both ultimately posit a hope for middle ground. DuCille speaks of her hope for a "complementary theorizing" involving collaboration of white and black interpreters. Similarly, Abel offers guidelines for white feminist critics who undertake critical interventions in black fiction. She urges white women readers to take a "self-conscious and self-critical relation to black feminist criticism" and engage in a dialogue with black scholars (843). Ultimately, Abel holds out the intriguing possibility that white intervention in black women's texts can "deepen our recognition of our racial selves and the 'others' we fantasmatically construct" (120).

Abel's notion that engaging in a multicultural community influences the white reader has also been suggested by other critics. In *Learning from Difference*, Richard Moreland proposes that reading across racial lines is an "interactive relationship" (7) with the potential to "remake the reader" (5). Turning to no less an authority than Toni Morrison to support this contention, he cites the scene in *Jazz* when the narrative voice—seemingly the book itself—addresses the reader as a lover with whom the book has engaged in a reciprocally transformative relationship: "I love . . . how close you let me be to you," the book says to the reader (229). Moreland goes on to argue that the writings of Henry Louis Gates Jr.,

Houston Baker, and Ralph Ellison all attest to the ways different historical and cultural traditions have influenced African American literature, even as an "Africanist presence" has shaped and remade American culture in countless ways. Ultimately, Moreland's argument that cross-racial relationships can be transforming and enabling is compelling, but still the question lingers: in this mutually transformative relationship, isn't one cultural body likely to dominate the other? How do we deal with the problem of domination?

The problem of domination within a relationship is a subject of debate among theorists of identification. The fundamental premise of identification theory today is that bonding with others is both constitutive of a self and dangerous to the self. On the one hand, theorists of identity development insist that raced, gendered, ethnic, national, and other identities arise out of identifications with a group. Diana Fuss maintains that identification "instantiates identity" (2) in that all the historical and cultural experiences we have with others shape our identities. In the words of Teresa de Lauretis, we become interpellated into a social identity through a "process whereby a social representation is accepted and absorbed by an individual as her (or his) own representation" (12). At the same time, identification theorists posit that joining with others is also fraught with peril to the self. In fact, Fuss goes so far as to write that "to be open to an identification is to be open to a death encounter" (1). At one level, she means that the self dies in the sense that the self is transformed and reformulated. At another level, bonding with others also poses the risk of being appropriated by another. Given these dangers, how does one maintain socially and historically formed differences while still engaging with others? Who or what enables one to make a dangerous crossing over without dominating another or being dominated by another?

To answer this question, I have turned to the work of four major fiction writers, William Faulkner, Richard Wright, Flannery O'Connor, and Toni Morrison, all of whom write across racial and gender boundaries, and the answer I have found in the texts of these white and black, male and female writers largely overlaps: father figures introduce new subjects to boundaries that both divide and attach, and these porous boundaries enable an individual to have commerce with others while still maintaining a different ethnic, raced, and gendered identity. In what follows, I briefly outline the view of the father figure's boundary-making function as it is variously developed in the texts of Faulkner, Wright, O'Connor, and Morrison.

Boundaries are commonly thought of as the site where different identities are supported by exclusion; that is, boundaries are the place where a subject or a group subject shuts out another or others. But boundaries do not solely exclude; rather, boundaries both divide *and* connect. A boundary is the site where difference is marked, but it is also the place where oppositions come together, where, for example, inside meets outside; and this definition highlights that different ethnic, raced, or gendered identities arise not by exclusion alone, but by a tension between an alliance and a pushing back against this alliance. As Bakhtin points out in "Discourse in the Novel," all dialectical meanings are based in a tension between related terms, and this relationship, together with a resistance to it, works to distinguish different identities. Take the binary opposition high and low. High is the opposite of low, but high is high only in relation to low. Without a low there is no high. High and low are different, but high and low also share a commonality: both are markers of elevation. Similarly, raced, gendered, and other identities are defined by their difference within a relationship. Male and female share an identity: they are both gender identities, but they are differently configured gender identities. Likewise, white and black racial identities are both socially constructed racial identifications, which have been socially and historically distinguished differentially in relation to one another.

The authors I examine continually drive home that boundaries are a point of both contact and division. Boundaries achieve this seeming contradiction by being not one thing or the other but a composite of both. The boundary between North and South, for example, is a place that is both North and South, and, because it is both, it is identical with neither. By being composite, the boundary enables both contact and division. In the fiction I look at, father figures enable a new subject to bond with others and still retain a culturally specific identity by acting like a boundary. Like a boundary, the father figure shares a relation with both the one and the other, but is identical with neither; and, by positioning her/himself between the one and the other, he/she sets a boundary that allows for both cultural exchange and cultural specificity. In other words, the father figure's presence marks a difference so as to prevent total assimilation of the one by the other, but the father figure also links the one with the other to enable socialization. A scene in Toni Morrison's *Beloved* images this paternal boundary-making function. When Paul D arrives at 124, he takes Denver and Sethe to a carnival, and as they walk there, their shadows appear to be holding hands, with Paul D positioned between Sethe and Denver. This positioning illustrates the father's boundary-marking role. Because Paul D's shadow intervenes between Sethe and Denver, they are separated by him; but, because the shadow holds each of their hands, they are still linked, but now this intervening presence marks a difference in their relationship. In other words, the father's presence introduced a connecting-dividing boundary between the one and the other.

In the preceding paragraph, I refer to the father figure as she or he because in the fiction of all four writers the father's boundary-setting role is ongoing work in culture that is taken up by others beside the biological father, and, in the works of O'Connor and Morrison, this function is performed by females as well as males. The use of the term "father" for this figure is admittedly confusing, then, because the appellation "father" suggests that, like the biological father who must be male, this intervening father figure must likewise always be gendered male. This point is well taken, and for this reason Julia Kristeva refers to this mediating figure as the "third party." At the same time, however, there is cause to refer to this boundary-forming figure as the father, because the role seems to originate with the father, who is usually the first to intervene in the undifferentiated mother-child attachment.

As Jessica Benjamin observes, whatever theory of identity development you turn to, in the beginning, the "father" is the way into the world of cultural differences (103–5). In the beginning, the infant perceives no difference—no gender difference, no ethnic or racial difference, and no difference from the mother's body—and the father introduces a world outside the mother-child relation because he is usually the first outsider the child recognizes and because he is different from the mother. But while the biological father *is* different from the mother and child, he is *also* related to them: indeed, by definition, a father is father by virtue of a relationship with the mother and child. Calling this boundary-setting figure the father, then, seems appropriate because the biological father— or, in his absence, whoever takes his place—models the combination of relatedness and difference that distinguishes a boundary.

There is yet another reason for a traditional association of the father figure with boundary introduction: the cultural father's socializing role seems to be modeled after the biological father's act of insemination. If you think about it, in the act of conception, the biological father intervenes in a same-same relationship, and his intervention introduces a difference, but his intervention also connects him to the mother and child. To be more specific, in the beginning, the genetic code of the mother's ovum is identical with the mother's. There is no difference between mother and ovum, and there is no child. A new and different life form arises when a male weds his genetic material to the genetic code of the ovum, and this merging transforms it, making it now different from both the mother and the father even as it shares relationships with both. The father's act of insemination is the original differentiating act, and it distinguishes by a blurring of different identities—by combining his DNA with the DNA of the mother. This biological model of fatherhood maps onto the cultural role I find outlined in the texts of the four authors. In the fiction, a similar process is ongoing in culture, as the child is introduced into different ethnic, race, gender, and other group identities by someone whose presence, like the original biological father, intervenes in a way that allows for both connection and individuation.

The conception of the father's socializing role that I find in the texts of Faulkner, Wright, O'Connor, and Morrison revises a traditional psychoanalytic narrative of individuation in ways that roughly align not only with one another but also with models proposed by some recent feminist and postcolonial theorists. For example, postcolonialist Homi Bhabha insists that boundaries are instrumental in the construction of social identities by being sites of hybridity. According to Bhabha, cultural identities are defined differentially, not by essences or centers but by various and dynamic boundaries or interactions with other identities (1–18). Bhabha's description of identity formation as dependent on liminal boundary spaces corresponds to the fictional representations of these complex dynamics, but Bhabha stops short of answering the question, who or what keeps these changing, differentially related boundaries in check? Likewise, most feminist theorists also have not addressed this question. While feminist thinkers have a long history of critiquing and correcting a male-centered Freudian/Lacanian model of identity, because feminists have been intent on redressing a male bias in this theory, they have tended to focus intensively on the mother's role in forming different subject positions, and, for the most part, they have not revised a traditional Freudian/Lacanian view of the father.[2] In this standard interpretation, which continues to influence even many of the French feminists, the mother and the father are polarized figures. The mother offers the child closeness and intimacy, but this maternal attachment threatens the child's individuation. The father introduces independence and separation, but this individuation is achieved by excluding others, beginning with the mother. Two feminists who, to some extent, have addressed the double bind produced by defining the mother and father oppositionally are Jessica Benjamin and Julia Kristeva, and their theories have helped me to interpret the paternal boundary-making role in the fiction of Faulkner, Wright, O'Connor, and Morrison.

Benjamin's project is to find an answer to the problem of domination, which she argues compellingly derives from oppositional thinking, in which, "one is always up and the other down, one is doer and the other done-to" (220). For example, an exclusionary, either-or model of identity holds that, because male is defined as the opposite of female, for the male to be powerful, the female has to be powerless. According to Benjamin, this oppositional thinking "is the basic pattern of domination"; it "thoroughly permeates our social relations, our ways of knowing, our efforts to transform and control the world"; and "it is set in motion by the denial of recognition to the original other, the mother who is reduced to object" (220). She argues for "a new logic—the logic of paradox, of sustaining the tension between contradictory forces" (221). According to the "logic of paradox," a difference between self and other is constituted not by exclusion alone, but by an "alternation between the oneness of harmonious attunement and the two-ness of disengagement" (50). In this theory, raced and gendered identities are grounded in a tension or balance between attachment and a resistance to attachment. Benjamin does not specifically address boundary formation, but such a tension or balance is the defining characteristic of a boundary, which anchors different identities in one another. As for the role of the father in socialization, Benjamin adamantly rejects a mother-father dichotomy, along with other dichotomizations. For Benjamin, the father represents "otherness," "a striving . . . for autonomy, but this striving is realized in the context of a powerful connection" (105–6), and this combination introduces the child to socialization as a "simultaneous process of transforming and being transformed by the other," "a tension between sameness and difference, . . . a continual exchange of influence" (49).

In a number of ways, the theory advanced by Julia Kristeva overlaps with Benjamin's. Like Benjamin, Kristeva issues a challenge to either-or, dichotomous distinctions and maintains that sexual, ethnic, racial, and other differences are not "founded only on difference, [they are] also founded on sameness" (Interview, *Women Analyze Women* 142). Kristeva's theory stresses that the borders between mother and father, self and other, the cultural and the precultural are always fluid, porous, and precarious, but Kristeva's theory moves beyond Benjamin and other theorists both because she analyzes the in-between, the site of a border, and because her central theoretical project is to investigate the process by which a child can balance a specific culturally formed identity even as the child engages with communities of others. The words of Kristeva quoted in my epigraph set out her principal objective and challenge other feminists to join her in this project. She insists that feminists are asking the wrong question: "The question . . . is not . . . what must be done in order that women be happy"; rather, the question to be asked is, "what is to be done in order that children have a development . . . which permits them to accede to the various elements of human culture?" (*Women Analyze Women* 139). And, in considering this question, Kristeva points out that a critical player in the child's accession to individuation within a multicultural community is the father, whose role has been widely culturally misrepresented: "And I think what interferes with that access is the underestimation of the paternal function" (139).

Kristeva's theory examines the dangers and possibilities of border spaces. She holds that, to constitute a social identity, a child must negotiate a threatening, paradoxical border space that stabilizes always unstable dualities in a fluid zone of inmixing. Kristeva names this in-between site the abject. The abject, she writes, is "the in-between, the ambiguous, the composite"; "it is something rejected from which one does not part"; it is "the impossible within [that] constitutes [one's] very being" (*Powers* 4, 5). Kristeva seems to allude here to the traditional exclusionary identity-narrative, which holds that exclusion constitutes a separate self, starting with severing the mother-child attachment. But Kristeva argues that exclusion fails to fully exclude and the abject is the slippage that threatens to "disturb identity, system, order" (*Powers* 4), even as these cultural identities owe their existence to the abject. Kristeva describes the abject as "pre-identity, presubject, preobject" (Oliver, *Reading Kristeva* 57), an unbounded fluidity associated with the original undifferentiated mother-child relation. The terrors of the abject must not be understated. Kristeva devotes an entire book, *Powers of Horror*, to a detailed account of the horrific nature of the abject. She writes that the abject is "death infecting life" (4); it is a zone of "meaninglessness" that "annihilates" subjectivity (2) and is anathema to the subject. Nonetheless, it is precisely this zone of borderlessness that a child must negotiate to make the passage from the mother's body to the external world; and to enable this border crossing, a third party must intervene.

In *Beloved*, Baby Suggs says, "Nobody could make it alone. . . . You could be lost forever, if there wasn't nobody to show you the way" (159). Baby Suggs is speaking of fugitive slaves who are trying to find their way to a free state, but her words apply equally well to a child struggling to disengage from the mother-child relation and to enter into relations with others as an independent social subject. This passage too requires a guide. According to Kristeva, the guide who enables this border crossing is what she calls the imaginary father or the third party. This third party introduces a boundary by acting as a "filter" or "threshold" (*Desire* 238). More specifically, the third party intervenes in a site where there is no boundary between mother and child, where all is fluidity and amorphousness, and this presence constitutes "a moment of stasis, a boundary, a symbolic barrier" (*Revolution* 102). The third party enables this boundary negotiation by substituting him- or herself for the mother, that is, by "stand[ing] in as support for the place of the mother" (Oliver, *Reading* 78). This boundary is the place "where mother and father meet," "a thoroughfare, a threshold where 'nature' confronts 'culture'" (*Desire* 249, 238). In Kristeva's theory, unlike the traditional psychoanalytic narrative, the father is not the mother's opposite; he is like the mother because he takes her place, but he is not the mother. He is what Kristeva calls "the father-mother conglomerate," "a conglomerate that already condenses two into one" (*Tales* 40, 222–23). And this overlap—the imaginary father's intervening presence—is the "threshold" that enables a new subject to conceive of itself as both different from others and like others. Kristeva writes, "Without someone on this threshold . . . then every speaker would be led to conceive its Being in relation to some void . . . [,] a nothing opposed to Being" (*Desire* 238).

In assuming this mediating role between mother and child, the father figure faces grave risks to an independent identity. The third party's intervention is a bond with the mother, and this relation is a return to a precultural condition before the rise of a centered self. If a male, the father who shares a relation with the mother risks his masculine difference, and Kristeva alludes to this blurring of gender difference by calling the father figure "the imaginary father" or the "maternal father" (*In the Beginning* 45). Likewise, the father figure risks other culturally made differences. In positioning him- or herself at the threshold, the father figure risks a breakdown of alterity, what Kristeva calls abjection, "a universe of borders, seesaws, fragile and mingled identities" where "agency becomes ambiguous, grows hollow, decays, and crumbles" (*Powers* 135). As the mediator between self and other, this third party is "at the border of my condition as a living being" (3) where there is only "heterogeneous flow" (11), and risks the death of the "I." Kristeva insists, however, that this dangerous third-party role is "productive" (*Revolution* 16). While the father figure's intervention in the mother-child relation is a return to the "source in the non-ego, drive and death" (*Powers* 15), the third party's presence constitutes "a combinatory moment" (*Revolution* 102) that is "a resurrection that has gone through death (of the ego). It is an alchemy that transforms death drive into the start of life, of new significance" (*Powers* 15). In sum, the intervention of "the third party, eventually the father" (13) instantiates a new social subject aware that "the 'I' is heterogeneous" (10).

The father's role in negotiating the fearful self-other border relation, which Kristeva reconceptualizes, is the focus of my project and the central subject of the fiction I analyze. Each of the works I examine is the narrative of a youth's induction into a social order of differential cultural identities, and in each of these narratives, father figures play pivotal roles. For example, Faulkner's novel *Intruder in the Dust* charts a young white boy's introduction to a white-racist Southern community, and, to make this passage, the boy, Chick Mallison, must choose between two father figures: his uncle, who is the spokesperson for a white, Western exclusionary model of identity, and Lucas Beauchamp, who is "not black nor white either" (13), and refuses Western culture's polarized oppositional logic. Wright's *Native Son* is also an initiation story. Whereas Chick Mallison is a privileged white boy in the American South in the 1940s, Bigger Thomas is a desperately poor black boy in the slums of Depression-era Chicago, in a white-dominant, racially polarized community. For Bigger to make his way into a multicultural community a father figure must straddle the border between black and white, and in *Native Son*, Max assumes this mediating role. O'Connor's short stories almost obsessively rehearse the same paradigm: a young woman or man feels trapped by a too-close mother-child relation, and then a dangerous male intrudes on this intimacy. Many of these paternal interventions fail, I argue, because these father figures solely exclude, leaving the youth to conceive itself, in Kristeva's terms, "in relation to some void . . . [,] a nothing opposed to Being" (*Desire* 238). Toni Morrison's *Beloved*, the last fictional work I analyze, narrates two parallel initiations. At one level, *Beloved* is the story of Denver, a young woman who still shares an unmediated relation with her mother, and the work of the novel is to chart Denver's progress into a community of others. More generally, though, *Beloved* also is the story of ex-slaves, who are trying to find a place for themselves in the white-dominant American culture that systematically tried to appropriate them as objects under slavery. For both Denver specifically and the ex-slaves more generally, to become social subjects in a mixed-race culture, someone, a father figure, must show them the way, or, as Baby Suggs wisely warns, they "could be lost forever" (159).

I turn now to the obvious question: why look to these particular authors for an account of the father's acculturating role? Initially, I selected these authors because they represent different culturally defined raced and gendered subject positions and because all four authors focus on the father's role in introducing social relations. But, from the outset, the choice of Faulkner, Wright, O'Connor, and Morrison seemed almost ineluctable because, while these writers are different, they are also related.

They are all quintessential American writers who share and respond to an American literary tradition, which, according to Morrison, emphasizes romance, flight, individualism, "solitude," and "separate confinement" ("Unspeakable" 1, 12). More than this, each of these writers has been forged by and examines the legacy of a Southern history in slavery and Jim Crow. Of course, each of these writers experiences differently and writes differently about the effects of racial slavery and segregation, but they are all responding, albeit differently, to the *same* history and culture. While the "Southernness" of Faulkner, Wright, and O'Connor, each of whom was born and raised in the crucible of the American South, is indisputable, some might challenge my inclusion of Toni Morrison in this grouping, and, admittedly, Morrison is an outlier in that, unlike Faulkner, Wright, and O'Connor, hers is not a distinctively Southern voice. But Morrison, who was born and raised in Ohio, has ties to the South: she is descended from Southern slaves and sharecroppers. Her parents and grandparents were part of the great migration out of the South. Her father's family emigrated from Georgia, and her mother left Alabama as a child with her family. And Morrison's fiction, like the fiction of Faulkner, Wright, and O'Connor, issues out of a Southern past. In *Beloved* and *A Mercy,* her subject is slavery, and her other novels, most notably *Song of Solomon* and *Paradise,* trace the lingering effects of slavery and Jim Crow on the lives of subsequent generations of African Americans.

With the exception of Morrison, these writers also overlap in that they share a particular historical and cultural moment. Faulkner, Wright, and O'Connor are contemporaries of one another. The publication of Faulkner's later novels is largely contemporaneous with the publishing careers of Wright and O'Connor. The relationship between Faulkner,

Wright, and O'Connor is self-evident. They shared the same time and space. We know that Faulkner, Wright, and O'Connor read one another's fiction, and it could be said that O'Connor and Wright wrote in the Nobel Laureate's shadow. As for Morrison, who belongs to a subsequent generation of writers, her inclusion is justified, I argue, because she is the literary heir of Faulkner, Wright, and O'Connor. She continues their tradition in a new postmodern world. Her first novel, *The Bluest Eye*, was published in 1970, just five years after O'Connor's last publication, eight years after Faulkner's, and nine years after Wright's; and of course Morrison, an omnivorous reader, read the fiction of her three predecessors and has pointed out the figurative uses of race in the fiction of Faulkner and O'Connor (*Playing* 14, 40–44).

My purpose here is not to argue that these writers influenced one another. Each of these writers is a stunning original, and each forcefully protests his or her originality. In fact, often when these writers speak of one another, their purpose is to deny influence. Morrison has famously said, "I am not *like* Faulkner" (Interview with Nellie McKay 152); similarly, many of O'Connor's comments about Faulkner seem aimed at distinguishing herself from Faulkner. In a letter written in 1958, O'Connor responds to a friend's question about Faulkner by saying, "I keep clear of Faulkner so my own little boat won't get swamped" (*Habit* 273).

The writers' denial of influence, however, is intriguing in that their very need to protest their difference suggests a sense of relatedness among them. While Flannery O'Connor never missed an opportunity to deny a Faulknerian influence, she also admitted that "the presence alone of Faulkner in our midst makes a great difference in what the writer can and cannot permit himself to do. Nobody wants his mule and wagon stalled on the same track the Dixie Limited is roaring down" (*Mystery* 45). For his part, Faulkner expressed admiration for O'Connor's fiction. When Maurice Coindreau, who translated into French many of Faulkner's works, told Faulkner he was translating *Wise Blood* into French, Faulkner "raised his head, pointed a forefinger at him and stated emphatically, 'That's good stuff'" (Gooch 308). Like O'Connor and Faulkner, Wright and Faulkner were keenly aware of one another's writerly presence. Wright did acknowledge a kinship with Faulkner. He referred to Faulkner as "a fellow Mississippian," and when asked what literary generation he identified with, Wright answered that he belonged to the generation "formed in 1929" (the year of the publication of *The Sound and the Fury*), which, he said, included Faulkner, among others (Ward and Butler 10, 32). In turn, Faulkner seemed to take an almost fatherly (some might say patronizing) interest in Wright. Following the publication of *Black Boy*, the famously reclusive author made a point to write Wright to praise *Native Son* and to caution the African American writer about writing in a narrowly autobiographical form, rather than "as an artist, as in *Native Son*" (*Selected Letters* 201). As for Morrison, while she has said that she is "typical of all writers who are convinced that they are wholly original and that if they recognized an influence they would abandon it as quickly as possible," she also states that "in a very, very personal way, in a very personal way as a reader, William Faulkner had an enormous effect on me, an enormous effect" ("Faulkner and Women" 296).

By way of conclusion, I propose to present a more detailed rationale of my choice of each of these particular authors and texts by outlining the different approach each takes to the father's role as boundary setter.

In novel after novel, William Faulkner (1897–1962) focuses on father-son relationships. For Faulkner, a culturally defined white Southern male, the great-grandson of a Confederate colonel, the question seems to be, what are the grounds for the father's authority? Faulkner's novels interrogate the notion that the father's authority is secured by an oppositional logic. According to this binary model, "white" is defined by an opposition with African Americans; similarly, masculinity is defined as the opposite of femininity; and the father's role is to prevent any overlap. In his masterwork, *Absalom, Absalom!*, Faulkner exposes the destructiveness of the Southern patriarchal "design," a social hierarchy built on exclusion and domination. The novel's pivotal scene, when young Sutpen is turned away from the planter's front door, is Sutpen's initiation into this exclusionary model of patriarchal authority, which he subsequently adopts. He elects to become the planter at the door, and turns away, one after another, his first wife, Eulalia; his son, Charles Bon; Miss Rosa; Millie; and his daughter by Millie. Sutpen fails, Faulkner knows, if Sutpen doesn't, because this model of father as excluder is both destructive to others and self-destructive. When asked about Sutpen's demise, Faulkner explained that Sutpen is destroyed because he was "completely self-centered," and added that "I think that people like that are destroyed sooner or later, because one has got to belong to the human family, and to take a responsible part in the human family" (*Faulkner in the University* 80–81). According to Faulkner, then, Sutpen's ambition to father a dynasty is doomed because he fails to be a father who "take[s] a responsible part in the human family"; Faulkner's words point to a different paternal role, a father who shares a relation with "the human family."

In my chapter on Faulkner, I select to examine a less well-known later work, his 1948 novel *Intruder in the Dust,* because it focuses on a father figure, Lucas Beauchamp, who models fatherhood as a way into an endlessly culturally diverse "human family." *Intruder* is an unconventional narrative, with dense, clause-laden, nearly unpunctuated sentences that make it challenging to read. Relatively few scholars have attempted to interpret the novel, and the critics who have offered readings have tended to focus on the boy Chick Mallison, the narrator who refers to himself oddly with the third-person pronoun "he." At one level, the novel certainly *is* the story of Chick's initiation into a white-dominant Southern culture. But when Faulkner was asked about this novel, he insisted that the novel's central figure is Lucas Beauchamp. Asked if *Intruder* "start[ed] . . . with the idea of a single character," Faulkner explained that the novel started with Lucas: "I thought of Beauchamp, then he took charge of the story" (*Faulkner in the University* 141–42). *Intruder,* I propose, is the story of Lucas Beauchamp, a father figure who achieves the unfailing paternal authority that always eluded Thomas Sutpen. Whereas Sutpen sought to be a father by relentlessly patrolling the boundaries of Sutpen's Hundred—the symbol of his patriarchal authority—Lucas Beauchamp is a liminal father figure, who blurs without obliterating white-black difference. While he is culturally defined as black, the text insists that Lucas "is not black nor white either" (13). Precisely because he does model overlap, Lucas is threatening to a white-dominant community, which seeks to "make a nigger out of him" (31). My chapter on Faulkner examines Lucas Beauchamp's alternative to a Western exclusionary model of paternal authorization.

Richard Wright (1908–1960), the grandson of former slaves, who grew up in the segregated South of the early twentieth century and chronicled that crucible in his biography *American Hunger/Black Boy,* always writes about the problem of racial oppression, but the destructive effects of American racism are perhaps most intensively analyzed in his greatest and most controversial novel, *Native Son* (1940). As a racialized male in a white-dominated culture, Bigger Thomas is "radically excluded" and is threatened with abjection. Bigger's lawyer, Max, expresses this same idea in non-psychological terms. In his courtroom defense of Bigger, Max characterizes the boy as a "corpse" that whites "buried" and that "returns to raid [their] homes" (456). Throughout the novel, Bigger is driven by two seemingly competing desires—a desire for community with others and a desire for independence and autonomy. These are the desires that drive every subject, but they are exacerbated in Bigger because he is a racialized subject in a racially polarized culture. Told by whites that he is inferior because he is black, Bigger longs to "be at home" in the world and to "merge with the men and women about him" (316). At the same time, however, he fears his own desire for solidarity with others because racial intermixing is forbidden by whites and because male-female bonding seems to threaten his male difference. The work of the novel, I contend, is to find a way to reconcile Bigger's conflicting needs for individuation and for integration, to find "another orbit between two poles that would let him live" (317). The last third of the novel focuses on Max, a father figure who straddles the border between white and black and introduces a boundary that enables individuation and social relations.

Flannery O'Connor (1925–1964) may seem like an unlikely writer to look to for a revisionist reading of the father's role in introducing a child to individuation within a heterogeneous community of others. O'Connor, of course, insisted on being interpreted in terms of Roman Catholic theology. She never tired of repeating that her fiction "has to do with the Divine life and our participation in it" (*Mystery* 111). But critics and readers alike have struggled to reconcile the signature violence in O'Connor's texts with her stated spiritual purpose. For example, a reader is hard put to see the connection between the action of grace and the work accomplished by violent male figures such as the Misfit, who murders the grandmother and her family; or Tom T. Shiftlet, who abandons the helpless Lucyknell Crater Jr. far from her mother; or Manley Pointer, who seduces Joy/Hulga and steals her prosthetic leg. Not surprisingly, feminist critics have taken issue with this male violence against women. Claire Katz writes that "actual fathers rarely appear in O'Connor's fiction; when they do, they are usually sadistic figures, their aggressiveness associated with the sexual role of the male as penetrator" (63), and Louise Westling contends that O'Connor writes about a "male-dominated culture" (513), where women are "tricked, taken advantage of, jilted and misused" (518). Yet in *Mystery and Manners*, O'Connor strangely suggests that these violent, disturbing male figures are somehow making grace accessible to others.[3]

My interpretation of O'Connor's fiction attempts to align the theological with the psychological. In her stories, the same paradigm seems to be reformulated. As the story begins, a young man or woman desires to break free of a static mother-child intimacy; then a third figure appears, and this outsider separates mother and child, leaving the youth stranded, shattered, and helpless. Claire Katz and James Mellard have argued that O'Connor's stories figure an account of the child's socialization as outlined by a Freudian Oedipal model. I propose that these third-party figures are called to be fatherly border figures, but, out of fear of the abject in-between, they often resist the father's mediating role and introduce only alienation and loss. Even though these third-party figures often fail to accomplish the father's role, Christ imagery attends them, I suggest, because, for O'Connor, the figure who risks straddling the middle serves as intermediary both between self and other and between human and Divine. In O'Connor's terms, the border figure is a prophet.

Whereas my choice of O'Connor for this grouping might seem unexpected, my turn to Toni Morrison (1931–), I think, will appear self-evident from the outset. As the first African American Nobel Laureate and author of *Playing in the Dark: Whiteness and the Literary Imagination*, Morrison seems to be the preeminent figure in the discussion of racial and gender politics in America today. Magali Michael points out that Morrison's novels "reimagine community within an increasingly multicultural and multi-racial America" (2), and scholars who have wrestled with the problem of racial and gendered specificity within cross-racial and cross-gendered relationships have repeatedly turned to Morrison's novels for her perspective on this double bind. While all of Morrison's novels engage with the contemporary debate about the need for and risks of identification within a community, a consideration of all of her stunning novels is outside the scope of my project. For the purposes of this study, I look to *Beloved* (1987) because, with its focus on slavery in America, it bears the closest analogies to the other texts I consider, all of which issue out of the American South, and because it represents her most profound and searching exploration into the dynamics of acculturation in a mixed-raced America.

In my reading, Morrison's *Beloved* tells the story of former slaves who are trying to forge social identities in an American culture, where, as Morrison argues in *Playing in the Dark*, "American means white" (47). Morrison's fictional account of slavery exposes the institutionalized terror tactics used by white slave owners to rob black women and men of a sense of a self-identity. In this way the novel strikingly illustrates scholar Hortense Spillers's theory that captured Africans were "culturally unmade" (72). The work of *Beloved* is to chart a way for these "culturally unmade" ex-slaves to take their place in American culture—the same white-dominant culture that systematically worked to appropriate them as objects. My investigation finds that, for these ex-slaves to form social identities, someone, a father figure, must be the intermediary who introduces a border that allows both for culturally different identities and for cultural relations.

In the concluding chapter, I move from theory and fiction to the real world of material culture, and I point to how, in material culture as in fiction and theory, social identities depend on a threshold figure who is double, that is, who shares a relation with both the one and the other. In this chapter I argue that the interfacing performed by the border figure is constantly going on in culture to distinguish social identities, but that the in-between role of the mediator is often wholly controlled by the dominant culture and used to create polarized identities. More specifically, I focus on two American cultural/historical examples of figures who straddle the in-between boundary site: the nineteenth-century blackface minstrel, a working-class immigrant who "blacked-up" to impersonate an African American for the entertainment of an all-white and mostly male audience; and John Howard Griffin, a journalist who in 1959 chemically darkened his skin and passed for a person of color so as to find out for himself the "truth" of race relations in the American South. In both these cases, a white-passing-for-black constitutes the needed two-sidedness of a boundary, and in both cases these double figures influenced race relations in America.

I choose to focus on these two instances of border figures to distinguish between a boundary setting that co-opts the other and a boundary configuration that introduces a balance between self and other. In the case of the blackface minstrel, the dominant culture devised an encounter between their idea of "white" ethnicity and their own degrading caricature of African American ethnicity. This white-dominated symbolization of the middle, where culture's binaries are interdependent, produced the effect the ruling class desired: at a time in America's history when it wasn't clear who was white and who was not-white, blackface minstrelsy insured an either-or dichotomy between "white" Americans and people of African descent; it also secured white domination of this binary. In the second half of the conclusion, I turn to John Howard Griffin's experience as a culturally defined white man passing for black, and I argue that in the early days of his "racial experiment" (175) he appropriates the racial middle in a way comparable to the nineteenth-century entertainer in blackface. When he first darkens his skin, he experiences no real solidarity with people of African extraction. Rather, like the blackface minstrel, he works to maintain total white control of the racial crossing and feels that the black identity he assumes is radically foreign to his "real" white identity. But, unlike the minstrel in a blackface mask, who performs a fiction in accordance with the dictates of white desire, Griffin for more than a month lives the life of an ethnically African man in the American South; he experiences daily humiliations from whites; he comes to know how it feels to be an African American in the segregated South; and this proximity becomes a racial border-crossing that, I argue, transforms Griffin. Because he crosses the color line, Griffin does not "become Negro" (175) as whites claim, but he is also not the same white man he was before, as he readily acknowledges. Like Lucas Beauchamp, who is "not black nor white either" (13), Griffin defies dichotomization; he is not the one thing or the other, because he shares a relation with both. Whatever our socially constructed identity, this relatedness frightens us because it threatens and transforms self-identity, but the third party's duality, his/her relation to both the one and the other, enables boundary negotiation. This doubling, then, is the answer to the question with which I began: How can we bond with others and still retain our cultural specificity? Because the fatherly threshold figure is both related and different, she or he *both intervenes and connects,* and this interfacing grounds different identities in one another. A sharing of different identities is not the end of different social identities; rather, it is the formula for new multicultural coalitions.

1 Beyond Oedipus

William Faulkner's *Intruder in the Dust*

But it is not enough to stand on the opposite riverbank, shout-
ing questions, challenging patriarchal, white conventions. . . . At
some point, . . . we will have to leave the opposite bank, the split
between the two mortal combatants somehow healed so that we
are on both shores at once.

GLORIA ANZALDÚA, *Borderlands/La Frontera*

Read for its latent meanings, *Intruder in the Dust* traces the cause
of racial lynchings to a model of identity formation based in exclusionary
tactics. At this symbolic level, the novel's two central developments, the
mob frenzy to lynch Lucas Beauchamp and the murder of Vinson Gowrie, appear to be driven by an oppositional, either-or logic. Disguised by
doubling and distanced by undeveloped characters and a convoluted plot,
the novel's project is to mount an inquiry into the fundamental problem
at the crux of the psychoanalytic master narrative of identity, namely,
that the boundaries that support self-identity—in particular, white, male
identity—appear to be insecurely secured by the dialectics of domination.
Stripped to its essentials, this identity narrative works from the premise that one term's ascendancy is guaranteed by the marginalization of
another. But Faulkner's novels accept no first principle as a given; rather,
they relentlessly expose and question a system of signification that exalts
the domination of others—like the lynching of Lucas Beauchamp—as the
foundation of cultural meanings.

Faulkner's bewildering novel *Intruder in the Dust* is a fiction about
burial and retrieval. By my count, various bodies are buried and exhumed
five times, and the novel's narrative technique mirrors this plot motif;
that is, the text withholds or buries meanings, retrieves them, and quickly
reburies them. For example, ostensibly, *Intruder in the Dust* is a murder

mystery, but few who have read it can recall the identity of either the murderer or his victim. In fact, the murderer is Crawford Gowrie, and he kills his brother, Vinson—a murder that should horrify us but does not, because the text works to withhold or bury this fratricide. In effect, their story is never told; or, more accurately, it is displaced onto another, the narrative of a relationship between a fourteen-year-old boy, Chick Mallison, who is identified as white, and an elderly, dignified man, Lucas Beauchamp, who is both father figure to Chick and culturally defined as "black." This narrative of a father-son relationship, like its double, the murder of Vincent Gowrie by his brother, also centers on burial and retrieval. As the novel opens, Lucas is about to be lynched. His offense, the novel insistently tells us, is refusing "to be a nigger" (18), that is, refusing to play a culturally assigned subordinate role that is defined by the word "nigger." The work of the novel is to avert this lynching; and, in a move that seems to defy credibility, Chick can only save Lucas by digging up a buried corpse.

These events, burial and disinterment, are, I suggest, symbolic. Specifically, they symbolize the way we compose polarized meanings in language. Binary meanings seem to depend on exclusionary tactics: we advance one term in a binary by subordinating, or burying, another. Burial symbolizes an effort to displace and deny so as to construct dominant and subordinate positions in a polarized opposition. Disinterment, on the other hand, symbolizes an end to burial in a restoration to a former equal footing that burial disturbed. In psychological terms, burial figures repression, and disinterment signifies the return of the repressed. The psychoanalytic account of identity formation exalts repression (a shutting out) as enabling self-identity and differential cultural meanings, even as it neatly sidesteps, or represses, Freud's finding that repression always instigates the return of the repressed, no matter the resistance.

If we read the events of *Intruder in the Dust* for a symbolic meaning, then, the text's improbable insistence that Chick must dig up a buried corpse to stop a lynching seems to suggest that this lynching and, by implication, all socially repressive acts like lynching can only be averted when we retrieve the buried term—that is, when we stop socially enforcing exclusive either/or oppositions. Of course, the alternative to cultural meanings defined by domination seems to be a leveling sameness. The word "equal" appears to imply "the same" or undifferentiated. And what is a "white identity" if it is equal to and not separate from a "black identity"? In *Intruder in the Dust*, this threat of a collapse of a white/black binary is personified in the character of Lucas Beauchamp, whom the narrative voice, unlike the characters in the novel, never identifies as a "black" man. Rather, the text insistently repeats that Lucas is "not black nor white either" (13) and thus a threat to discrete white and black identities.

In *Intruder in the Dust,* Faulkner attempts to find a way to think beyond the marginalization of others as the guarantee of cultural boundaries. As numerous critics have noted, the novel is the account of Chick Mallison's initiation into manhood. In making this passage, Chick must choose between two models of male gender identity formation, which are represented, respectively, by his uncle and Lucas. In the second half of the novel, Lawyer Stevens garrulously makes the case for white, male autonomy defined by the dialectics of domination; set against Stevens's voice is the commanding presence of Lucas Beauchamp, who presides over the first half of the book and shows Chick another way to compose cultural boundaries.

The Lynching of Nelse Patton

The subject of *Intruder in the Dust* is an averted lynching, or, put another way, the novel instructs us in a way to stop practices like lynchings. By way of beginning, I want to suggest that Faulkner's fiction rewrites an appalling actual event, the lynching of Nelse Patton, which took place in Oxford in 1908 when Faulkner was eleven. My notion that Faulkner's fiction represents a revisionary return to a historical lynching is supported by a number of curious correspondences between the fictional and the tragically real.[1]

The most notable parallel between the fictional lynching and the actual lynching is the vital roles played in both by adolescent boys. In *Intruder,* two sixteen-year-old boys, Chick and Aleck Sander, accompanied by an elderly white lady, Miss Habersham, prevent the lynching of Lucas Beauchamp, accused of the murder of a white man. In Oxford in 1908, two young white boys, the fifteen-year-old John B. Cullen, a friend of Faulkner's, and John's younger brother, Jenks, captured and delivered over to a white posse Nelse Patton, a black man accused of the murder of a white woman.[2] Nor did the involvement of the Cullen boys end there. Patton was jailed, and later that evening a frenzied mob gained entry to the jail by passing through the jail windows the sons of guards, among them John and Jenks. Inside, the sons held their fathers and flung open the jail doors to the mob. Still, the mob could not enter Patton's cell, and from eight o'clock that night until two in the morning, as the boys watched, the mob worked to cut through the jail wall. When they finally broke into the cell, they shot Patton twenty-six times, scalped him, castrated him, tied him to a car, and dragged his body around the streets of Oxford. Then they hanged him from a tree in the town square, two blocks from Faulkner's home (Blotner 113–14; Doyle 326).

In 1935, in response to a suggestion that he write a lynching story, Faulkner abruptly retorted that, because he had never witnessed a lynching, he could not write about one (Doyle 326; Williamson 159). Of course, in 1935 he had already published two works, "Dry September" (1931) and *Light in August* (1932), that powerfully evoke lynchings; and, as numerous commentators have observed, Faulkner, whose bed was not more than a thousand yards from the scene of the lynching on that fateful September night, had to have heard the fevered mob and the shots fired at Patton. Surely he also saw the mutilated body. The *Lafayette County Press*'s account of the lynching states that on the day after the lynching, the body of Nelse Patton was publicly displayed in the public square for every passerby to view (Cullen 96). If Faulkner did not himself actually witness the lynching of Nelse Patton (and he may well have), he unquestionably knew about it,[3] and I propose that his novel of an averted lynching, *Intruder in the Dust,* represents Faulkner's fictional transformation of a lynching that was not prevented.[4] More specifically, Faulkner's transformation revises racial boundary formation. *Intruder in the Dust* both exposes the Oedipal model of white self-identity that drove Patton's lynching and replaces it with another model of boundary formation, one that risks the in-between space of a border.

Revising Oedipus

Because *Intruder in the Dust* withholds its meanings, it fails spectacularly as a detective fiction, a genre that, at least at the conclusion, offers full disclosure. For example, in *Intruder,* the murderer of Vinson Gowrie is finally identified as his older brother, Crawford, but the stated rationale for the murder does not explain it. We are asked to believe that Crawford murdered his brother to ensure the lynching of Lucas Beauchamp, who threatened to expose him as a thief. As Gavin Stevens points out, this solution to the mystery poses another one: "But why Vinson? Why did Crawford have to kill Vinson in order to obliterate the witness to his thieving? . . . Why . . . this bizarre detour?" (219). Stevens's question haunts

the novel, but is never addressed. Not only does the reason for the fratricide seem to be withheld, but the murderer, Crawford Gowrie, and his
murdered brother, Vinson, also seem to be banished from the text. Unre-
alized as characters, they are merely names in the novel, whose histories
are summarily sketched in at the novel's end. They are as shadowy as
figures in a dream, and their shadowiness is our clue to their secret meaning: they are shadows in Chick's dream, the disguised, returned, unwanted
feelings of a boy who is being inducted into manhood.

As the returned trace of an unthinkable meaning, which Chick refers to elliptically as "something shocking and shameful out of the whole
white foundation" (135), Crawford Gowrie is barred from the novel; and,
displaced, the forbidden meaning returns in the form of disguised substitutes. Unidentified and practically invisible, Crawford appears once as a
"shadow" at the novel's pivotal graveyard scene. Specifically, he appears
on the night when Chick, Aleck Sander, and Miss Habersham exhume the
body of the murdered man, Vinson Gowrie, in an attempt to produce evidence to prove Lucas's innocence. This unthinkable violation of a grave
is the novel's axis, to which I will return, but, for now, I want to focus on
the trace of Crawford Gowrie's ghostly presence. As Chick and his com-
panions approach the graveyard in the "inky" night, Aleck Sander hears
a mule coming toward them on the road. They hide, and, as the mule
passes, Chick sees only "a darker shadow than shadow against the pale
dirt of the road" (98). This "shadow" carries "something" indistinguish-
able on the saddle in front of him, but the rider's identity and the nature
of his burden are not divulged at this time. Crawford never appears again
in the text, but the mule that he was riding on that night does. On the
morning after the late-night exhumation, Chick and Aleck Sander return
to the gravesite, this time accompanied by Uncle Gavin Stevens and the
sheriff, who takes with him two black prisoners. As they are about to dig
up the grave again, old Nub Gowrie, the father of the clan, arrives, and
with him are two sons, twins, who ride a mule with a rope burn, the same
mule that the night before had carried Crawford and his dead brother,
Vinson. This repetition—the same mule with two Gowrie brothers on
it—signals doubling: the Gowrie twins are substitutes for Crawford and
his brother, Vinson, whose corpse Crawford carried across his saddle the
night before.

Apparently, the substitution of the Gowrie twins for Crawford and
Vinson does not sufficiently disguise the refused meaning, because the
text now generates two sets of doubles for the twins. The first of these

doubles is the pair of black prisoners whom the sheriff takes with him to the gravesite. The sheriff appears at the gravesite with "the two Negroes"; Nub Gowrie arrives "with the two identical wooden-faced sons" (167). The sheriff orders the two prisoners to dig up the grave; Nub insists that the twins do the digging in their place. Most to the point, the Gowrie twins stand in the same relation to their father that the black prisoners bear to the sheriff. Both pairs are called "boys"; both are submissive son-figures; and both are notably silent while the sheriff and Nub Gowrie speak.

Even this substitution, however, still seems to leave the rejected meaning unacceptably close to home, because the two hounds that follow Nub Gowrie to the gravesite function as another set of doubles for both the prisoners and the twins. Like the twins and the prisoners, the dogs are a pair and are utterly submissive to their master, and Nub indiscriminately refers to both the dogs and the sons as "boys."

These doubles are the scrambled, returned trace of a refused, unthinkable meaning, the answer to the question that haunts the novel: why did Crawford choose to kill his brother so as to rid himself of Lucas? The rejected meaning takes form when old man Gowrie menaces the convicts. He draws his gun on them as they, terrified, whirl and run for their lives. The denied impulse surfaces again when the old man violently assaults the cringing hounds:

> The old man shouting and cursing and the yelping of the hounds and the thudding sound a man's shoe makes against a dog's ribs . . . and old Gowrie still kicking at them and cursing. . . . "Hold up, Mr. Gowrie," the sheriff said. . . . But the old man didn't seem to hear him. He didn't even seem aware that anyone else was there; he seemed even to have forgot why he was kicking the dogs: . . . still hobbling and hopping after them on one leg and the other poised and cocked to kick even after they had retreated . . . and were merely trying to dodge past him and get out of the ditch into safety, still kicking at them and cursing after the sheriff caught him by his one arm and held him. (170)

Nub Gowrie, "the fiery old tyrant of a father" (160), vents a terrible fury on the hounds and the prisoners, figures for the twins, who are, in turn, substitutes for Crawford and Vinson. In other words, a homely dread, a fear of the father, appears in the text as a threat not to his own sons, but to distanced son figures—the prisoners and the hounds. In a novel full of father figures—Lucas, Uncle Gavin, the sheriff, and Chick's shadowy father—Nub Gowrie, who keeps his grown sons "boys," is the threatening father figure out of a boy's nightmare. When Chick opens the grave of Vinson Gowrie, it is Nub that he fears, and it is Nub that the town expects to lead the lynch mob. The specific threat that old man Gowrie poses appears as an image. Nub, who clamps a gun to his side with the stub of an arm, is a one-armed man. This missing member functions as a scarcely veiled image for the dismemberment that the son fears as the father's punishment. And this image provides the veiled answer to the question, why did Vinson kill his brother? The image suggests that the dialectics of domination drove this murder. In other words, a desire to be the powerful father out of a Freudian myth drives Vinson to kill his brother, as a displaced substitute for the father he fears.

At this point in my symbolic reading, it might seem that Faulkner's novel, with its fearful father figure and murderous son, should be read in terms of Freud's Oedipal logic, which narratizes the dialectics of domination. But Faulkner's novel evokes this Oedipal theory of identity to discredit it by revealing that our Western model of either-or oppositions, which Freudian theory codifies, drives social violence, like the murder of Vinson, the narrowly averted lynching of Lucas Beauchamp, and the actual lynching and castration of Nelse Patton, which the novel revises. In the Freudian/Lacanian Oedipal narrative, the father authorizes boundaries by threatening the son with castration. For Freud, the fear of castration is literal. For Lacan, the threat is symbolic and "the father" is whoever or whatever represents the law that decrees exclusion of, first, the mother, and then others. But, in both, the father is identified with a profoundly disturbing act of evisceration that is deemed necessary as enabling boundary formation.[5]

In *Intruder in the Dust,* Faulkner takes issue with this interpretation of the paternal function and suggests another way to interpret the father's boundary-making role. While initially Nub Gowrie appears to represent the disturbing father out of Freud's nightmarish Oedipal theory of development, in a subsequent scene, Faulkner's text exposes this figure as a reification of a child's fearful fantasy. In a novel where burial signifies marginalization and exhumation symbolizes a return to an undemarcated condition, Nub Gowrie eschews the repressive, dominating role that establishes the position of father in the Oedipal narrative when he willingly buries himself to exhume the buried body of his son.

In the last of a series of exhumations in the novel, Nub Gowrie risks losing himself in deadly, enveloping quicksand to retrieve his dead son.

The quicksand, which is described as "without demarcation . . . an expanse of wet sand as smooth and innocent and markless of surface as so much milk" (172), aptly figures a fearful obliteration of culture's boundaries. In particular, we cling to exclusion out of fear of a loss of an autonomous self, and Nub's relinquishment to powerlessness is also figured in the quicksand image. When Nub jumps into the "bland surface," he "half-disappear[s] . . . with no shock or jolt: just fixed and immobile as if his legs had been cut off at the loins by one swing of a scythe, leaving his trunk sitting upright on the bland depthless milklike sand" (173). As in the psychoanalytic narrative, in this image too, a loss of distinguishing difference is identified as a return to an early precultural undifferentiated mother-child relation; the quicksand is a "milklike," "markless surface" into which Nub "half-disappears," and the freeing of Vinson's dead body from the sand is described with an image that suggests the emergence of a child from vaginal lips: "the body coming out now feet first, gallowsed up and out of the inscrutable suck, to the heave of the crude tackle then free of the sand with a faint smacking plop like the sound of lips perhaps in sleep and in the bland surface nothing: a faint wimple wrinkle already fading then gone like the end of a faint secret fading smile" (173). And when the one-armed Nub, who had formerly seemed like the personification of Freud's castrating father, leaps into the quicksand, the scene images another breakdown of alterity, a merging of the mother and father.

In a scene that pictures the blurring of defining cultural boundaries—the two Negro prisoners, for example, now work hand in hand with the Gowrie twins to raise the corpse—the most remarkable border crossing occurs when Nub caresses his dead son in an archetypal gesture that unmistakably defines the loving intimacy of the maternal role: "The old man stooped and began to brush clumsily with his one hand at the sand clogged into the eyes and nostrils and mouth, the hand looking curious and stiff at this which had been shaped so supple and quick to violence; to the buttons on the shirt and the butt and hammer of the pistol: . . . as kneeling now the old man jerked out the tail of his shirt and bending to bring it close, wiped the or at the dead face with it then bending tried to blow the wet sand from it as though he had forgotten the sand was still damp" (174). Grieving over and ministering to his dead son, Nub is the very image of the Pietà, the often reproduced image of the Virgin Mary holding and mourning the dead body of Christ, her son. The image of the Pietà captures the quality of maternal identification that, according to the psychoanalytic narrative, threatens autonomy and social hierarchy. In the image, the mother, who contains the corpse of her son in her lap, is, as it were, claiming her dead son as her own. This identification of the maternal womb with death is a ceaselessly recurring theme in Western literature. As pictured in the Pietà, however, it is not a fearful or threatening image; rather, the image venerates an identificatory love that is undaunted by death.

Faulkner's stunning substitution of the father for the mother in the Pietà archetype revises the psychoanalytic narrative, which defines the mother and father as dialectical opposites: the father represents the law that decrees exclusion; the mother stands for a fluid, unbounded intimacy that threatens individuation. In this master narrative, love is suspect because love fosters union. In the words of the Lacanian commentator James Mellard, "The Oedipal law of alienation into language (Lacan's version of Freud's castration) . . . , alas, exists on the side of Thanatos, not Eros. The drive toward subjectivity, therefore, is always toward death and the Symbolic; the contrary drive—toward loss of subjectivity—is always toward love and the Imaginary" (*Using Lacan* 32). Translated, the passage means that love threatens the boundaries of the self: "the ego loses itself in the loved one" (32). Because love crosses boundaries, in Freudian and Lacanian theory, the mother is outlawed, and the father is himself absent. In Faulkner's image also, the mother is absent, but the father replaces her—not with an empty signifier as Lacan holds, but with his presence—and this paternal substitution is both different from the mother and the same: he is not the mother, but he is like her in that he loves his son. Both different and the same, he is the mother's double. In this image, the father's boundary-setting role is rewritten. The father risks the terrible in-between, "the border of my condition as a living being" (Kristeva, *Powers* 3), where the difference between the one and the other breaks down, and his presence distinguishes. Nub's intervention delivers his son. Of course, in this case, Nub's loving intervention comes too late, and his son is, as it were, born dead, the victim of an Oedipal rivalry with his older brother. After this appearance, Nub Gowrie fades from the novel, but in the character of Lucas Beauchamp the text explores a father figure who introduces social identity, not by social domination, but by straddling the border between self and other.

Straddling Culture's Oppositions

Lucas Beauchamp is a father whose authority is not defined by an Oedipal threat.[6] While he is evoked in the text as unmistakably a father figure—Chick insistently compares him to his own grandfather and obeys him because "like his grandfather the man striding ahead of him was simply incapable of conceiving himself by a child contradicted and defied" (8)—he is a father who refuses the dialectics of domination. On the one hand, *Intruder in the Dust* tirelessly repeats that Lucas refuses "to be a nigger" (18); at the same time, he refuses the dominant role in the master/slave binary. For example, when a white man attacks Lucas because he does not "act like a nigger" (48), Lucas responds with "calm speculative de-tachment" (19). Similarly, in a memorable early scene, he thwarts Chick's attempt to establish white supremacy through the tactics of domination. When Chick throws money on the floor and commands Lucas, "Pick it up!" (15), in response, he is "nothing." "And still nothing, the man didn't move, hands clasped behind him, looking at nothing" (16).

Simply put, Lucas rejects a system of signification based in either-or dichotomies. To apprehend Lucas's subversive strategy, a comparison/contrast with Joe Christmas, the ultimately castrated protagonist of *Light in August* (1932), is instructive. Joe's unique dilemma—he does not know if he is black or white—serves to underscore the problematics of a selfhood defined by exclusion. Joe ricochets back and forth between ag-gressor and victim, master and slave, white and black, but he can never get outside this dialectic: when he rejects one position as untenable, he knows no way to define a self other than by assuming the opposite role. In marked contrast to Joe Christmas, Lucas rejects both terms of the dialec-tic. A curious, insistently repeated description of Lucas seems to register his resistance to culture's binary ordering: "What looked out of [his face] had no pigment at all, not even the white man's lack of it, not arrogant, not even scornful: just intractable and composed" (7). This description of Lucas as "not black nor white either, not arrogant and not even scornful" (13) but simply "intractable and composed" (43) is twice repeated, and the reiterated phrases underscore that Lucas is not one thing or another. Joe Christmas vacillates between black and white, between domination and submission. Lucas, on the other hand, assumes a position in between culture's oppositional meanings.

Of course, the question then arises: outside of culture's system of either-or meanings, how does Lucas signify? According to language theorists, refusing language's differential meanings is not merely difficult, it is impossible. Lacan writes, "Man speaks, . . . but it is because the symbol has made him man" (*Écrits: A Selection* 65). What Lacan means is that our signifiers signify. We make meaning and we make ourselves in culture by enforcing artificial, arbitrary boundaries between the self and what we name the not-self, that is, what we reject (or bury). Lucas does not accept this either-or exclusionary logic; the threat that he courts is that he will cease to signify. Yet the text insistently observes that Lucas is "composed."

Through Lucas, the text suggests that the feared, fluid middle that threatens a loss of distinctions also plays a part in the introduction of boundaries that distinguish a social identity and social meanings. Freud's discovery of the unconscious mind led to his theory that mental processes are a function of a dynamic interaction between repression and the return of the repressed. While both the Freudian and the Lacanian theories of identity formation generally read this return as dangerous, Freud's recognition that repression is inseparable from return argues that both processes work together to produce subject formation. In fact, Lacan's mirror stage, an intermediate phase in his theory of subjectivity formation, provides a model of identity that depends on an oscillation between fluid inmixing and resistance. As an alternative to meanings constructed solely by exclusion, Lacan's mirror stage, which has been the focus of much study by feminist theorists, may help us to understand Lucas's model of paternal authority.

In Lacan's mirror phase, identity is composed of the interplay of separation and relatedness. Lacan describes the mirror stage as a developmental phase between two registers of being: the imaginary and the symbolic. Lacan's imaginary or pre-Oedipal phase is an early point in the infant's development when no distinctions exist, and the child perceives itself as one and continuous with the mother's body and the world; Lacan's symbolic is the condition of the post-Oedipal subject whose separate identity depends on an always unstable repression (ordained by the father) of a desire for maternal identification. The mirror phase is notable because it allows for both individuation and relationship. In the mirror phase, the child has a sense of self, but this self is both separate from the mother and related to her. More specifically, in this phase the mother functions like a mirror or identificatory imago that reflects back at the child a unified, intact body image. A blurring of mother and self, outside and inside, still obtains, since the child continues to identify with the mother, but this identification does not impede a sense of self; rather, it enables identity. Like a mirror, in which we find our image, Eagleton explains, the mother or identificatory image "is at once somehow part of ourselves—we identify with it—and yet not ourselves, something alien" (164–65). This process by which we locate a self in the mirror phase sounds strikingly like doubling, since the mother of the mirror phase is a double, both eerily the same and also different. This mirror phase, which enables a boundary by doubling and which Lacan sidelines as a mere way station in the development of a fully formed self, may, in fact, more accurately reflect the way we make social meanings and ourselves in culture. All well and good, but the father, the representative of difference, is curiously absent from Lacan's account of this intermediate phase. What part does the father play in this alternative identity narrative? In *Intruder in the Dust,* Faulkner introduces a father who authorizes boundaries by becoming the mother's double.

As the novel opens, Lucas appears in a symbolic birthing scene that radically reinterprets the father's role in introducing cultural boundaries. The scene takes the form of a memory: Chick recalls meeting Lucas for the first time four years earlier when he was twelve. While hunting, Chick falls off a footlog into the icy cold water of a creek; Chick's immersion in and emergence from the water figures a move from preexistence to existence in the world of cultural meanings. As he climbs out of the creek, he and the reader see Lucas for the first time, and Lucas, who looms over "the boy" and carries an ax over his shoulder, appears to represent the threatening father out of Freud's script. But, like Nub Gowrie later in the text, Lucas also dispels the myth of the father as a fearful figure who introduces the child to dialectical meanings enforced by domination. Lucas's first words in the novel articulate a rejection of what Lacan calls "the phallic distinction." He says to Aleck Sander, who has extended a long pole to Chick, "Get the pole out of his way so he can get out" (6). Lucas's words signify a revision of a masculinist identity script. Lucas does preside as individuation takes place, as symbolized by Chick's emergence from the water, but Chick emerges on his own, buoyed by the water, a symbol for a precultural fluidity. This scene seems to emblemize the feminist theorist Jane Gallop's variant reading of the relationship of the imaginary and the symbolic orders. Gallop argues that the relationship is not an oppositional one, that "the paths to the symbolic are thus in the imaginary" and that "the symbolic can be reached only by not trying to avoid the imaginary, but knowingly being in the imaginary" (60).

Lucas's revision of an exclusionary Oedipal model of identity is the figurative meaning of not only the immersion scene but also the events that immediately follow. He summons Chick to follow him home to Molly, an ancient mother figure, "a tiny old almost doll-sized woman" (10). In this context, "home" signifies as both a return to a precultural existence and a return of the marginalized mother, the first to be made other. Whereas in the psychoanalytic narrative the father and mother are oppositional figures, in this scene Lucas is the key figure as Chick experiences a breakdown of alterity associated with the pre-Oedipal mother. Within Lucas's house, in a scene marked by images of enclosure and incorporation, Chick strips naked and is "enveloped in [a] quilt like a cocoon" (11); then, his thoughts flow back to his early years, which are described in terms evocative of an early undifferentiated stage. He recalls times "spent . . . in Paralee's, Aleck Sander's mother's cabin . . . where . . . Paralee would cook whole meals for them halfway between two meals at the house and he and Aleck Sander would eat them together, the food tasting the same to each" (12).

The scene within Lucas's house suggests a model of boundary formation based in a tension between inclusion and exclusion. In the psychoanalytic narrative of our induction into a social order, the father represents difference (he is different from the first figure with whom we identify, the mother) and introduces separation (the mother is excluded). In this scene, the same paradigm applies in a reinterpreted form. Lucas is unmistakably a father figure—his gold toothpick and beaver hat make him the image of Chick's grandfather, the personification of paternal authority—and he replaces the mother: throughout the scene, "there stood over him still . . . the man" (12); however, this induction into culture is not so much the complete break that binary logic demands as it is a substitution. The images of incorporation, the enclosing house, and Molly's presence in the background all argue that an original attachment to the mother is not completed banished. But that maternal identification is not threatening precisely because the father, Lucas, is there, and his presence marks a difference. Lucas marks a boundary that both divides and attaches: he introduces difference—he is different from Molly—but he is also allied with Molly. While, in the Western script too, the father sets a boundary, this revisionary interpretation recognizes that a boundary, a marker of difference, is also a point of contact.

Taken together, these memory scenes of Chick's introduction to Lucas offer an alternative to the definition of fatherhood proposed by a Western mind-set intent on establishing exclusive, polarized meanings. In Lacan's identity narrative, for example, curiously, the father, who replaces the banished mother, "can only be the effect of a pure signifier" or "the dead father" (199) in that he represents only absence. This definition arises out of the seeming need for a vacuum to allow for absolute separation between binary meanings; and this, according to Lacan, is the father's role. This scene in *Intruder* suggests an alternative reading of the same paradigm—namely, that the father is the mother's uncanny double. In this scene, while Lucas clearly is father, he is a father who shares a relation with Molly, an ancient maternal figure. His relationship with her is symbolized in the text by the hearth fire, which he lit on the night of their wedding and which has burned continuously all the years since, an outward sign of their commitment to one another; and, throughout the scene in the house, Lucas stands "straddled before the fire" (14). The word "straddled" here points to the father's role in the development of a separate identity and differential meanings: like a boundary, the father "straddles" culture's polarities like male and female, black and white. Difference does not have to be a function of absence. Transformation and substitution also mark a difference, the difference necessary for meaning in culture; and the father is the first substitute, the figure who introduces us into the realm of culture and language, where the sign is both not the signified but related to the signified.

Because Lucas straddles culture's binary ordering, he is difficult to read. His way of making meaning is fearful to us, because the fluid, transformative in-between threatens autonomy and self-identity. But, at this point in the narrative, the text insists that the father introduces boundaries by risking the in-between where his presence marks a boundary in a contact zone. A compelling illustration of Lucas's variant interpretation of boundary formation appears in the form of a rambling, clause-laden, nearly unpunctuated description of Lucas's house:

> and now they were in no well-used tended lane leading to tenant or servant quarters and marked by walking feet but a savage gash half gully and half road mounting a hill with an air solitary independent and intractable too and then he saw the house, the cabin . . . the paintless wooden house, the paintless picket fence whose paintless latchless gate the man kneed open still without stopping . . . , the four of them walking in what was less than walk because its surface was dirt too yet more than path, the footpacked strip running plumbline straight between two borders of tin cans and empty bottles and shards of china and earthenware set into the ground, up to the

paintless steps and the paintless gallery along whose edge sat more cans but larger—empty gallon buckets which had once contained molasses or perhaps paint and wornout water or milk pails and one five-gallon can for kerosene with its top cut off and half of what had once been somebody's (Edmonds' without doubt) kitchen hot water tank sliced longways like a banana—out of which flowers had grown last summer and from which the dead stalks and the dried and brittle tendrils still leaned and drooped, and beyond this the house itself, gray and weathered and not so much paintless as independent of and intractable to paint so that the house was not only the one possible continuation of the stern untended road but was its crown too as the carven ailanthus leaves are the Greek column's capital. (8–9)

Houses, Freud tells us, are a symbol for the self; Lucas's house functions as an identificatory imago. Reading the image, one immediately remarks a correspondence: the same words used repeatedly to describe Lucas, "independent and intractable," also describe his house. We note as well that the house is repeatedly and emphatically characterized as "paintless." The metaphor is easily worked out. Like his house, which is "independent of and intractable to paint," he is proof against culture's exclusive either-or oppositions. How, then, does he distinguish a self? Like a disguised meaning out of the unconscious mind, the image of his house points the way to differential meanings that arise in a site of interplay.

The passage appears to be an attempt to wrench language, the medium of the symbolic order, so as to simulate the in-betweenness of a border zone. The description is characterized by teeming, even overwhelming presence. Nothing is left out, and no single item dominates. Because of a lack of containment, there is disorder, overflow, blurred distinctions. For example, the description of Lucas's house is both what it is and something else; that is, it is at one and the same time a description of the house and a description of the path, the hill, the fence, the gate, the walkway, the tin cans, the empty bottles, the shards of china, and much more. In this same way, the road, the gate, and the walkway also do not seem to be coincident with themselves. The road to the house is "half gully and half road"; the gate is both gate and "latchless"; the walkway is "less than walk . . . yet more than path." Each item is an item in a series, a part of an overarching whole. The key point, however, is that while continuity blurs distinctions, it does not efface them: the road, gate, walk, and house do not cease to signify. Cultural meanings are produced by a difference within a relationship. The image signifies that, contrary to our fears, the "I" can be "I" and still acknowledge relationships, like the child in the mirror stage who locates a self by means of a mirroring m/other; like Lucas's house, which is both "the one possible continuation of the stern untended road" and "its crown"; like Lucas himself, who "straddles" the fearful in-between where culture's exclusive either-or oppositions interface, but who is nonetheless "composed" (13).

The Uncanny Double

Lucas's rejection of a Western notion that exclusionary tactics alone preserve cultural boundaries is the veiled meaning of the "job" of exhumation, which he "offers" to Chick. Critics have frequently faulted Lucas for refusing to take action (Weinstein 125; Morris and Morris 235); these critics have overlooked the enormity of the central act of the novel, the exhumation of the dead, which is ordained by Lucas. The retrieval of the buried body signifies a fearful breakdown of self-defining boundaries. Whereas, according to the psychoanalytic narrative, the father is father by dint of ordering exclusion (or burying), Lucas is a father who directs Chick to reclaim (or exhume) what has been shut out. As the text has revealed, a binary model, which creates dominant and subordinated positions, engenders Oedipal violence, such as the murder of Vinson and the mob frenzy to lynch Lucas.[7] The "job" of disinterment symbolizes the way out of this deadly cycle: it symbolizes both an unburying of unthinkable fears and desires and an opening of the self to the excluded other. But Lucas's alternative to the dialectics of domination poses deadly risks to subjectivity. In effect, Lucas summons Chick to confront the borderline, "where meaning collapses" (2), and risk a breakdown of alterity. In the scene of the midnight graveyard exhumation, all of the horrors of what Kristeva calls the abject, "the place of banishment" (*Powers* 2), are strikingly dramatized.

Prior to this point in the narrative, the text has critiqued the psychoanalytic identity narrative, which is based in the dialectics of domination, but, arguably, when it becomes Chick's "job" to imitate Lucas and to be the go-between between self and other, this work seems to be fictively rendered in accordance with the Freudian perspective. For Freud and Lacan, the breakdown of alterity is anathema; it threatens psychic stability and prefigures only death. Previously in the text, we have seen Lucas and Nub Gowrie face this threat with equanimity: for example, on the night when the whole town is awake and awaits the imminent lynching, Lucas sleeps peacefully in his jail cell; similarly, without a thought for himself, Nub Gowrie leaps into deadly quicksand to save his dead son. However, when Chick is called to disinter the buried term in the dialectic and, in effect, faces what Kristeva calls "the erotic, death-bearing unconscious . . . a projection . . . of the death drive" (*Strangers* 192), the text envisions this opening of the self to the other in accordance with the Freudian/Lacanian script, which equates border transgression only with annihilation and which makes of the mother a figure out of a child's nightmare.[8]

Throughout the graveyard scene of disinterment, a troubling alignment of the mother with death persists. The retrieval of the buried corpse, which symbolizes a return to the borderline, "at the border of my condition as a living being" (*Powers* 3), begins promisingly with the appearance of Miss Habersham. In a novel where maternal figures are shadowy, marginalized figures, in this scene of disinterment, Miss Habersham, who, in her old-fashioned hat, reminds Chick of his dead grandmother, is foregrounded. Thereafter, however, this recognition of the mother's presence seems to be evoked as a dissolution of subjectivity in a gruesome maternal embrace. The portrait of Miss Habersham in *Intruder* bears comparison with her previous incarnation as Miss Worsham in *Go Down, Moses*. In that novel's closing section, "Go Down, Moses," Miss Worsham crosses culturally defined racial boundaries to join with Mollie Beauchamp and her family members as they mourn the death of Mollie's grandson in a grieving, unbroken circle around the hearth fire, "the ancient symbol of human coherence and solidarity" (361). In striking contrast to Gavin Stevens, who ignominiously runs from this death observance, Miss Worsham signals her acceptance of a solidarity that threatens cultural boundaries when she says to Stevens, "It's our grief" (363). In *Intruder*, once again Stevens and Miss Habersham are contrasted, and again this paradigm applies. By presiding over the opening of the grave, symbolically Miss Habersham bravely risks a dissolution of the I that Stevens, who asks, "how risk it?" (79), fearfully refuses.

This same maternal willingness to cross the boundary between self and other, even if it means risking death, is pictured in the Pietà, but whereas that image honors a love that is not daunted by death, in this graveyard scene, the mother figure inspires terror and seems to be blamed for the breakdown of alterity. While the text recognizes that Miss Habersham is braver than Stevens, that she seeks to protect the boys from death, that, in fact, she attempts to substitute herself for them as she asks them to walk behind her, nevertheless, in this scene, the effect of her willingness to take death on herself is a troubling identification of the mother with death, the same identification that is inscribed in the Freudian/Lacanian master narrative.[9] For example, as Chick and his black foster brother dig, they are described as "children" standing waist-deep in a pit, which is imaged as a maw that threatens to devour them: they stand "invisible to one another above the pit's inky yawn" (127). The message that the mother is the bearer of death is suggested again when Chick trains his flashlight on a tombstone and reads the engraved name of the mother of the corpse as if the dead man were buried in her. It is implied yet again when Chick "look[s] up out of a halfway rifled grave" and "see[s] as always Miss Habersham in motionless silhouette on the sky above him" (101). A "motionless silhouette" and the object of Chick's gaze, Miss Habersham is represented as Chick's double, his mirror image. This doubling is comparable to another: the doubling of the mother and the father that occurs when Nub Gowrie takes on the mother's role as he embraces his dead child. But the similarity only calls attention to a striking contrast: whereas Nub fearlessly risks himself when he leaps into quicksand to retrieve his dead son, Chick seems gripped by horror as he digs up the body of another buried son.

The text also seems to reinscribe the masculinist Lacanian interpretation of border crossing when the opening of the casket is evoked as a sexual climax. Aleck Sander "thrust[s]" the board into the dirt with increasing rapidity, in a repeated motion that is accompanied by his accelerating breathing: "and [Chick] could hear the *chuck!* and then the faint swish as Aleck Sander thrust the board into the dirt and then flung the load up and outward, expelling his breath, saying 'Hah!' each time—a sound furious raging and restrained, going faster and faster until the ejaculation was almost as rapid as the beat of someone running: 'Hah! . . . Hah! . . . Hah!'" (101). This sexual imagery, the hallmark of Lacan's notion of *jouissance,* seems to record rather than to revise the traditional male narrative of subjectivity. *Jouissance,* in French, literally means sexual orgasm, and Lacan employs the sexual term to describe the satisfaction of what Freud calls the death instinct. Lacan's appropriation of the sexual term seems to equate sexual intercourse with death for a man. For Lacan, *jouissance,* the act of identification with the alienated other/mother, is always "de trop" (323), too much; that is, it is the death gasp of the dissolving subject.

Finally, a disturbing symbology attends the opening of the coffin. To enter the coffin, Chick lowers himself into the hole, stretches himself out above the coffin, "balanc[es]" himself above it, and "straddle[s]" (102) it. Posed in this way, when Chick raises the lid, the corpse becomes his mirror image or double. The "straddling" that Chick is called to here is the father's role as modeled by Lucas when he stood "straddled" (14) before the hearth fire, the symbol of his relationship to Mollie. But when Chick attempts to assume the middle ground where binary meanings interface, this border crossing is evoked as an all-unwelcome Freudian uncanny moment, when a disguised formation of the unthinkable—our own death-bound existence—is recognized and is banished even in the moment of recognition.

In this uncanny moment, the novel's central meaning, which is buried under layer after layer of denial, is recovered—transformed like a dream image. When Chick figuratively merges with the corpse of the stranger, Jake Montgomery, they are doubled, and this doubling signifies that the stranger is not strange, but the disguised, returned trace of feelings that Chick disowns. To recover these denied feelings, we must resolve a series of displacements. Jake, who is Chick's double, is a displaced substitute for Vinson, since Jake's corpse has replaced Vinson's. Vinson, in turn, is Crawford's double, the figure of what he denies, since Crawford kills Vinson as a way to act out his Oedipal fears and desires. If we work our way through this series of displacements, we see that, by way of Jake and Vinson, Crawford is Chick's double twice removed. Crawford, who figures in the novel only as a "shadow" seen by Chick, is Chick's shadow. Crawford, the malevolent son who kills his brother, is the double of Chick *Mallison;* and this doubling suggests that Crawford's story, itself all scrambled in the manner of a dream image, is Chick's story, the disguised return of Chick's own will to power and dread of powerlessness, which he must either consciously own or bury again, a repression that, in Freud's words, "produces substitute formations" (*SE* 14: 154).[10]

Gavin Stevens and the Rhetoric of Race

In a novel that buries and retrieves meanings, in its last third, the text seems to rebury what Lucas and Chick have labored to uncover as it now foregrounds Lawyer Stevens, who counters the text's subversive content with a thinly veiled argument for enforcing racial polarization. Taking for his subject the timely issue of integration in the South—in 1948 President Truman was urging Congress to adopt his civil rights program—Stevens, in a seemingly interminable stream of convoluted rhetoric, argues the "Go slow, now" delay tactics of Southern resistance to integration. At a symbolic level, his running commentary works to reassert the dialectics of domination, which, up to this point, the novel has critiqued.

Because of correspondences between Stevens's pronouncements and Faulkner's own public statements on racial issues, from the time of its initial publication, many reviewers and critics of *Intruder in the Dust* have read Gavin Stevens as Faulkner's spokesperson.[11] For his part, Faulkner denied that Stevens is an authorial surrogate;[12] and a number of scholars have quite rightly warned against "read[ing] backwards from the public statements into the fiction" (Polk 140), a questionable and problematic move in any case and particularly in this instance, since, within the text, Stevens's line of reasoning is arguably discredited. That said, how do we account for the striking similarities between Stevens's pronouncements and Faulkner's? In my reading, this similarity is the effect of a common intent: both Faulkner's political statements and the lawyer's intrusive rhetorical posturing issue the same defense of a racial hierarchy composed by advancing the one by subordinating the other, which in earlier scenes the text has challenged. To counter that critique and to restore white dominance in a racial binary, Faulkner draws on the specious rhetoric he uses in public forums to argue to postpone integration, a delay tactic that masks an argument for racial segregation as the support of white identity. As Wesley and Barbara Morris write, "It is the logic of difference that justifies (like a myth) the 'not yet ready' argument of modern racism" (235). Because both Stevens and Faulkner are mounting a similar argument, a veiled defense of enforcing polarized racial relations, and *not* because I mean to suggest that correspondences between the character's and the author's arguments privilege Stevens's voice, I interpret together the latent content of Faulkner's and Stevens's "not yet ready" rationalizations.

If we read Faulkner's and Lawyer Stevens's convoluted and coded language for disguised meanings, we find that both are making the case for an autonomous, separate, Southern identity. For instance, the emphatically repeated message of both voices is a rejection of Northern "interference" as a threatening incursion by "outlanders" (199) on an intact, separate South. In his interview with Russell Howe, for example, Faulkner adamantly insists that the South must "be let alone" (Meriwether and Millgate 263) to deal with racial injustice in its own way and on its own terms: "don't force us," he says (259). Similarly, in *Intruder*, Gavin Stevens expostulates, "I only say that the injustice is ours, the South's. We must expiate and abolish it ourselves, alone and without help, nor even (with thanks) advice" (199). It should be noted that, in his public statements, Faulkner expressed the opinion that "inequality was artificial" ("On Fear" 99) and that "equality is inevitable, an irresistible force" (Meriwether and Millgate 260). At the same time, however, the defensiveness of Faulkner's and Stevens's emphatic insistence on non-intervention from "outsiders," suggests both a fear of this "irresistible" equality and a desire to resist it. Perhaps the starkest example of this defensive, separatist posture is Faulkner's statement, made during the Howe interview and later publicly recanted, that if he were forced to by interfering outsiders, he would "fight for Mississippi against the United States even if it meant going out into the street and shooting Negroes" (261).[13]

That Faulkner and Stevens are, in fact, arguing to preserve white dominance in a racial binary is the veiled subtext of a frequently reiterated theme of their discourse: both invoke regional loyalty to a "homogeneous South" to justify postponing racial equality.[14] In the following passage, the "homogeneous South" functions as a code word for "white South":

> It's because we alone in the United States (I'm not speaking of Sambo right now; I'll get to him in a minute) are a homogeneous people. . . . So we are not really resisting what the outland calls (and we too) progress and enlightenment. We are defending not actually our politics or beliefs or even our way of life, but simply our homogeneity from a federal government to which the rest of this country has had to surrender. . . . Only a few of us know that only from homogeneity comes anything of a people or for a people of durable and lasting value. . . . That's why we must resist the North: not just to preserve ourselves. (150–51)

Stevens contends that racial integration poses a threat to Southern homogeneity. "Homogeneity," of course, refers to a uniform people. In what sense are diverse Southerners uniform? Stevens's intrusive parentheses and his offensive term "Sambo" provide the answer. In describing Southern homogeneity, Stevens must bracket off "Sambo" because it is "Sambo's" very exclusion that defines a "Southern" homogeneous identity. Within the context of a binary opposition, certain Southerners can be identified as homogeneous, that is, white, if others are characterized as different from them because these others are like "Sambo." "Sambo" is of course a racial stereotype, a white man's image of a black man as care-free, irresponsible, and childish. In a text where Lucas has refused to be "a nigger," "Sambo" seems to function as a euphemism for "nigger." With this racial stereotype, Stevens uses language to create a racial binary, a white man/"Sambo" polarity, and, in this last third of the novel, as Stevens builds a world of words, we see the terrible power of representations to characterize and even determine identity.

Fear of a loss of white dominance in a racial dialectic drives Stevens's and Faulkner's "go slow" rhetoric. In the lawyer's impassioned advocacy of Southerners' "homogeneity," a fear of common ground is thinly masked by a negative construction. Freud explains that a prohibited meaning may make its way into consciousness if it is negated (*SE* 19: 239). An illustration of such a negative construction is Stevens's assertion, "That's why we must resist the North: not just to preserve ourselves." Disavowed by "not," Stevens voices his fear that racial integration will signify the obliteration of an autonomous white identity. This same fear emerges in Faulkner's public statements on race. In the aptly titled essay "On Fear," for example, in a sentence so convoluted and clause-burdened as to obscure his meaning, the fear that racial equality will mean the end to white identity appears buried in a negative construction: "White people in the South . . . will—must— . . . grasp at such straws for weapons as contumely and threat and insult to change the views or anyway the voice which dares to suggest that betterment of the Negro's condition does not necessarily presage the doom of the white race" (95). Even more explicitly, the fear of white annihilation surfaces in the course of the Russell Howe interview, when Faulkner blurts out, "Shall we obliterate the persecutor?" (Meriwether and Millgate 261). In this context, we see why Southern "homogeneity" is so prized; the homogeneous South is code for the dominant white race. Whereas integration threatens white hegemony, homogeneity—that is, a white ruling class distinguished by the dialectics of racial domination—holds out the promise of white supremacy, as Stevens claims in the course of a panegyric to homogeneity: one, uniform, and homogeneous, he says, the South will "present a front not only impregnable but not even to be threatened" (153).[15]

Faulkner's conflicted novel, however, does not let stand uncontested Stevens's claim for white invincibility through an artificial racial dialectic. The critical difference between Faulkner's public statements and Stevens's fictional monologue is that, within the text, repressed meanings return reconfigured. The meaning that Stevens refuses returns in the form of an example of his lauded homogeneity, the Gowrie clan, the living embodiment of Stevens's notion of "homogeneity":

> [The Gowries are] integrated and interlocked and intermarried . . . not even into a simple clan or tribe but a race a species which before now had made their hill stronghold good against the county and federal government too, which did not even simply inhabit . . . but had translated and transmogrified that whole region of lonely pine hills . . . where peace officers from town didn't even go unless they were sent for and strange white men didn't wander far from the highway after dark and no Negro at any time—where as a local wit said once the only stranger ever to enter with impunity was God and He only by daylight and on Sunday—into a synonym for independence and violence: an idea with physical boundaries like a quarantine for plague so that solitary unique and alone out of all the county it was known to the rest of the county by the number of its survey co-ordinate—Beat Four. (35)

"Interlocked and intermarried," the Gowrie clan epitomizes a homogeneous identity produced by exclusion; and, within the clan, the Gowrie twins are a subset who even more strikingly represent homogeneity. No two human beings could be more alike than the identical Gowrie twins. They are as "identical as two clothing store dummies" (159); as "identical as two clothes pins on a line, the identical faces even weathered exactly alike" (160). When they dismount a mule, "they got down as one, at the same time even" (160). As the text's leading example of "identicalness," we might expect them to model the invincibility that Stevens hopes issues from uniformity; instead, through doubling, the twins function to undercut the homogeneity argument. The Gowrie twins, who ride double on the same mule that, on the night of the murder, carried Crawford Gowrie with his murdered brother flung across the saddle, are doubles for the murderer and his victim. This doubling of the two pairs of brothers formulates the unspeakable meaning that Vinson was not murdered by a rejected "outlander," but by someone as like him as Gowrie twin is like Gowrie twin.

Through this doubling, the novel leaks the message that, no matter how exclusively we draw the boundaries that define "us," we are never safe; a murderous impulse always lurks inside the border, engendered by the very binary logic that encourages us to exclude and dominate in the name of self-preservation. The text of *Intruder in the Dust* withholds or buries the knowledge that Vinson was murdered by his brother, because this fratricide suggests that a Western model of binary thinking, which seeks to empower the one by dominating or, to use Freud's term, "castrating" the other, does not make us "invincible," as Gavin Stevens idly dreams; rather, it incites a power struggle among brothers.

Ned Barnett and Lucas Beauchamp

Intruder in the Dust, which begins so promisingly, ends disappointingly. In the end, the text's critique of a white, male difference—Lacan's "phallic difference"—defined by the dialectics of domination is buried along with Vinson's corpse and the newly dead Crawford Gowrie, who is disposed of with a brief reference to his jail cell suicide. Former boundary transgressions are swept aside, and the status quo is restored. The sign of this restoration is a change in Chick, who, in the final scene, seems almost to metamorphose into his uncle. The novel has always been the story of Chick's induction into manhood and the social order, a rite of passage that he navigates with the guidance of two father figures: Uncle Gavin Stevens, the spokesperson for maintaining racial polarization, and Lucas Beauchamp, a borderland father who straddles the risky middle between culture's black and white identities. In the end, Chick must choose between them, and he chooses whiteness secured by dichotomization, as we expected he would, since, for Chick, unburying, symbolizing a border transgression, always seemed to be tantamount only to death.

The novel's end recalls its beginning. In both the opening and the concluding scenes, Lucas is the object of Chick's gaze, and this similarity focuses our attention on a striking difference. In the opening pages, Chick, who has fallen into a creek, "look[s] up" (6) from the icy water to see "a man" (7) above him. In the final pages, he "look[s] down into the Square" (229) from his uncle's office window and sees Lucas below him. Perhaps even more to the point, Chick and his uncle now have a shared perspective: "And that was when they saw Lucas crossing the Square, probably at the same time" (234). The symbolism is transparent: Chick, who formerly had opposed his uncle's racial views and had accused him of "defend[ing] the lynchers" (199), now has internalized his uncle's way of seeing.

The last chapter, which brings together Lucas, Stevens, and Chick in Stevens's law office, seems designed to reassert the dialectics of racial domination, which formerly had been subverted in the text. Whereas, in the opening scene of the novel, Chick repeatedly identifies Lucas as "a man" (7–16), in the closing one, Stevens works hard to deny manhood to Lucas. For example, before Lucas can speak, Stevens tries to take command: "You didn't come here for me to tell you what to do so I'm going to tell you anyway" (235). By "tell[ing]" Lucas "what to do," Stevens is claiming agency for himself, at the other man's expense. Lucas has come to the law office as a client to pay his bill, but Stevens refuses payment because both men know that, were the lawyer to accept money from the other man, he would be treating Lucas as an equal. Finally, to get rid of Lucas, Stevens accepts a token payment, but he treats it as a joke. He explains that he will take two dollars to pay for a pen point found broken when "[he] came to again" after repeatedly "trying . . . to get . . . sense out of . . . all the different things you finally told me" (239). The scene takes a turn for the worse when Lucas attempts to pay part of his bill with a sack of fifty pennies, and Stevens insists that Lucas count the pennies. As Chick and the amused Stevens observe, Lucas counts each coin, "one by one moving each one with his forefinger into the first mass of dimes and nickels, counting aloud" (240). The purpose of this penny-count clearly is to make the old man look like the "Sambo" of Stevens's racial stereotyping, and we see now, if we hadn't already, that Stevens is no different from all the other "homogeneous" white men in Jefferson, who are driven by a compulsion to "make a nigger" out of Lucas so as to establish their own high estate as white men.

Despite Stevens's best efforts to do so, the novel does not conclude with the dialectics of domination reaffirmed, because Lucas is proof against the lawyer's wordplay just as he was proof against the lynch mob's tactics. While Chick, now a member of a white community defined by racial exclusion, has changed, Lucas remains "unchanged." When Lucas enters the law office, Chick sees "the same face which he had seen for the first time when he climbed dripping up out of the icy creek that morning four years ago, unchanged, to which nothing had happened since not even age" (235). Lucas is the "same" figure of authority whom, four years ago, the boy "could no more imagine himself contradicting . . . than he could his grandfather" (8), and the difference between the first and last scene is a function of Stevens's and now Chick's refusal to acknowledge Lucas's paternal authority. This denial is shockingly illustrated in the final pages as Stevens uses a racial slur to refer to Lucas: "you violated a white grave to save a nigger" (236), he says to Chick. Set against this attempt to demean him is Lucas's claim of a receipt, a tangible token of their acknowledgment of him as a man and an equal (Millgate 220; Gwin 96; Moreland, "Faulkner's Continuing Education" 67–68; Dussere 54; Towner 33).

I want to conclude by suggesting that Lucas's paternal authority, which Stevens and other white men in the novel work to deny, is itself a signifier for the paternal status of the widely recognized source for Lucas Beauchamp—Ned Barnett. According to Faulkner family lore, Ned Barnett was "a retainer for generations" (Blotner 538); recently, however, Joel Williamson, who has studied census records and other legal documents, disputes the family claim. We know with certainty that Ned Barnett was born in 1865; in 1910 he lived in the village of Ripley just a few doors away from the old colonel's "shadow family"; and from the 1930s until his death in 1947, he worked for William Faulkner, first as a tenant farmer, then as a household servant (Williamson 260–61). Like Lucas, Ned Barnett was a man of notable, unbending dignity, who seemed ageless. But the trait that unmistakably identifies Ned Barnett as the inspiration for Lucas Beauchamp is his practice of wearing the old-fashioned clothes that he inherited from Faulkner's father, grandfather, and great-grandfather (Blotner 52–53). In *Intruder,* the outdated clothes that Lucas wears prompt Chick to identify him with his grandfather. In his semi-autobiographical essay "Mississippi" (1954), Faulkner provides an extended reminiscence of "Uncle" Ned and makes this same identification: "Ned, born in a cabin in the back yard in 1865, in the time of the middleaged's great-grandfather and had outlived three generations of them, who had not only walked and talked so constantly for so many years with the three generations that he walked and talked like them, he had two tremendous trunks filled with the clothes which they had worn . . . so that, glancing idly up and out the library window, the middleaged would see that back, that stride, that coat and hat going down the drive toward the road, and his heart would stop and even turn over" (*Essays* 39). Faulkner recalls here an uncanny experience, a moment when repression breaks down and a denied meaning is recognized. In this reminiscence, the denied meaning that returns is the recognition of Ned Barnett's paternal authority. In the uncanny moment, Faulkner sees that Ned is the double of his dead grandfather. This same meaning, I argue, is the disguised center of *Intruder in Dust.* More specifically, at the center of *Intruder* is the continually banished and returning knowledge that Lucas Beauchamp, who is modeled after

Ned Barnett, achieves patriarchal authority by eschewing a master/slave dialectic and bravely straddling the fluid, transformative middle ground between culture's polarized identities.

Does *Intruder in the Dust* successfully challenge a dominant Western system of meanings defined by exclusion? Because Faulkner's novel is deeply conflicted, the reader, I think, must judge. On the one hand, the novel exposes the deadly cycle of violence generated by the dialectics of domination, and, in the person of Lucas Beauchamp, suggests that the father figure marks a boundary by both attaching and dividing. At the same time, however, the text also opposes Lucas's revisionary inscription of boundary formation. First, as we have seen, Gavin Stevens speaks for the white men in the novel who are committed to a white, male autonomy defined by marginalization of others. In addition, even when Chick emulates Lucas and risks a breakdown of alterity, this border crossing is imagined as solely deadly—a ghoulish envelopment in the nightmare figure of Freud's pre-Oedipal mother. Perhaps more to the point, the novel's subversive content—a critique of a phallic authority defined by domination—is buried under layer after layer of displacement and substitution. One might argue that Faulkner uses an exclusionary system of differential meanings to demonstrate its instability, but it is also possible that, unlike Lucas, Faulkner can find no way to signify outside of culture's either-or meanings. Indeed, the novel's most troubling exclusion may be Faulkner's refusal to acknowledge Ned Barnett's contribution to his work. "Uncle" Ned's widely noted dignity marks him as unquestionably the model for Lucas Beauchamp; and his death in late December of 1947 appears to have prompted Faulkner, in January of 1948, to set aside the novel he was working on to compose *Intruder in the Dust* (Blotner 1243–44, 1246). Similar circumstances, the death of lifetime Faulkner family servant Caroline Barr in 1940, had moved Faulkner to dedicate to her his novel *Go Down, Moses* (1942), which, in many ways, appears to be the counterpart of *Intruder*.[16] Yet despite this precedent and despite the long shadow that Ned Barnett casts over *Intruder in the Dust*, Faulkner did not dedicate it to him. Instead, the novel conspicuously lacks a dedication. It would be ungenerous of readers, however, to fault Faulkner for this omission since, in novel after novel, he rethinks the problem of differential meanings defined by exclusion. Even if *Intruder in the Dust* does not publicly acknowledge its debt to Ned Barnett, still it pays tribute to a man who is not daunted by the risky in-between where culture's polarities interface and where the father's intervention marks a boundary. In the end, perhaps the best we can say is, while *Intruder in the Dust* may fail to challenge a system of meanings based in domination, the novel nonetheless gives us Lucas Beauchamp/Ned Barnett, who unquestionably succeeds in issuing this challenge.

2 Crossing a Racial Border

Richard Wright's *Native Son*

I felt that without a common bond uniting men there could be no living worthy of being called human.

RICHARD WRIGHT, *American Hunger*

Richard Wright's *Native Son* has long been read as a powerful indictment of the warping effects of racial oppression in America. While the fiction's status as one of America's foremost racial protest novels is uncontestable, still the widely accepted interpretation that it denounces racial victimization and condemns a "white American society" that drives Bigger to "a futile, murderous, and self-destructive rebellion" (Kinnamon, "Native Son" 70) leaves unanswered questions.[1] Specifically, Bigger Thomas does not think that the murders of the white woman and the black woman are "futile, murderous, self-destructive" acts. On the contrary, Bigger goes to his death feeling empowered by this violence against women: "I didn't know I was really alive in this world until I felt things hard enough to kill for them," he says to his lawyer, Max. "What I killed for must've been good" (501).[2] Bigger's sense that the murder of women is self-affirming has elicited charges of misogyny. Barbara Johnson, for example, puts the question bluntly: "Does racism explain away the novel's careless misogyny?" (120). And Sherley Anne Williams accuses Wright of fathering "a bastard line, racist misogyny—the denigration of black women as justification for glorifying the symbolic white woman and male narcissism" (395).[3]

My project is to argue that Bigger feels empowered when he kills Mary and Bessie because they threaten him, but we readers have not accurately assessed the threat that each woman poses to him. Of course, Bigger himself insists that he kills to preserve himself, and scholars have often countered that Bessie, who is black and a victim like Bigger, does not seem to pose an imminent, credible threat.[4] I propose that Bigger's sense of urgent danger issues from a psychological threat that Bigger is unable to articulate. Both women trigger Bigger's own feared desire for a "supporting oneness" with others (420), but this drive poses a threat both to his life and to his male identity. The consummation of his sexual desire for the white woman, Mary, constitutes miscegenation, a transgression of black-white boundaries, which is prohibited by the dominant white culture: "They kill us for women like her" (405), Bigger tells Max. And his desire for sexual intercourse with both women, as an inmixing of male and female, threatens his male difference. Both Mary and Bessie invite a desire for sexual union that seems to obscure or even obliterate self-defining borders. This disintegration of the borders between me and not-me is what Julia Kristeva terms abjection. Abjection, she writes, is "the in-between, the ambiguous, the composite." It is "the breaking down of a world that has erased its borders" (*Powers* 4). According to Kristeva, this crossing of borders, as Bigger intuits, is a "real threat"—"it annihilates me" (*Powers* 4, 2)—but at the same time Kristeva insists that this death of the "I" in the other is also "productive" (*Revolution* 16). "'I' am in the process of becoming an other at the expense of my own death. . . . I give birth to myself amid the violence of sobs, of vomit. . . . I abject myself within the same motion through which 'I' claim to establish myself" (*Powers* 3). How is abjection, the breakdown of alterity, "productive"? According to Kristeva, when properly negotiated with the help of a "third party, eventually the father" (*Powers* 13), abjection shatters a sense of individuation and then transforms it so as to allow for cultural exchange, cross-fertilization, and the production of new social identities.

In *Native Son*, Wright explores how racial oppression in America inflects a drive for solidarity with others. Throughout the novel, Bigger Thomas is torn between two seemingly conflicting compulsions. Repeatedly, he expresses a desire to "blot out" (384) a threat; alternatively, he speaks of a desire to be "at home" with others in the world (316, 411). I argue that the threat Bigger is driven to "blot out" is precisely his own deep urge to ally himself with others. As Kristeva points out, a desire to identify with others is fearful to every subject because identification threatens the engulfment of the I in the other that "pulverizes the subject" (*Powers* 5). But for Bigger, a black man in America, the threat is particularly terrifying. As a racialized subject in a white-dominant culture, he is reviled, excluded, and shamed: "They kill you before you die" (409), he tells Max. Given that whites insist on keeping racialized subjects separate and unequal, he senses that his own urgent need to bond with his fellow men and women is deadly. When he kills Mary and Bessie, he is futilely trying to deny or "blot out" a drive to cross boundaries—like the boundary between white and black or male and female—that his sexual desire for them evokes.

Wright's extensive familiarity with Freud is well documented—indeed, his friend Margaret Walker states that Wright was "obsessed with psychoanalysis" (245)—and, in *Native Son*, he reinterprets Freudian theory in a way that bears comparison to Kristeva's feminist revision of Freudian paradigms.[5] In "Beyond the Pleasure Principle," Freud identifies a powerful "organic instinct" to return to an "old state of things" prior to the rise of cultural formations. Determining that this instinct is the "final goal of all organic striving" (45), he calls this drive "the death instinct" and grimly concludes that "the aim of all life is death" (46).

Whereas for Freud this impulse to return to an early stage before individuation represents the triumph of death over life, in *Powers of Horror*, Kristeva seems to rewrite this regressive impulse as a pull toward what she calls "a heterogeneous flow" (10), which is "the death of the ego," but it also precedes "new life, new significance" (15). In *Native Son*, Bigger's urgent need for "a wholeness, a oneness" (490), for a return to a time before, as Bigger puts it, "fear made him live in an element which he reckoned as 'them'" (100) seems to correspond to the regressive instinct that Freud describes and that Kristeva seems to reconceive as abjection. In what follows, I argue that Wright's representation of this urge toward inclusivity seems to anticipate Kristeva's more hopeful interpretation.

From the beginning, women in Wright's fiction must die. When Wright's friend Jane Newton questioned his plotting of Bessie's death in *Native Son*, his response was immediate and unequivocal: "'But I have to get rid of her. She must die!' he insisted" (Fabre 121). The deaths of Bessie Mears and Mary Dalton in *Native Son* conform to a pattern in Wright's fiction that began very early. In *Black Boy*, he describes an early attempt to write a story about "an Indian maiden, beautiful and reserved, who sat alone upon the bank of a still stream." He then admits that, "not knowing how to develop the story, I resolved that the girl had to die" (141); accordingly, he has the Indian maiden commit suicide: she walks out into the water and is engulfed in a "dark stream" (141). Barbara Johnson has addressed this pattern of killing off women in Wright's fiction and attributes it to a lack of "available models for plots" (122) for women of color. Wright biographer Michel Fabre hypothesizes that the female deaths in the fiction are traceable to Wright's mother's lifelong invalidism and her expressed longing for death (31–32). Fabre's invocation of Wright's mother in this context seems to point to Kristeva's theory of abjection.[6] According to Kristeva, an early mother-child intimacy threatens the individual with the collapse of self-defining boundaries. Interpreted in terms of Kristeva's theory, the fates of these women must be death, because, like the mother, who once carried a child in her body, they seem to threaten individuation. The Indian maiden, for example, straddles oppositions: she is neither black nor white; she is associated with "eternal twilight" (141) and with a surrender to a deadly fluidity. In Kristeva's terms, the Indian maiden is a borderline, in-between figure; that is, she invokes "the border of my condition as a living being," "the place where I am not and which permits me to be" (*Powers* 3). As the embodiment of a desire to straddle divisions, the girl "must die" because this straddling is socially proscribed and because the author himself senses that this buried desire to elide culture's polarized oppositions, which continually erupts in his fiction, must be "blotted out" (*Powers* 159).[7]

The Indian maiden is among the first in a series of women in Wright's fiction who seem to figure a pull toward a breakdown of alterity that Kristeva, among others, analyzes.[8] In my reading, this drive, as it is inflected by race, is the focus of *Native Son*. Interpreted this way, Wright's novel engages with a central project of feminist criticism and pushes it in a new direction—so as to consider the effects of racial marginalization. In what follows, I suggest that Mary Dalton and Bessie Mears die because they evoke in Bigger a desire to ally himself with others that threatens gender and race boundaries. This desire is both the subject of *Native Son* and a central thread throughout all of Wright's autobiographical writing. As Fabre suggests, the "hunger" in the original title of Wright's autobiography, *American Hunger*, refers to a lifelong yearning to participate in an American culture that separates white from black (xviii-xix, 97–98). And in "I Tried to Be a Communist," Wright also stresses his need to be "at home" with people of different races and ethnicities. In the essay Wright explains that Communism attracted him because Marxist ideals spoke to the "possibility of uniting scattered but kindred peoples into a whole. It seemed to me that here at last, in the realm of revolutionary expression, Negro experience could find a home, a functioning value and role" (118). In *Native Son*, Wright explores this desire as Bigger seeks to come to terms with his own urgent need to break down the "wall" (120) between white and black and forge a "union" with others that will, at last, "end fear and shame" (130) and confer "identity" (420). While the novel's ending—Bigger's proclamation that "what I killed for must've been good" (501)—articulates a deeply disturbing resolution to the conflict between his desire to be "at home" (316) with others and a need to deny this desire, as I will propose, the novel also maps out an alternative to Bigger's choice, and this other way can be interpreted in terms of Kristeva's theory of the borderline abject.

A White Blur

From the beginning, Wright makes clear that Mary threatens Bigger because she transgresses boundaries. With "her face some six inches from his," she says, "I scare you?" (71); and, while Bigger mumbles "Oh, no'm" (71), Mary does scare him precisely because she is trying to close the gap between them. At a physical level, she wedges herself next to him in the front seat of the car so that their bodies touch. At a psychological level as well, she disturbs him because "she waded right in" (67). Bigger notes the difference between her screen image, which he had viewed in the movie theater before meeting her, and her living presence. On the screen, that is, as imagined in his mind, he has total power over her and she is "not dangerous," but in life she is powerful: "she walked over everything" and "put herself in the way" (62). Repeatedly, he observes that Mary is getting too close, so close that she seems to be inside him: "he felt that she knew every feeling and thought he had" (74); "she was looking inside him and he didn't like it" (92). Throughout the scene that leads up to and precipitates Mary's death by suffocation, distinctions between outside and inside, white woman and black man are breaking down, and this is deeply threatening to him.

Bigger fears Mary because she evokes his own outlawed desire to cross racial boundaries. Repeatedly, he expresses a desire to be "the equal of others" (419) and to find "an identification with some part of the world in which he lived, and this identification forming the basis for a new hope that would function in him as pride and dignity" (317). He longs to reach out and touch others, and "in that touch, response of recognition, there would be union, identity; there would be a supporting oneness, a wholeness which had been denied him all his life" (420). This identification would seem to be precisely what Mary and Jan offer. Jan, for example, reaches out to shake hands with Bigger and insists, "You're a man just like I am; I'm no better than you" (80). Similarly, Mary tries to overpass the cultural interdiction that separates them: "She responded to him as if he were human, as if he lived in the same world as she. And he had never felt that before in a white person" (74). At the same time, her closeness inspires in him fear and an urgent need to "blot out": "Suddenly he wanted to seize some heavy object . . . and in some strange way rise up and stand in naked space above the speeding car and with one final blow blot it out—with himself and them in it" (80). With their terror tactics, a white racist culture has instilled in Bigger a dread of his own desire for closeness with whites, and it is this desire, which Mary and Jan have elicited, that Bigger wants to "blot out" so as to create a "naked space" between him and them.

In addition to invoking a forbidden desire for a transgression of racial boundaries, Mary's closeness to Bigger endangers gender difference. This danger is also posed by the women who are closest to him. Just as Bigger resents Mary because she transgresses boundaries, he rages against the females in his family for being "too close." On the morning after Mary's death, he wakes early and tries to leave, but "the bed on which his mother and sister slept stand[s] squarely in the way" (112). Like Mary, who "put herself in the way" (62), his mother and sister are "in the way"; and, like Mary, they inspire in him a desire to "blot out": "Goddam! He wanted to wave his hand and blot them out. They were always too close to him, so close that he could never have any way of his own" (112). As if to drive home the parallel, his anger with his mother and sister seems to turn his thoughts to his decapitation of Mary: "There hovered before his eyes an image of Mary's head lying on the wet newspapers, the curly black ringlets soaked with blood" (112). The proximity of this image to his urge to "blot out" his mother and sister suggests that, like his mother and sister, Mary represents a female fluidity that threatens "a way of his own."

When Bigger suffocates Mary, he is trying to exorcise his own socially proscribed desire to couple with the white girl. As JanMohamed explains in his Freudian reading of the scene of Mary's "accidental" death, Mary is "the highly desirable sexual object [who] is simultaneously proffered and prohibited to the general public but particularly prohibited to black men." Accordingly, when Bigger initiates sex with the white girl, Jan-Mohamed rightly observes that Bigger is violating "a racialized Oedipal injunction" (83) or, alternatively stated, crossing a forbidden white-black border. Certainly the scene in Mary's bedroom is unmistakably moving toward a desired sexual climax. With his arms "tight" around Mary and his lips "pressed tightly against hers," Bigger feels "her body moving strongly" against his. And then this intercourse is aborted and Mary is killed because of the appearance of the "white blur," the spectral form of Mary's blind mother who enters the room. For JanMohamed, the white blur is the racialized gaze that transforms the sex drive into a death drive, because "the racialized production of [Bigger's] subjectivity" has caused "eros" to be "totally displaced by the fear induced by thanatos," with the result that Bigger "has, in effect, been totally captured by the death drive" (100–101).

Unlike JanMohamed, who proposes that a white culture has so terrorized Bigger that "fear and hate are the only affects that provide the cathectic glue that binds and, hence, produces Bigger as a subject" (*Death-Bound Subject* 100), I would argue that eros and fear—or a desire to open the self to the other and a fear of this dangerous desire—are continually in conflict in Bigger, and the war between desire and fear is metaphorically represented in "the white blur." As JanMohamed points out, the white blur produces the sexualized scene of Mary's death. Just as Bigger is about to act on an overwhelming desire for intercourse with Mary, when he "was aware only of her body now," he suddenly "stiffen[s]" as a "hysterical terror seized him," and this terror takes the form of a "white blur . . . standing by the door, silent, ghostlike" that "filled his eyes and gripped his body" (97). In the ensuing deadly, sexualized scene, Bigger acts in the "grip" of a "terror" of a "white blur" and the desperate need to rid himself of the suffocating fear that the white blur might "touch him" (97). Driven by fear, Bigger smothers Mary in an act that simulates sexual intercourse. Certainly the text suggests that the "white blur" is Bigger's own fear of whites; "his eyes were filled with the white blur" (98), and clearly the fear is white because Bigger fears a white world. Moreover, in "How Bigger Was Born," Wright describes his own experience with a white blur, "a mental censor . . . draped in white," and he defines it as an internalized dread of whites, "product of the fears which a negro feels from living in America" (523). But Wright also stresses in *Native Son* that this fear is experienced as a "blur," and the word "blur" suggests that Bigger fears the blurring of self and other, black and white, male and female that intercourse with the white girl signifies. In the scene, Bigger seems to split up the desire and the fear of this desire, and he seems to project on Mary his forbidden desire for the white girl, while he projects on her mother his terror of this desire. In this way, Mrs. Dalton comes to represent "the white blur," his own terror of transgressing the boundary between white and black. This interpretation opens up the symbolic level of Bigger's fear of being touched by Mrs. Dalton even as he is touching her daughter. At a literal level, Bigger fears that the blind woman's touch will reveal his presence; at a symbolic level, he fears her touch because touching represents the feared and desired bonding with others that is forbidden to him by the dominant white culture.[9]

I propose that, in a perverse way, Mary's sexualized murder works temporarily to address Bigger's conflict between desire and fear. The accidental combination of sex and death satisfies both his needs, his desire to couple with Mary and his compulsion to disown—or kill—this feared desire. As countless critics have noted, the suffocation of Mary is described in terms evocative of sexual intercourse—Mary's body "surge[s]" and "heave[s]" (98) beneath his own as he pushes downward on the pillow. At the same time, his need to resist an insupportable fear is also evoked in sexually suggestive terms: "Frenzy dominated him. . . . Mrs. Dalton was moving slowly toward him and he grew tight and full, as though about to explode" (97). Then, when he accidentally kills Mary, he finds himself free of fear—"He felt that he had been in the grip of a weird spell and was now free" (99)—and his freedom from fear is also described in terms suggestive of detumescence following an ejaculation. After Mary's death at his hands, he is "relaxed," "crouched," and "bent" (86). For the first time in his life, Bigger has banished fear, because he has worked out on Mary's body his conflicting needs to transgress social boundaries and to "blot out" this same forbidden desire.

The reprieve from fear that Bigger experiences following Mary's death, however, is short-lived. Assessing the effect on him of the accidental or unconsciously motivated murder, he finds that "the thought of what he had done, the awful horror of it, . . . formed for him for the first time in his fear-ridden life a barrier of protection between him and a world he feared" (118–19). Mary's death forms "a barrier of protection" because he has made her the site of his own desire and then symbolically disowned his desire with the incineration of her body. But this displacement only represses an urgent need for engagement with others.[10] According to Freud, repressed material always returns in a new, altered form (*SE* 14: 154). In the case of Bigger's fear, "the white blur" returns in the form of Mrs. Dalton's white cat, which trails him as he decapitates and incinerates Mary's body. For example, when Bigger has to lift Mary's dead body, he is brought to the edge of existence, where "death infect[s] life" (*Powers* 4), and his fear again takes the form of the white blur: as he takes the corpse in his arms, he "involuntarily jerked his head round and saw a white blur . . . and his body was instantly wrapped in a sheet of blazing terror and a hard ache seized his head and then the white blur went away" (102). The last appearance of the white cat, which has been cast in the text as "the white blur," drives home that the white blur is a projection of Bigger's own fear of self-annihilation. In this final image, the white cat "leaped upon Bigger's shoulders and sat perched there like a second head" (257) as the newspaperman snaps a picture. As Bigger's second head, the cat/white blur is Bigger's double or alter ego, the representation of his own denied fear of border crossing that shadows him.

"A White Thread Stretching Out over a Vast Black Gulf"

Readers and scholars of *Native Son* have been appalled and bewildered by Bigger's seemingly deliberate rape and murder of Bessie. Whereas Mary is the very symbol of a white world that terrorizes him so that he cannot live, Bessie, like Bigger, is black and a victim of white oppression. And whereas Bigger is not consciously aware that he is murdering Mary, textual evidence—such as the mental note he makes of the brick in the room of the empty tenement building—suggests that he plans Bessie's murder. Also, as previously noted, his insistence that he has no choice but to murder Bessie is unconvincing and seems to mask a subliminal motivation. In my reading, Bigger is moved to rape and kill Bessie so as to project on her the conflict between his desire and his fear of his desire.

Because Bessie evokes in Bigger an urge to be "at one" with others, he is driven to act out on her body his conflicting feelings. She triggers in him a desire to overpass boundaries between self and other: sex with Bessie "made him feel that he did not need to long for a home now" (154). While intercourse with Bessie fulfills his need to be "at home" with others, coitus also seems to collapse the gender distinction between him and her and thus to threaten abjection, a loss of self-defining boundaries. In addition, Bigger fears his desire for Bessie because in her he sees embodied a haunting sense of a lack of self-coherence, which a dominant white culture seeks to project on the racialized other. These conflicting feelings explain Bigger's sense that there are two Bessies: "one a body that he had just had and wanted badly again" and the other, which he associates with her face and wants to "blot out, kill, sweep away" (159–60). Bessie's body becomes for him the site of his overwhelming need for solidarity with others; her head becomes the image of his resistance to this need.

Bigger's rape and murder of Bessie simultaneously satisfies and punishes a dreaded, forbidden desire to transgress boundaries. Once again, like Mary's "accidental" death, the scene of Bessie's murder joins sex and death. Whereas Bigger metaphorically rapes Mary as he suffocates her, Bigger literally rapes Bessie and then murders her. And once again, in this configuration of a scene of sex and death, a "white blur" drives Bigger to kill, but this time the observing witness, the "white blur," is Bigger's own fantasy image. More specifically, to bring himself to kill Bessie, he has to call up in his mind the white blur: "He had to stand here until that picture came back, that motive, that driving desire to escape the law. . . . A sense of the white blur hovering near, of Mary burning, of Britten, of the law tracking him down came back. Again, he was ready" (273–74). The imagined nature of the witness to the scene is telling. To drive himself to kill, Bigger has to feel once again the terror of imminent self-annihilation, but in this instance there is no witness. Bigger is both transgressor and censor, and this double role acts out his conflicting desires. In this way Wright makes clear that when Bigger rapes and kills Bessie, he displaces onto her body both his compulsion to transgress the boundary between them and his equally urgent need to "blot out" this forbidden, terrifying desire.

This interpretation of Bigger's drive to rape and kill Bessie is also implied in the text by imagery that connects her with the white cat, which had been cast in the text as a "white blur" (105). After killing Bessie, Bigger dreads looking at her and finding "those round large black eyes, her bloody mouth open in awe and wonder and pain and accusation" (259). This description allies her with the white cat, which in the newspaper photograph had "perched upon [Bigger's] right shoulder, its big round black eyes twin pools of secret guilt" (259). This pairing of Bessie with the white cat, Bigger's "second head" or double, supports Bigger's contention, at the novel's end, that when he killed, he "was trying to do something else" (496). When he pounds Bessie's head with a brick, he is trying to stamp out his own seemingly life-threatening desire for a blurring of culture's oppositions that is symbolized by the white blur.

At a latent level, the text suggests that Bigger's tactic of projection and displacement of a dangerous desire is the means not to self-preservation but to self-destruction. After raping Bessie, Bigger waits for her to fall deeply asleep before he carries out his plan to kill her. In the darkness, he listens to her breathing. When she stirs and her "deep, regular breathing had stopped," he "stiffened" with fear and thinks of her breath "as a white thread stretching out over a vast black gulf and felt that he was clinging to it and was waiting to see if the ravel in the white thread which had started would continue and let him drop to the rocks far below" (272). On the surface, Bigger seems to mean that he will be lost if she wakes because he needs her to sleep so that he can kill her. At a metaphorical level, however, the image suggests that Bessie's breath, the symbol of her aliveness, supports him; it keeps him from falling into "a vast black gulf." Strikingly, the image reverses the conventional cultural identification of woman with a black pit, a symbol for maternal engulfment. Instead of representing the pit, with its threat of incorporation, Bessie is identified with the white thread that keeps Bigger from the engulfing abyss. Throughout the novel, whiteness has been associated with the feared dominant white culture and with social hierarchy, and this image aligns Bessie with acculturation, or what Lacan calls the symbolic order. This alignment suggests that the desire for alliances with others that Bessie evokes in Bigger is not tantamount to the dissolution of a separate gendered and raced identity, but instead supports identity articulation and socialization. This image prefigures Kristeva's notion of the borderline in-between as the "safeguard" of culture (*Powers* 2) and points the way to the final third of the novel, which charts the culturally productive possibilities of border crossings that Bigger has been determined to resist.

The Borderland Father

Wright frames Bigger's subsequent flight from annihilation at the hands of pursuing white men in terms that suggest resistance to abjection. Kristeva describes the abject as "the jettisoned object" at "the border of my condition as a living being" (*Powers* 2, 3). The radical exclusion of the abject is linked to the maternal body—Kristeva writes that "if it is a jettisoned object, it is so from the mother" (*Powers* 73)—and to fluidity, since abjection "dissolve[s]" the subject in "a mobile discontinuity" (*Revolution* 104). In *Native Son*, Wright turns to water imagery to image this pursuing threat of abjection. More specifically, to break down Bigger's resistance, the white men train on him the spewing water from a fire hose, and his "hardness" (312) is no match for the power of the water. As the feminist theorist Luce Irigaray notes, water "eludes placement and identity" (*This Sex* 117). Water, then, is evocative of a fluid blurring of distinctions that Bigger both desires and fears and that he associates with women. And, as Klaus Theweleit has documented, this male fear, which drives Bigger, is widespread across cultures. In *Male Fantasies*, Theweleit shows that a male association of a threatening fluid formlessness with the "endlessly flowing woman" (380) has a long history in art, literature, history, and popular culture. At this point in Wright's novel, this male fear of an identity-blurring maternal body seems to be reinscribed. To save himself from a threatening fluidity, Bigger clings to a "white looming bulk" (308). The "white bulk," which at first Bigger can't identify, turns out to be a water tower covered in snow. In describing the snow-covered water tower, the text stresses both its whiteness and its phallic shape. The male imagery is readily explained. Throughout the novel, women have been associated with a border-dissolving fluidity and men have been identified with a resistance to this breakdown of cultural divisions. In the case of the water tower, the phallic nature of the tower again suggests a definition of a "phallic difference" as the attempt to contain a drive toward a breakdown of alterity, just as the water tower contains the power of the water. But the whiteness of the "looming bulk" seems baffling. Given that Bigger is running from white men intent on killing him, why is the tower, which he clings to as the instrument of his salvation, insistently described as white? The answer, I suggest, is that, throughout the novel, white men seek to enforce rigid hierarchy and socially inscribed gender and raced identities, and this is part of Bigger's dilemma. His desire for "a way of his own" (112) paradoxically aligns him with the white men who would kill him.

When Bigger is captured by white men, he surrenders to the abject borderline he has struggled against all his life. Abjection is the "place where meaning collapses" (*Powers* 2), and Wright depicts Bigger's surrender as a fall into "nothingness" (318). Bigger, who refuses to speak or drink water for three days, is "swallowed in darkness" (314); he is "dumb, driven, with the shadow of emptiness in his eyes" (317). Kristeva insists, however, that this "place where I am not" is also the place "which permits me to be." The borderline space of "the inaugural loss that laid the foundation of its own being" is where "any being, meaning, language or desire is founded" (*Powers* 3, 5). Similarly, in Wright's text, Bigger's surrender to a deathlike state seems to represent a stage on the way to developing a new social self. In fact, like Kristeva, who writes that abjection is both the "death (of the ego)" and "a resurrection" (*Powers* 15), Wright turns to Christian resurrection imagery to describe Bigger's experience as a captive. Bigger's surrender to the white men is compared to a crucifixion: "Two men stretched his arms out, as though about to crucify him" (314);

and, like Christ, who rises from the dead after three days, in three days Bigger also "c[ame] out into the world again" (319).

To describe the three days of Bigger's figurative death, Wright again turns to water imagery. Here, however, as if anticipating Kristeva's theory, he suggests that this fluidity is both creative and destructive: "[Bigger] turned away from his life and . . . looked wistfully upon the dark face of ancient waters upon which some spirit had breathed and created him, the dark face of the waters from which he had been first made in the image of a man with a man's obscure need and urge; feeling that he wanted to sink back into those waters and rest eternally" (316). While Wright's use of water imagery invokes a masculinist identification of women with the dissolution of cultural formations, at the same time, in this passage, the fluidity associated with the maternal body suggests both birth and dissolution. Water, like the mother, is the life-giving source. This meaning is more fully developed earlier in the text, when Bigger's sexual intercourse with Bessie is similarly depicted as a restorative return to primal waters:

> and the thought and image of the whole blind world which had made him ashamed and afraid fell away as he felt her as a fallow field beneath him stretching out under a cloudy sky waiting for rain, and he slept in her body, rising and sinking with the ebb and flow of her blood, being willingly dragged into a warm night sea to rise renewed to the surface to face a world he hated and wanted to blot out of existence, clinging close to a fountain whose warm waters washed and cleaned his senses, cooled them, made them strong and keen again to see and smell and touch and taste and hear, cleared them to end the tiredness and to reforge in him a new sense of time and space. (154)

Water imagery, a symbol for a powerful drive toward inclusion, describes both Bigger's surrender and sexual intercourse. When Bigger gives himself up to the white men, he relinquishes to a fall into "nothingness" (318). Intercourse is rendered in similar terms because it too is a border transgression, a flowing together of self and other. But Wright describes both sex and Bigger's abject state as an oscillation in a cycle, a fall back into an original formlessness that precedes transformation.

According to Kristeva, the "start of new significance" requires the intervention of a third party, a father figure. To enable a child to move beyond "what, having been the mother, will turn into an abject," a father figure must "serve as go-between for [the child] to become autonomous and authentic in its turn." She explains that the "fashion[ing] [of] the human being occurs as a result of a *mimesis*, by means of which [the child] becomes homologous to another, in order to become himself" (*Powers* 13). This mimesis refers to the child's imitation or representation of a third party, the father. Formerly, the child was only like the mother, and this relation threatened the child's independence and individuation. But through an imitation or representation of the father, who is different from the child and the mother, the child becomes "homologous to another," that is, shares a relation with someone who is different from the child and the mother. This new bond displaces the mother-child relation but does not erase it; rather, it triangulates it. And because the father-child relation replaces the mother-child relation, the father becomes the mother's double, in that he is like the mother, but not the mother. This first new bonding with someone outside the self paves the way for relationships with a series of others, and each new relationship affects but does not obliterate self-identity.

Without this threshold figure, Kristeva writes, "every speaker would be led to conceive its Being in relation to some void" (*Desire* 238). It is this paternal go-between, someone who can mediate between the outside world and the self that Bigger lacks. His biological father, who should have been the first to assume this role, was killed in a riot in the South, a victim of racism. In this context it is noteworthy that, like Bigger, Wright also lacked a father figure. Wright's own father deserted the family when Wright was four years old, and in *Black Boy (American Hunger)* Wright associates his father's absence with a feeling of emptiness. He writes that "the image of my father became associated with pangs of hunger" (22). While Wright is speaking of his literal hunger, the original title of his autobiography, *American Hunger*, refers to his lifelong metaphorical "hunger" for a sense of inclusion in American culture, which began with his father's absence.[11]

In *Native Son*, at a great cost to himself, Max, Bigger's Jewish lawyer, fills this void for Bigger. Max becomes the first to offer Bigger a long-denied paternal alliance that enables Bigger to negotiate his conflicting desires for "a supporting oneness" with others (420) and for black manhood. Max is a white father figure whose presence at the threshold between culture's racial polarities ends Bigger's inability to be "at home" in "a cold white world" (279). In Kristeva's terms, Max is the borderline figure, who is like the mother. He is a nurturing figure who provides Bigger with food and clothes. Whereas other white men have been like a "white mountain of hate" (333), Max offers the boy intimacy and solidarity. He is on Bigger's "side" (333), "fight[s] [his] battle" (416), sits close to him in the courtroom, and calls him "son" (425). Above all, whereas Lacanian theory insists that the place of the father is "both constitutive and empty" (Rose 32), the text repeatedly emphasizes that Max is a "tangible presence, white, solid real" (491) that made [Bigger] feel that there was "something he could cling to" (443). As Bigger puts it, when Max "fling[s] aside the curtain" (333) that has always separated white from black, he feels, for the first time, that "the word had become flesh" (333). In other words, because of Max's presence, the word ceases to be an empty floating signifier; it is attached to the signified, and Bigger begins to feel "at home" (411) in a white-dominant culture. Like Kristeva's third-party figure, Max, who offers Bigger closeness associated with the mother, is "the mother-father conglomerate" (*Tales* 40), the "bridge between nature and culture, between the drives and the symbolic" (Oliver, *Subjectivity* 74), "the pivot of sociality" (Moi 287). Most important, Max is a bridge between black and white. Of course, as a "bridge," he transgresses racial boundaries and puts at risk his white male identity. In Max's case, this threat is literalized: because he represents Bigger in court, white men call him a "dirty Jew" (403) and threaten his life. Because he crosses boundaries, he is "radically excluded"; he is scorned, hated, and exiled. At the "unruly border," he is "on the edge of non-existence" (*Powers* 22, 2).

Max straddles the border between himself and Bigger when he bears witness for Bigger. Kelly Oliver (*Subjectivity*) differentiates between two forms of witnessing, witnessing to one's own experiences and witnessing to another's. In *Native Son*, both forms appear. Bigger is a self-witness when he describes to Max the racial oppression that he has endured, much like a Holocaust survivor testifying to the horrors of the Holocaust. The psychoanalyst Dori Laub, who has examined the effects of witnessing on Holocaust survivors, writes that the Holocaust eliminated witnesses, and this elimination made the annihilation of human life complete. To survive as subjects, he argues, survivors must pass on their stories to others so as to "live through testimony" (85). Like a Holocaust survivor, Bigger tells his story to Max, who "listen[s]" and "ask[s] questions," and Bigger feels "a recognition of his life, of his feelings, of his person that he had never encountered before" (417). For the first time, Bigger "trie[s] to see himself in relation to other men" (418). According to Oliver, this self-witnessing produces recognition, but this recognition is still based in a subject-object opposition, while witnessing for another obscures the boundaries between self and other and creates "an open subjectivity" (xvi). In *Native Son*, Max becomes the witness for another when he testifies in court on Bigger's behalf: "*I* shall bear witness for Bigger Thomas" (436), Max states. Whereas Bigger witnesses to his own experience, Max testifies to an experience that is not his own.

In testifying for Bigger, Max faces the problem of a common subject position that poses the danger of co-opting the other's story. Earlier in the novel, on the fateful night when Bigger served as chauffeur for Mary and Jan, the two whites had modeled a racial border crossing that was a takeover by the dominant culture. While Bigger listens silently, they speak of black culture in white stereotypes: "They have so much emotion! What a people! If we could ever get them going . . ." (88); they ask Bigger to sing a Negro spiritual for them; and they make Bigger feel that these whites, "having helped to put him down, having helped to deform him, held him up now to look at him and be amused" (76). Black culture and Bigger himself are alien to them, and they make no connection with Bigger, because they engage only with a racist caricature dictated by white ideology. I propose that Max's assumption of a common subject position contrasts starkly with Mary's and Jan's. Unlike Mary and Jan, who are privileged whites observing blacks, Max listens intently to Bigger's story, and when he bears witness for Bigger, he speaks not for Bigger, but as Bigger. Max, who is hated by whites for his defense of Bigger, relinquishes white privilege and occupies the risky, fluid middle between black and white. To make a white world no longer "No Man's Land" (402) to Bigger, but a culture in which he can find a home, Max cross-identifies and establishes common ground. That is, to testify for Bigger, without dominating Bigger, Max must relinquish "the mastery of the subject over itself" and put "the other first" (Oliver, *Subjectivity* 175). This relinquishment of self-mastery is a surrender to the in-between abject that "pulverizes" (*Powers* 5) the subject. In Faulkner's *Intruder in the Dust*, when Lucas asks Chick to exhume a corpse to save him, at a symbolic level, Chick is summoned to a similar risky border crossing, and this cross-identification is dramatized as a terrifying doubling with a corpse in a graveyard. In Wright's novel, by fearlessly confronting the same threat to ego boundaries, Max establishes a common ground between himself and Bigger that gives Bigger "faith that at bottom all men lived as he lived and felt as he felt" (493). As Oliver notes, testifying, "with its religious connotations" (174), suggests an act of faith. While it is impossible to know the other or to share the experience of another, through this act of faith, which "opens subjectivity to otherness and to experiencing the other otherwise" (176), communication and communion become possible.

A Male "Will to Kill"

In the final phase of his life, as he prepares for his death, Bigger seems to find a resolution to his conflicting desires for solidarity with others and for black manhood. The resolution had been modeled for him by Max, who demonstrates the possibility of a permeable racial identity. In the following passage, Bigger contemplates such an identity, and the incoherence of the passage reflects the risk that identification with others poses: "With this new sense of the value of himself gained from Max's talk, a sense fleeting and obscure, he tried to feel that if Max had been able to see the man in him beneath those wild and cruel acts of his, acts of fear and hate and murder and flight and despair, then he *too* would hate, if *he* were *they*, just as now *he* was hating *them* and *they* were hating *him*. For the first time in his life he felt ground beneath his feet, and he wanted it to stay there" (418–19). Discrete, different racial identities seem to break down in this passage, as the pronouns "*he*," "*they*," and "*them*," italicized as if to call attention to them, refer ambiguously to Bigger, Max, and "*them*." This pronoun confusion textually reproduces the boundary crossing that Max has modeled. Like Max's white-black alliance, the unclear pronoun references reflect the dangers of the borderline: unintelligibility and indistinguishability. At the same time, however, this ambiguity, the interplay of Bigger with Max and with *them*, functions to ground Bigger's identity in a community of others. For the first time, Bigger feels "ground beneath his feet"; that is, he feels anchored in the world by a relationship with others. While the borderline in-between, signaled by the confusing pronoun references, points to a feared overlapping of particular raced identities, at the same time, this elision with other men functions like an interfacing boundary as the grounds or basis for a community identity with other men, white and black.[12] This passage bears comparison with the description of Lucas Beauchamp's house in Faulkner's *Intruder in the Dust*. Like the ambiguous pronoun references that blur identities in Wright's text, the clause-laden, overburdened, nearly unpunctuated sentences that describe Lucas's house in Faulkner's novel evoke an interplay of culture's either-or meanings that threatens distinctions without effacing them. At this point in the text, like Faulkner, Wright offers an alternative to an exclusionary identity narrative. He suggests that risking a breakdown of white-black alterity *obscures but does not efface* culturally inscribed racial identities even as it enables cultural interchange.

In a subsequent series of images, the language of the unconscious, Wright seems to revise an exclusionary identity narrative that objectifies people of color. He begins with an image that pictures the central theme of *Native Son*, the warping effects of racial segregation: "[Bigger] saw a black sprawling prison full of tiny black cells in which people lived; each cell had its stone jar of water and a crust of bread and no one could go from cell to cell and there were screams and curses and yells of suffering and nobody heard them, for the walls were thick and darkness was everywhere" (419). Because the prison and the cells are "black," the image seems to figure the effects of a specifically racial exclusion. At the same time, the image may suggest that the alienation and objectification of others leave both black and white adrift. The "walls" that isolate create "darkness everywhere."

In the next image, Bigger pictures an end to such racial separation. He imagines a racially integrated society as a blurring but not an erasure of culturally specific identities: "If he reached out with his hands and touched other people, reached out through these stone walls and felt other hands connected with other hearts—if he did that, would there be a reply, a shock? . . . And in that touch, response of recognition, there would be union, identity; there would be a supporting oneness, a wholeness which had been denied him all his life" (420). In "How Bigger Was Born," Wright sums up the central meaning of *Native Son* with these words: "The most I could say of Bigger was that he felt the *need* for a whole life and *acted* out of that need; that was all" (527). All his life, Bigger has desired "wholeness," and in this image he seems to have achieved "a wholeness which had been denied him." The "touch" of others would supply "recognition . . . [,] union, identity." But the question remains: how has Bigger overcome his fear that solidarity with whites and with women will obliterate his black manhood? Here Bigger longs to be touched, yet formerly he was so terrified of the touch of a "white blur" that he killed Mary. Bigger fears "the white blur" because racial integration is forbidden by whites and because male-female closeness threatens his manhood. Furthermore, while Max modeled a straddling of culture's binary oppositions, Wright made starkly clear that "reaching out to touch other hearts" poses the threat of self-obliteration. When Max crosses racial lines to reach out and touch Bigger, he is cast out by other whites, and when he crosses gender lines to offer a relationship to replace a lost maternal connection, he puts at risk his masculinity. How can Bigger "touch" and be touched by others without risking his black manhood?

Apparently, the elision of self and other represented in these images is not threatening to Bigger because he pictures only a bonding of black and white men that would make him "the equal of others" (419), specifically white men. Two subsequent images stage scenes of identification, but both pointedly envision solidarity only with other men: "Another impulse rose in him, born of desperate need, and his mind clothed it in an image of a strong blinding sun sending hot rays down and he was standing in the midst of a vast crowd of men, white men and black men and all men, and the sun's rays melted away the many differences, the colors, the clothes, and drew what was common and good upward toward the sun" (420). The scene would seem to picture a fearful breakdown of alterity, since the difference between self and other is "melt[ing]" away, leaving, it would seem, only a leveling sameness. On closer inspection, however, it is clear that only certain differences have eroded: differences of "clothes," "colors," "white," and "black." The community identity that remains blurs class, ethnic, and racial differences, but male difference is emphatically intact. Wright's repeated use of the word "men" in this passage—"a vast crowd of men, white men and black men and all men"—suggests that maleness is what is "common and good" in this grouping and that female exclusion anchors this collective masculine identity. In other words, Bigger seems to picture a racially heterogeneous community identity composed exclusively of men.

With one final image, Wright moves toward a concept of a more pervious racial identity, but once again, as represented in the text, this inclusive racial and ethnic identity does not seem to include women: "He looked out upon the world and the people about him with a double vision: one vision pictured death, an image of him, alone, sitting strapped in the electric chair and waiting for the hot current to leap through his body; and the other vision pictured life, an image of himself standing amid throngs of men lost in the welter of their lives with the hope of emerging again, different, unafraid" (422). The passage appears to identify the socially productive element of the fearful borderline. An "in-between," "ambiguous," "composite" site (*Powers* 4) seems to be pictured as Bigger sees himself "standing amid throngs of men lost in the welter of their lives." While Bigger's culturally specific raced identity is temporarily "lost," he is hopeful that it will "emerg[e] again, different, unafraid." Insofar as Bigger pictures a coming together of men of different races and ethnicities in a transformative cultural exchange, his image seems to map onto Kristeva's theory of a "productive" (*Revolution* 16) shattering of a culturally specific identity. However, even as Bigger imagines straddling racial lines, he seems determined to enforce a gender divide. The passage is striking for its insistence on an exclusively male bonding. Bigger imagines losing himself "amid throngs of men"—not people and not men and women. The pointed absence of any references to women in his images of a community identity reinscribes a masculinist erasure of women. In accordance with the traditional Freudian/Lacanian model, female exclusion presumably defines a male presence. Throughout *Native Son*, Bigger has been cast in the role of the marginalized, uncanny stranger. When Max crossed racial lines to grant him "an openly designated relationship with the world" (471), he created an interracial space, and, for the first time, Bigger feels "at home," that is, no longer "unheimlich." Yet while recognizing that exclusionary racial practices had "buried" him (456), Bigger appears tacitly to collude with other men to exclude women. Whereas Max risked both gender and race ambiguity when he straddled the thresholds between mother and father and between black and white, Bigger's images of a racially mixed group identity picture crossing only color and class lines, not a gender line.

As the novel ends, in a move that appalls Max, Bigger appears to conclude that when he killed Mary and Bessie he joined a racially heterogeneous community of men who empower themselves by dominating others. Ironically, Max, who has himself sought to mediate culture's polarities, prompts Bigger to draw this conclusion. In his final meeting with Max before his execution, Bigger desperately seeks to overcome his lifelong sense that others scorn him because of his blackness, and so he asks Max, "I know the folks who sent me here to die hated me; I know that. B-b-but you reckon th-they was like m-me, trying to g-get something like I was . . . ?" (497). Max responds with a Marxist vision of class exploitation. He explains that the upper class "rule[s] and regulate[s] life" (500) by oppressing others: "The men who own those buildings want to keep what they own, even if it makes others suffer. In order to keep it, they push men down in the mud and tell them that they are beasts" (499). He insists that black people are not inferior but rather that these men (and Max repeatedly defines the exploiters as "men") "say that black people . . . [and] *all* people who work are inferior" (500) as a tactic to subordinate others. Bigger infers from the lawyer's words that he is not despised because of his race but because he is on the wrong "side" (500), the side of the victimized, and that when he killed Mary and Bessie he crossed to the dominant male side.

As the effect of Max's words, Bigger goes to his death convinced that the murders of Mary and Bessie were acts of male self-affirmation. While Max denounces those who victimize others, Bigger now sees himself as acting like the ruling class when he killed. As Cynthia Willett observes, Bigger's final acceptance of his "will to kill" (316) seems to evoke a Nietzschean celebration of a male will to power. Certainly, Nietzsche's description of the "glorious feeling of treating another human being as lower than himself" (2: 5) helps to explain Bigger's feeling of being truly "alive in this world" (501) when he killed.[13] Concomitantly, Freudian theory is applicable. When Bigger cries out, "But what I killed for, I am! It must've been pretty deep in me to make me kill!" (501), he implies that he expressed his innate or biological male nature when he killed. This assertion is consistent with Freud's theory that "men are not gentle, friendly creatures . . . , but that a powerful measure of desire for aggression has to be reckoned as part of their instinctual endowment." In *Civilization and Its Discontents*, Freud writes that men are tempted "to exploit [a neighbor's] capacity for work without compensation, to use him sexually without his consent, to seize his possessions, to humiliate him, to cause him pain, to torture and to kill him. *Homo homini lupus*" (85). Bigger's insistence that the murders tapped his essential nature seems to issue from a concept of manhood like Freud's, a notion of maleness as defined by aggressive drives. This interpretation would explain why in the closing scene Bigger calls out to Max and asks to be remembered to Jan. In particular, my reading is supported by Bigger's choice to address Jan, not as an inferior, but as an equal. As Max is walking away from the prison cell, his back to Bigger, Bigger calls after him: "Tell. . . . Tell Mister. . . . Tell Jan hello. . . ." With this changed form of address, Bigger, who smiles "a faint, wry bitter smile" (502), signals his sense that he is the equal of white men. Sadly, he appears to believe that they are joined by a common male aggressive instinct.

In the end, Max recoils in horror from the essentially Oedipal vision that Bigger now espouses. Max responds to this view with multiple negations: "No; no; no. . . . Bigger, not that . . ." (501). With this repetition of "no," Max expresses his denial of Bigger's valorization of violent domination as male strength, "hardness," and proud defiance. These denials prepare us for the Oedipal imagery in the novel's closing scene: Max "gropes for his hat" and "felt for the door" "like a blind man" (501). Oedipus blinds himself to sign outwardly his need to deny (that is, close his eyes to) his unwitting horrific deeds, his murder of his father and his incestuous coupling with his mother. Like Oedipus, Max also seeks to blind himself to an unbearable vision. Max turns away "in terror" (501) from Bigger's conviction that when he murdered he bonded with other men, who, like him, evince what Nietzsche calls a "will to power" or what Freud calls an Oedipal instinct, an instinctive drive to dominate others.

We must not underestimate the force of Max's "no" in this final scene, which serves as a powerful countervalence to Bigger's affirmation of a male "will to kill." Even more to the point, Bigger's capitulation to a masculinist ethic of domination runs counter to the central dynamic of *Native Son*, which—with the striking exception of Bigger's pride in killing—is to denounce the tactics of victimization. Of course, Bigger's celebration of a male will to power reflects Wright's extensive reading and keen interest in Nietzschean philosophy and Freudian psychoanalytic theory. But, contrary to Fabre's assertion that Wright possessed an "exaggerated reverence for books" and "too much faith in ideas" (531), in *Native Son*, the author questions and counters the ideas of Nietzsche and Freud. Arguably, the novel's conclusion critiques the aggressive, exploitative instincts that these thinkers advance. Bigger's sense of a shared male hardness does not create social bonds with other men, as he idly dreams. Instead, his valorization of murder drives away the man who crosses racial lines to offer him "a supporting oneness" (420), and, as the novel ends, Bigger is left alone in his cell as he awaits execution. The tactics of domination, Wright suggests, lead only to isolation and death. If Bigger joins ranks with anyone by adopting these tactics, it is men like Britten and Buckley, whom he hates.

Perhaps because Bigger's idealization of killing is so powerfully represented, scholars of *Native Son* largely have overlooked that the "truth" (501) Bigger articulates at the novel's conclusion is only one side of a dialectic in Wright's text. Throughout the novel, two ways of being a man in the world have been counterpointed. In the end, Bigger endorses the exclusionary logic of the Freudian/Lacanian narrative of male autonomy. But juxtaposed with this view is a definition of manhood/fatherhood that anticipates the theories of feminist thinkers such as Julia Kristeva and Jessica Benjamin. This critical counter-narrative also suggests that fathers play a foundational role in the acculturation process by distinguishing boundaries, but, contrary to Freud and Lacan, these boundaries are not defined solely by exclusion. Instead, boundaries are a fluid, terrifying "No Man's Land" (402). Men like Max, who assume the role of father or foundational figure, risk self-identity by straddling culture's polarities, and their presence marks a cultural boundary by being both "symbolic barrier" (*Revolution* 102) and point of contact.

Bigger's espousal of a masculinist exclusionary ethic should not blind us to the achievement of *Native Son*. Decades before contemporary feminist thinkers, Wright's powerful anti-racist novel anticipates their insistence that a desire for alliances with others plays a critical role in the acculturation process. More important, Wright's text shows how white America's refusal to grant a "home" to people of color increases the racialized subject's yearning for an outlawed inclusion even as it instills a warping, murderous fear of this forbidden desire. As Kristeva stresses in her exploration of abjection, the borderline, which is both the one thing and the other, is deeply threatening to every individual. Wright's accomplishment is to show how discriminatory racial practices in America, which seek to objectify black Americans and to induce a fear of boundary transgression, make the threat nearly insupportable. All his life Bigger has been so threatened with obliteration by whites that he dreads bonding with those in whom he sees his own fear of annihilation mirrored, like his mother, sister, brother, Gus, or Bessie. In addition, he comes to fear his own sexual drive as the occasion for a dangerous, forbidden border crossing with women. In sum, Bigger is undone because a dominant white culture has made anathema to him his own urgent desire to overcome racial alienation and to be the equal of white and black others. While Bigger's case serves as a cautionary example, Wright's novel also has mapped out a way to reconcile competing drives for culturally specific identities and for solidarity with others. Ultimately, Wright's text calls his readers, white and black, male and female, to "have the courage to call yourself disintegrated" and to welcome what seems like a "threat," "the apprehension [that] the other [is] at the heart of what we persist in maintaining [is] a proper, solid 'us'" (*Strangers* 192). Like Kristeva, Richard Wright also points to the social possibilities of welcoming the other as one's own, just as Max embraces Bigger as a son.

3 Flannery O'Connor's Prophets

These critics . . . see no connection between God's grace and
Africanist "othering" in Flannery O'Connor.

TONI MORRISON, *Playing in the Dark*

Flannery O'Connor famously insisted that the subject of her fiction "is the action of grace in territories largely held by the devil" (*Mystery*
118). While, as James Mellard notes, O'Connor largely has "had her way
with critics" ("O'Connor's *Others*" 625), her interpreters have been hard-
pressed to reconcile the signature violence in her fiction with traditional
religious beliefs. When called on to explain the violence in her fiction,
O'Connor always insisted that violence enables the action of God's grace:
"I suppose the reasons for the use of so much violence in modern fiction
will differ with each writer who uses it, but in my own stories I have found
that violence is strangely capable of returning my characters to reality
and preparing them to accept their moment of grace. Their heads are so
hard that almost nothing else will do the work" (*Mystery* 112). The opera-
tive word here is "strangely," and scholars have found very strange, even
inexplicable, the redemptive properties of murder, rape, and mutilation.[1]
Claire Katz writes that O'Connor "unleashes a whirlwind of destructive
forces more profound than her Christian theme would seem to justify"
(55); and Preston Browning observes that O'Connor's enigmatic fiction
calls for interpretations that go beyond religious orthodoxy: "If it was
Christian orthodoxy to which she subscribed, her work is manifest proof
that it was orthodoxy with a difference. For her persistent habit of finding
the human reality in the extreme, the perverse, the violent calls for closer
examination" (56).

My project is to interpret the violent action of grace in O'Connor's fiction by aligning the theological with the psychological and the social. As
scholars Robert Brinkmeyer and John Duvall have noted, the language

that O'Connor uses to describe the relation between violence and grace points us in the direction of ego construction or, more accurately, ego destructuring.[2] O'Connor writes that "violence is a force which can be used for good or evil," and, "for the serious writer, [it] is never an end in itself. It is the extreme situation that best reveals what we are essentially" (*Mystery* 113). Violence reveals "what we are essentially"; that is, it takes violence to break through to the "I" and reveal the true nature of identity. But what is the "I," and how does this violent destructuring and self-recognition move us closer to God? O'Connor's definition of grace, which foregrounds the idea of an encounter between the human and the divine, suggests an answer. Grace, she says, is the mystery of "the Divine life and our participation in it" (*Mystery* 111). It is always a violent "intrusion" (112) that enables a moment of "contact" (111) with the divine. For O'Connor, then, grace is an experience at the border of the self, the borderline place that is dual, where self and other or human and divine make "contact." In Kristeva's terms, the borderline is the abject, the place where self-identity is threatened and where we recognize the self's own hybridity—that is, that the self owes its existence to and is bound up with others. For O'Connor, it is at this borderline place, the edge of our existence as an I, where we are faced with "what we are essentially," that the human can access the divine.

The almost obsessively recurring pattern in O'Connor's stories is a shattering of alterity, which Kristeva calls abjection. To begin with, Kristeva describes abjection in terms that evoke the destruction endemic in O'Connor's world. Abjection, Kristeva writes, "pulverizes the subject" (*Powers* 5); it is "death infecting life," "the edge of non-existence" (*Powers* 3). Such terms aptly describe the deadly and near-death experiences that leave O'Connor's protagonists helpless, stunned, and altered at the end of each story. And both Kristeva and O'Connor insist that these deadly encounters are salutary. As Katz astutely notes, early and late in O'Connor's works: "Paradoxically, to be destroyed is to be saved" (61), while Kristeva describes abjection as "productive" violence (*Revolution* 16), and even applies to abjection terms that invoke Christian redemption: Abjection, she writes, "is a resurrection that has gone through death (of the ego). It is an alchemy that transforms death drive into a start of life, of new significance" (*Powers* 15). Violence in O'Connor's fiction seems to serve a similar transformative purpose. In story after story, O'Connor inscribes violent collisions or convergences: in "Greenleaf," the Greenleaf bull gores Mrs. May; in "The Enduring Chill," the fierce bird seems to pierce Asbury with its icicle; in "Revelation," Mary Grace slams Ruby Turpin with a book; in "Everything That Rises Must Converge," a title that underscores the signal importance of convergence, the African-American woman from the bus strikes Julian's mother with her pocketbook. In each of these instances, like abjection, the intrusive, bludgeoning violence "erase[s] . . . borders" (*Powers* 4) and gives rise to a sense that the self is shot through with the other. For O'Connor, this violent penetration of self-protecting borders opens the human self to the divine life; or, as O'Connor puts it, "violence . . . prepar[es] [my characters] to accept their moment of grace" (*Mystery* 112).

For both Kristeva and O'Connor, this disruption of borders is potentially self-annihilating; and, for both, it only enables a transforming recognition of what Kristeva calls "the impossible within" (*Powers* 5) and what O'Connor calls the divine life if properly negotiated with the help of an intervening-linking third party who straddles the border between self and other. This third party, Kristeva says, often is the father or a father-figure, because the father shares a relation with both mother and child but is also different from both. In terms of O'Connor's Roman Catholic theology, Jesus Christ is an example of such a dual figure, who is both the one and the other; Christ is both God and man, and by being both, allows for "contact" between the human and the divine or what O'Connor calls grace. In what follows, I propose to trace moments of self-shattering violence—or abjection—in O'Connor's fiction that are mediated by figures who are the instruments of grace because they are, like Christ, not the one thing or the other but a composite of both. And because they emulate Christ and are the channel through which God's grace can reach us, O'Connor calls these third-party figures prophets.

Artificial Race Difference

Beginning with its title, O'Connor's "The Artificial Nigger" is problematic. O'Connor repeatedly singled out this story, which foregrounds a racial slur in its title, as her "favorite" work (*Habit* 101, 209) and "probably the best thing I'll ever write" (*Habit* 209). In particular, she was pleased with the story's ending: "in those last two paragraphs," she says, "I have practically gone from the Garden of Eden to the Gates of Paradise" (*Habit* 78). Scholars have struggled to reconcile her admiration for the story with its racist title. When she submitted this fiction for publication in the *Kenyon Review*, the editor, John Crowe Ransom, suggested that she change the title, but O'Connor resisted. In her reply to Ransom, she wrote: "If this title would embarrass the magazine, you can of course change it." At the same time, however, she defended the title: "I don't think the story should be called anything but 'The Artificial Nigger'" (Fitzgerald 180, 181), and argued that she did not use the term "lightly" (Fitzgerald 182).[3]

The title refers of course to the central icon of the story, a lawn jockey, a racist, demeaning yard statue that, at the story's conclusion, mysteriously reconciles Mr. Head and his grandson Nelson. In the text itself, the racial slur is only used by the racist characters, Mr. Head and Nelson, while the narrator distinguishes her voice from theirs and substitutes the term, "artificial Negro." Why then abandon this careful narrative practice for the title of the work? In a letter to a friend, O'Connor addresses this question: " . . . to have sanitized the title," she writes, "would have robbed the story of its real power, the power to invert racist intention into antiracist redemption" (*Habit* 111). But how is her use of a racist term antiracist? As I see it, O'Connor elects to couple the disparaging racial epithet with the word "artificial" so as to underscore the artificiality of the term. Like the statuary it refers to, a white-constructed racist caricature of a real human being, the racist designation "nigger" is artificial; that is, it is fabricated by the dominant white culture so as to subordinate the real person of African ethnicity to an artificial construction, or, in the words of Lacan, to make the signified "disappear" under the weight of the signifier. More simply put, the pairing of the racist term with the word "artificial" suggests that the inferiority signified by the loaded label is artificial, a fiction or lie, but a lie that is the basis for white dominance in a binary construction of cultural meanings. The title points, then, to a poststructuralist definition of cultural meanings. Different cultures assign meanings to visible differences, like gender, race, and ethnic differences, but these meanings are man-made cultural productions, which are enforced by words and by domination.

The subject of "The Artificial Nigger," I propose, is the move into the world of culturally assigned boundaries, what Lacan calls the symbolic order, the realm of language and culture. As numerous critics have pointed out, the story seems to take the form of an initiation narrative: it recounts the introduction of a young boy, Nelson, to a community of others. Nelson's is a curious case. He has lived his life together with his grandfather in a remote rural region where he has never seen a person of color since, as Mr. Head explains, "we run that [last] one out twelve years ago and that was before you were born" (252); and apparently he has had little or no experience with women since Mr. Head's wife died long ago and Nelson's mother, Mr. Head's daughter, died shortly after the boy was born. With grandfather and grandson as sole and constant company, Nelson and Mr. Head have become copies of one another: "They . . . looked enough alike to be brothers and brothers not too far apart in age, for Mr. Head had a youthful expression . . . , while the boy's look was ancient" (251). The story, then, recounts Nelson's introduction to a wider world beyond this homogeneous white male outpost, a heterogeneous world of gender and race difference.

As the story begins, Mr. Head is a man on a mission. He is taking his grandson, Nelson, to Atlanta to teach him "a lesson." Nelson, Mr. Head explains, "is a child who was never satisfied until he had given an impudent answer" (250), and Head's stated purpose in taking Nelson to the city is to teach the child that "he was not as smart as he thought he was" (251). The trip to Atlanta is meant to showcase Nelson's "ignoran[ce]" (255) and Mr. Head's superior wisdom and worldliness (Mr. Head has been to Atlanta twice before) and to secure once and for all Nelson's submission to his grandfather's authority. In other words, Head wants to establish the dialectics of domination with regard to Nelson in much the same way that a white racist culture wants to secure the subordination of people of color. Thus Head's efforts to subordinate Nelson have the effect of aligning Nelson with the racial other. But, as numerous critics have observed, Mr. Head fails miserably to demonstrate his patriarchal prowess to Nelson; instead, in the big city, he is lost and helpless. He has to turn to people of color to help him, and, driven by fear of a group of women, he abandons Nelson when the boy turns to him for help.

The story explores more, however, than a particular white old man's failure to establish white male patriarchal authority through domination. The journey to Atlanta figures Nelson's initiation into Western culture's assigned polarized meanings, like the black/white dialectic. And this journey takes the two back literally to Nelson's place of origin, Atlanta, where Nelson was born. At a figurative level, Nelson and Mr. Head are also returning to the origin, that is, to the fearful borderline site where self-identity arises, unstable terrain that is not one thing or another.[4]

In O'Connor's story, Atlanta's underground system of sewers functions as an image for the boundaries that support culture's exclusive, either-or meanings. Soon after they arrive in Atlanta, Mr. Head and Nelson contemplate the mystery of "how the world was put together in its lower parts," the part that "underlined" the "entire city" (259). They allude, of course, to the Atlanta sewer system, but this language alerts us to symbolic implications.[5] Just as the upper world of the city is supported by subterranean depths, so also the dominant term in a dialectic is defined in terms of what it is not; i.e., male is not female; white is not black, and this not-white or not-male is what must be withheld or driven underground. But, as O'Connor figures these dualisms, she stresses that the two levels of the city, the upper one, symbol for the foregrounded term, and the negated, underground other one are counterparts; they channel one another through "tunnels" or "holes." This porousness, which Mr. Head and Nelson fear—"a man could slide into it and be sucked along down endless pitchblack tunnels" (259)—figures the site where culture's opposites converge. When Mr. Head and Nelson visit Atlanta, they fall through these "tunnels"; that is, they experience self-identity as fluid, in-between, and shot through with the other.

From the beginning of their journey to its culmination, when they behold the statuary that gives the story its title, Mr. Head and Nelson are confounded by a feeling of uncanniness, which Freud defines as a breakdown of the self/other division. For example, as they ride on the train to Atlanta, they are haunted by what O'Connor calls "ghosts." These ghosts are their own reflections in the train windows as they look out. O'Connor's insistent references to these doubles or other selves can be read as an instance of the uncomfortable feeling that what is strange haunts us, even exists within us. The sense of the self's own otherness is even more tellingly manifested in the story by Nelson's repeatedly rehearsed feeling that "black forms [are] moving up from some dark part of himself into the light" (264). This feeling of blackness buried in the white self is reiterated in each of Nelson's experiences with people of color in the city. For instance, the alterity between black and white seems to collapse when Nelson, who has never in his life seen a person of color, first views a "coffee-colored man" on the train, and he sees "a man" no different from himself. And again later, when Nelson and Mr. Head are lost in the city and Nelson asks an African American woman for directions, Nelson's odd response to the woman also seems to illustrate a borderline experience where black and white find common ground.

I want to focus briefly on Nelson's interaction with the African American woman because it seems to foreshadow the fiction's mysterious conclusion, the reconciliation of Mr. Head and Nelson through the mediation—or what we might call the intercession—of the racist yard statue of the story's title. As he approaches the large, dark woman, Nelson is overcome with desire: "He suddenly wanted her to reach down and pick him up and draw him against her and then he wanted to feel her breath on his face. He wanted to look down and down into her eyes while she held him tighter and tighter. He had never had such a feeling before. He felt as if he were reeling down through a pitchblack tunnel" (262). To understand Nelson's desire, we need to remember that, prior to his trip to Atlanta, his world has been empty of women and people of color. Face to face with the woman, he experiences aching loss. In psychoanalytic terms, we could call his desire for the woman a desire for incorporation; and, in the text, this drive is compared to the feeling of "reeling down a black tunnel," an image that recalls Atlanta's subterranean tunnels and Mr. Head's warning that a man could be lost forever in them. But in this instance Nelson desires the self-other identification signified by the tunnel image. This reading may help to interpret O'Connor's often-quoted gloss on Nelson's interaction with the woman. In a letter to a friend, she imputes a divine dimension to this encounter: "I meant for her in an almost physical way to suggest the mystery of existence to him . . . and I felt that such a black mountain of maternity would give him the required shock to start those black forms moving up from his unconscious" (*Habit* 78). O'Connor's remark connects the spiritual with the social. The "black forms moving up from [Nelson's] unconscious" are an image for the otherness at the center of the self, his own blackness, if you will; and in her letter O'Connor asserts a congruence between this fearful breakdown of alterity and "the mystery of existence," which for O'Connor is the penetration of the human by the divine through the action of grace.[6]

The central action of the narrative, Mr. Head's denial of his grandson, often has been read as an allusion to Peter's denial of Christ; I propose to interpret it as O'Connor's representation of the formation of otherness. Otherness, the episode suggests, issues out of a refusal to acknowledge kinship. To begin with, Mr. Head disavows his relationship to his grandson out of fear. When Nelson awakens from a nap and finds his grandfather gone, he becomes panic-stricken. He dashes down the street "like a wild maddened pony" (264) and knocks down an elderly woman. When his grandfather catches up with Nelson, he finds the boy and the woman lying on the pavement; the woman is yelling that someone will pay for her broken ankle; and a crowd of women are "milling around Nelson as if they might suddenly all dive on him at once and tear him to pieces" (265). These events trigger the grandfather's denial of his grandson. "His eyes glazed with fear and caution," he says, "This is not my boy" (265). Mr.

Head's denial reenacts how white Westerners construct binary meanings in culture by denying a relationship where there is a relationship. This denial, O'Connor suggests, is an attempt to stave off a threat to the self. Mr. Head disavows relatedness so as to save himself from being "t[orn] to pieces" by the women—that is, to secure his male boundaries. In O'Connor's text, however, alienation alone does not make Mr. Head safe or powerful. Without Nelson, the street ahead of him becomes the very "hollow tunnel" (265) that he was trying to avoid, and he now "wander[s]" in "a black strange place where nothing was like it had ever been before" (267). Exclusionary tactics alone have left him adrift in an alien, because alienated, universe in which he has no reference point: "He felt he knew now what time would be like without seasons and what heat would be like without light and what man would be like without salvation. He didn't care if he never made the train and if it had not been for what suddenly caught his attention, like a cry out of the gathering dusk, he might have forgotten there was a station to go to" (268). In denying his relation to his grandson, Mr. Head has lost the connection that supports discrete identities, like the relationships between light and heat, time and seasons, and man and salvation.

At the story's end, the enigmatic central icon, the lawn jockey of the title—a cruel, racist image of an African American—mysteriously reconciles Mr. Head and Nelson as they stand mesmerized before it. For O'Connor, the widespread Southern practice of decorating homes and lawns with grotesque plaster figures of African Americans embodies the problem of racial discrimination in the South. In a letter to a friend, dated August 28, 1955, she writes, "There is nothing that screams out the tragedy of the South like what my uncle calls 'nigger statuary'" (*Habit* 101). Susan Gubar points specifically to the lawn jockey in O'Connor's story as an example of a white appropriation of blackness that works to subjugate. Nevertheless, in this story, this racist artifact has a redemptive effect on the grandfather and grandson. Seeking to explain the sculpture's mysterious healing effect, critics have proposed that the grandfather and grandson are reconciled because this distorted, degrading caricature of an African American is so radically different from the white old man and boy that they are reminded of their similarity. Most scholars seem to agree that the racist yard ornament succeeds in uniting grandfather and grandson in their common whiteness,[7] and because this critical view has prevailed, a number of scholars have dismissed the story. For example, Jeanne Perreault ruefully observes, "What is actually achieved in the celebrated end of 'The Artificial Nigger' is a reiteration of the old, sad split between mind and body, male and female, black and white" (410).

While Gubar is unquestionably right that this racist caricature is a white appropriation of blackness that works to reify positions of dominance and subjection, at the same time, as John Duvall has perceptively observed, Mr. Head's and Nelson's encounter with the racist statue constitutes a "figurative blurring of racial binaries" (65) that provokes a crisis for their whiteness that, in turn, supports the action of grace. How can we reconcile these seemingly opposed positions? I propose that the eponymous statue is a boundary-making figure that mediates between culture's polarities but that, in the case of this statue (which issues out of the tradition of blackface minstrelsy, discussed in the final chapter), a white-dominant culture demeans the cross-racial figure so as to support white racial dominance.

The figure "prepar[es] them to accept their moment of grace" because the dark form, which might be "young or old," "happy" or "miserable" (268), is a third-party mediating figure. As Frederick Asals, Duvall, and Burkman and Meloy have observed, the figure of the African American is Mr. Head's and Nelson's black double, the uncanny stranger in whom they see the lineaments of the self.[8] While the racist yard decoration is designed to exaggerate racial difference and Nelson and Mr. Head are mesmerized by its strangeness, at the same time the text is also at pains to point out that the statue is the image and likeness of Nelson and Mr. Head. For example, Nelson is described as a "small figure" (268) only a few sentences before the statue is introduced as a "plaster figure . . . about Nelson's size" (268). The statue is a mysterious black form, and, throughout the story, Nelson has been feeling a "black mysterious form" (267) rising within him. And, as I have noted, Mr. Head wants Nelson to submit to his superior authority in the same way that a segregated South sought to subordinate African Americans. The plaster figure's "wild look of misery" (268) reflects the "ravaged and abandoned" (267) expression on Mr. Head's face. It leans forward at an angle that mirrors the stance of Mr. Head and Nelson; and, like the statue, which might be young or old, Mr. Head and Nelson have been described as seemingly indeterminate in age.

Because the lawn statue is both like the white grandfather and grandson and strange to them, it enables boundaries, in particular, racial boundaries; and this purpose explains the widespread proliferation of these decorative images in the homes of whites in the American South in the fifties and sixties, a time of racial upheaval. In a time of social change, to stabilize racial identities, the dominant culture turns to a threshold figure that can interface between culture's racial binaries; but this racial crossing is designed by whites so as to denigrate blackness and assert white superiority. Accordingly, while O'Connor emphasizes similarity in difference in describing the yard statue, she is ever aware that racist artifacts like this one "scream out the tragedy of the South" because they reveal how whites attempt to dominate and degrade the cross-racial figure.

Nonetheless, the yard statue, as racial intermediary, helps the white old man and his grandson to negotiate the terrifying borderline between self and other and between human and divine. As Mr. Head and Nelson stand transfixed before this mysterious dark form, they experience what Kristeva calls abjection, a violent dissolution of ego boundaries: "They could feel it dissolving their differences like an action of mercy" (269). The act that saves them, the action of grace, is a dismantling of the difference between the I and the other. Near the end of the story, Mr. Head re-experiences the feeling that the white-constructed figure of the African American triggers in him, and, as O'Connor spells out more clearly the "action of mercy," it seems to work like Kristeva's abjection, which is a "destruction and construction" of the subject (*Revolution* 16). For example, in a final paragraph that O'Connor described as approaching "the Gates of Paradise," the action of mercy seems to dissolve culture's identifying labels: "Mr. Head stood very still and felt the action of mercy touch him again but this time he knew that there were no words in the world that could name it" (269). In Kristeva's terms, there are "no words in the world" for this action because this moment is a "destruction of the sign and representation, and hence of narrative and metalanguage" (*Revolution* 103). For Kristeva, this disintegration of either-or meanings is a "dangerous and violent crucible." "Going through this experience," she writes, "exposes the subject to impossible dangers of relinquishing his identity" (104). In O'Connor's story, Mr. Head experiences this disintegration and change as he now sees himself with new eyes and "burn[s] with shame": "He stood appalled, judging himself with the thoroughness of God, while the action of mercy covered his pride like a flame and consumed it. He had never thought himself a great sinner before but he saw now that his true depravity had been hidden from him lest it cause him despair" (269–70). Stripped of the veil of artificial signs, Mr. Head, in O'Connor's terms, is now face to face with "reality," with "what [he is] essentially" (*Mystery* 112, 113), and deconstructed in this way, grace can reach him.

To survive this dissolution of cultural formations, there must be some-one who stands between, and this buffer enables transformation. I propose that, at a time when Mr. Head and Nelson are without moorings to locate a self, the lawn statue restores them to each other and to themselves by mediating between self and other, God and human. The statue makes possible both contact and distance by being like a hyphen. A number of scholars have suggested that the lawn jockey is a Christ figure in that it functions as a scapegoat.[9] I would push this suggestive analysis further. Like Christ, who is both human and divine—not the one or the other but both—and therefore can be the conduit for grace, the yard sculpture is similarly double, a figure that O'Connor calls a prophet, whose presence is saving.

In a letter to a friend, O'Connor suggests that "the action of mercy" has a transformative effect on Mr. Head. She writes, "Mr. Head is changed by his experience even though he remains Mr. Head. He is stable but not the same man at the end of the story. Stable in the sense that he bears his same physical contours and peculiarities but they are all ordered to a new vision" (*Habit* 275). O'Connor's words point to a confounding pairing of sameness and difference. Mr. Head is the "same" and "not the same."[10] This description, the same and different, is the formula for transforma-tion; it enables us to break out of static sameness; it is a leap forward to the new. At the same time, this coupling of oppositions, the same and not the same, inspires terror because it threatens a sense of a stable, es-sential self-identity and social hierarchies. O'Connor's fiction recognizes both the fearfulness and the transformative possibilities of the borderline place, the place where self and other converge. After viewing the figure of the African American, Nelson turns to his grandfather and says, "Let's go home before we get ourselves lost again" (269). For the first time, the boy describes his grandfather and himself as "we," a compound identity. This new sense of togetherness with his grandfather suggests a produc-tive sharing of identities that promises to open onto wider identifications with others. At the same time, when the story closes and Mr. Head and Nelson are safely home, the boy also says, "I'm glad I've went once, but I'll never go back again" (270). With these words, Nelson gives voice to a dread of the middle, the place that is both the one thing and the other. In "The Artificial Nigger," O'Connor narrates Kristeva's message that the borderline place both destroys and saves; and, for O'Connor, this fearful in-between place is the "the mystery of existence" (269), the place where

Nelson and we all "come from" (259), and the place where mercy can act on us.

A Different Kind of Difference: "Greenleaf"

"Greenleaf" provides a textbook example of the redemptive violence that is the signature characteristic of O'Connor's fiction. At the story's conclusion, Mrs. May, a farm owner, is gored by her farm worker's bull, and O'Connor's use of Christ imagery to describe the wounding unmistakably suggests that it is Christ who penetrates the dying woman: the bull's horn "pierce[s] [Mrs. May's] heart" (333), and earlier the farm worker's wife, Mrs. Greenleaf, in the act of faith healing, had called on Christ to "stab [her] in the heart" (317). Aside from this allusion to Christ, however, the violence in the story seems to exemplify domination. Throughout the fiction, Mrs. May has been struggling to assert her class superiority to her farm laborers, the Greenleafs, by "k[eeping] [her] foot on [Mr. Greenleaf's] neck" (321); but, despite her efforts, the class difference between the Mays and the Greenleafs is eroding, and, according to the prevailing reading of the fiction, the penetration of Mrs. May by the Greenleaf bull at the story's end signifies their domination of her.[11] Of course, such an interpretation works from the premises of exclusionary logic; that is, the Mays' upper-class status is determined by the marginalization of the Greenleafs. This reading, however, overlooks the story's revisionary inscription of boundary-making, which is modeled by the Greenleaf twins, who are both alike and different. While Mrs. May has devoted her life to the dialectics of domination to establish her family's class difference from the Greenleafs, at the story's end, when she is pierced through the heart by the Greenleaf bull, the violent goring graphically depicts Kristeva's insistence that the self is shot through with the other.

In "Greenleaf," the Greenleaf twins model boundary making as a combination of sameness and difference. As twins, they are doubles of one another—both alike and different. Contrary to the deeply entrenched Western conviction that such a pairing of oppositions is tantamount to indeterminacy, "Greenleaf" depicts how difference can exist within similarity as the twins model social identity as like brother and sisterhood. This notion of social identities, which I find dramatized in "Greenleaf," has been formulated as a theory by Jessica Benjamin. Benjamin writes that identity differentiation is a "simultaneous process of transforming and being transformed by the other," "a tension between sameness and difference, . . . a continual exchange of influence" (49). In what follows, I propose to show that O'Connor's story "Greenleaf" and, in particular, the Greenleaf twins seem to exemplify Benjamin's abstract theory.

Unlike the Mays, who marginalize others, the identical Greenleaf twins accept that we can share identities with others and still retain culturally specific identities. Their names, O.T. and E.T., suggest this combination of sameness and difference. They share an identity: the last half of their names is identical, while the first half is different. And because they understand that difference can exist within similarity, they are not afraid to risk indistinguishability. For example, when Mrs. May addresses one of the identical twins, she never knows to whom she is speaking: "They were twins and you never knew when you spoke to one of them whether you were speaking to O.T. or E.T., and they never had the politeness to enlighten you" (317). Mrs. May condemns as rudeness an individuality that is foreign to her, that is, a subject position that does not fiercely guard its borders, but instead submits to its own porousness. O.T. and E.T. seem to personify Benjamin's theory that a "striving for autonomy . . . is realized in the context of a powerful connection" (105–6). And this understanding that difference can coexist with similarities, O'Connor suggests, is the answer to the problem of domination. When Mrs. May asks the Greenleaf's hired man, "Which is boss, Mr. O.T. or Mr. E.T.?," he replies, "They never quarls. . . . They like one man in two skins." In turn, she flatly rejects this answer: "Hmp. I expect you just never heard them quarrel" (326). Mrs. May's rejection assumes that individuation and autonomy are contingent upon a power struggle. Without domination, there is no margin and no center. But O.T. and E.T. do not struggle. Neither is "boss"; rather, they are equals in a relationship that oscillates between subject and object positions.

The Greenleaf twins accept a shared identity not only with one another but also with those who are culturally defined as racially other. This white-black alliance begins with Mrs. May's relentless efforts to derogate them in the same way that she disparages people of color. But the slippage between the Greenleafs and African Americans is not only the effect of Mrs. May's insistence on her whiteness and their difference from her. For example, unlike Mrs. May, whom we first see with egg-white paste on her face, the Greenleafs are described as less exclusively white. Mr. Greenleaf's face, we are told, is "dark" (329), and the Greenleaf twins are characterized as "red-skinned" (317). More important, not only are the

Greenleaf twins doubles for each other, they also have a black double, their African American hired man. We never see O.T. or E.T. in the story; instead, they are represented by their worker, "a light yellow boy dressed in [their] cast-off Army clothes" (325). When their hired man answers Mrs. May's question about the Greenleaf bull, he consistently refers to himself and the Greenleafs together as "we": "*We* ain't knowed where he was. . . . He done busted up one of *our* trucks. *We* be glad to see the last of him" (325–26, emphasis mine). Wearing the twins' clothes and speaking for them in the first-person plural, the black young man is both similar to and different from the Greenleafs, the definition of the double, and this doubling sets a permeable boundary that both distinguishes and allows for cross-cultural exchange.

Throughout the story Mrs. May struggles to divide the Mays from the Greenleafs, but all her efforts to shut out the Greenleafs have the effect of blurring the Greenleaf-May distinction. For example, Mrs. May recalls that the Greenleaf boys grew up on her place and that "they wore my boys' old clothes and played with my boys' old toys and hunted with my boys' old guns" (328). Mrs. May's purpose is to remind the Greenleafs of their inferiority to the Mays, but, in the act of forming a boundary, her boys and the Greenleaf twins become doubles. Reinforcing this connectedness, the May sons, Scofield and Wesley, impersonate the Greenleafs and speak in what they call "Greenleaf English" (327). While the May sons' objective is to demean the Greenleafs and to establish a boundary between them, their mimicking of the Greenleafs suggests that they turn to doubleness to set a boundary.

The blurring of identities recurs insistently throughout the story and is epitomized in the figure of the Greenleaf bull. Their bull, I propose, embodies the father's doubling or boundary-making role. Just as the Greenleaf twins father children who are mixed (with French mothers, the children speak both French and Greenleaf English), their bull keeps finding its way into Mrs. May's herd and breeding with her cows. To perform the father's mediating function, the father figure, like a boundary, has to share a relation with both the one and the other. Accordingly, like the identical Greenleaf twins, who are described as "one man in two skins," the Greenleaf bull is also two-in-one, not one thing or another, but composed of both. For example, with a hedge "wreath across his horns," he is "like some patient god come down to woo [Mrs. May]." On the other hand, Mrs. May addresses the animal in a "guttural" tone "as if . . . to a dog" (311). The bull is identified with the Greenleafs—Mrs. May says,

"That's a Greenleaf bull if ever I saw one" (323); and he is also linked to people of color: when Mrs. May first sees the stray bull in her yard, she refers to its owner with a racial slur. This duality enables the father's mediating role; at the same time, this doubleness aligns the bull with Christ, who is also double, both God and man, and this parallel seems to suggest, paradoxically, that the bull that wounds Mrs. May is also the instrument of grace.[12]

The terrible wounding of Mrs. May by the bull, which is also the bull's violent death, graphically depicts the interdependence of the Greenleafs and the Mays that Mrs. May has resisted all her life. Even in O'Connor's earliest musings about "Greenleaf," she seemed to envision the story's centerpiece, the goring of a woman by a bull, as a site of doubleness. Announcing to a friend that she was working on the story, O'Connor wrote, "I am very happy right now writing a story ["Greenleaf"] in which I plan for the heroine, aged 63, to be gored by a bull. I am not convinced yet that this is purgation or whether I identify myself with her or the bull" (*Habit* 129). Even this brief encapsulation of the story's climactic wounding describes it as ambiguous, both the one and the other: it may be "purgation" or an identification, and, if an identification, it may be an identification with the bull or Mrs. May. O'Connor's comments point out that this story of a woman gored by a bull blurs alterity. Most strikingly, the wounding seems to elide sex and death. The unmistakably sexual language used to describe the goring—"the bull . . . buried his head in her lap, like a wild tormented lover" (333)—compares this double-death to a sexual union, a union of maternal and paternal figures in a *liebestod* or dying of the ego into the other. As well, this language, which aligns love and death—"One of his horns sank until it pierced her heart and the other curved around her side and held her in an unbreakable grip" (333)—echoes Mrs. Greenleaf's cry during her faith healing: "Oh Jesus, stab me in the heart" (317); and this association of the bull with Christ suggests that this love-death may be the means to Mrs. May's salvation.

On the surface, the death of Mrs. May on the horns of the bull might seem to invite a Freudian interpretation of male individuation. According to Freud, to achieve autonomy, a son must sever his attachment to his mother. But "Greenleaf" clearly revises this exclusionary paradigm. While the goring of Mrs. May suggests that she is the "radically excluded" (Kristeva, *Powers* 2) mother, whose exclusion makes way for a new order, at the same time this story also insists that exclusion never fully excludes and that this death by penetration is also a bonding of maternal and paternal and of May and Greenleaf. As O'Connor's gloss on the story suggests, the wounding of Mrs. May by the bull is ambiguous: it might be a purgation or merely an identification. If a purgation, the union of May and Greenleaf, symbolized by the Greenleaf bull's penetration of Mrs. May's heart, is the occasion for a saving encounter, a moment of grace; in Kristeva's terms, an abjection that shatters the self and enables transformation. On the other hand, it is also possible that, by ordering Mr. Greenleaf to shoot his sons' bull, the saving, mediating figure, Mrs. May has doomed herself along with the bull and erased the opportunity for the new life that the Greenleaf name promises. While Mrs. May's salvation may be in doubt, the "discovery" that she makes as she dies seems unmistakable. Surely, as she is pierced to the heart by the horn of the dying Greenleaf bull, she discovers the interdependence of the Mays and the Greenleafs.

Prophets and Borders

Flannery O'Connor's *The Violent Bear It Away* (1960) seems to narrate a search for intact, self-containing borders. In the novel, young Tarwater seeks to be autonomous and self-determined, but he finds himself "with barely an inch to move in, barely an inch in which to keep himself inviolate" (162). More specifically, the boy resists incursions on his identity from two father figures, his great-uncle, old Tarwater, a prophet whose identical name suggests the threat of identicalness, and his uncle, an atheist. Each of these father figures would make the boy the image of himself. The "trap" (159) that Tarwater finds himself in is that all of his efforts to keep himself separate seem to turn into the opposite, acts that connect him to another. For example, the uncle's child, Bishop, is unbaptized, and his great-uncle Tarwater has ordered young Tarwater to baptize the child and so begin his calling as a prophet, like his great-uncle. To erase the occasion for identification with the old man, young Tarwater drowns the child, but "the one thing" becomes "another" (157), as the act of drowning Bishop becomes its opposite, the baptism of Bishop. For young Tarwater, this merging of either-or oppositions seems to signal indeterminacy, the obliteration of distinguishing differences.

For O'Connor, this breakdown of alterity is the precondition for the action of grace. For example, in the final scene of *The Violent Bear It Away,* O'Connor suggests that the dissolution of self-defining boundaries can be transformative in a way that touches on the divine. The novel ends with an allusion to Christ's multiplication of the loaves and fishes to feed a multitude. This miracle, like the Roman Catholic doctrine it prefigures, the Transubstantiation (the conversion of bread and wine into the body and blood of Christ), exemplifies the productive possibilities of the deconstruction of a single, intact identity: the one loaf surrenders its self-containing borders; it becomes many, and it nourishes a community. This allusion suggests that human access to the divine is achieved through a surrender of self-identity comparable to the self-other convergences that Tarwater has resisted throughout the novel.

In this closing section, I want to focus on the figure of the prophet in O'Connor's fiction. My purpose is to show that O'Connor's prophet figure plays the role of Kristeva's third party or buffer. For both O'Connor and Kristeva, the role of the prophet or third party is crucial. By sharing a relation with both the one and the other, this mediating figure regulates an encounter between self and other so that self-identity can survive identification. O'Connor's prophets are called to follow Christ; and Christ, like the third party, is a threshold figure, who shares an identity with human beings and with God and serves as an intermediary that allows for exchange between the human and the divine.

Like *The Violent Bear It Away*, O'Connor's story "The Enduring Chill" (1958) explores the borderline in-between that threatens subjectivity but is also somehow the precondition for the action of grace. In the story, another young man, Asbury Fox, faces a dilemma like Tarwater's. Like Tarwater, Asbury struggles to be separate and autonomous; and, like Tarwater, all of Asbury's efforts to distance himself from others turn into the opposite, moments of convergence. Whereas Tarwater sought to differentiate himself from father figures, Asbury seeks to detach himself from his mother. Like so many of O'Connor's protagonists, Asbury still seems to be attached to his mother. He is described as his mother's "little boy" (366), and he compares his imagination to a bird that his mother has "cage[d]" and "pinion[ed]" (364). He feels as if he is her "slave" (364) and believes that his autonomy is contingent upon separating totally from his mother. As the story opens, Asbury, a young, aspiring writer, has left the big city and returned home to his mother's dairy farm because he is sick and thinks he is dying. In fact, Asbury seems to be looking forward to death. In death he expects to be "liberat[ed]" (364) from his mother by a transcendent, male god figure, like a Jesuit priest he once met who had a "superior expression" and looked "over the heads of the others" (360). At the conclusion of "The Enduring Chill," the deathly experience arrives, and out of this destruction arises "the New Man" (360), a new transformed Asbury; but the father figures who "assist" (360) this transformation are not the "mysteriously saturnine" (374) figures that Asbury pictures, but homely figures who are like his mother. Whereas Asbury anticipates an intervention that will separate him from his mother, what occurs at the story's end is a reunion, like the homecoming Asbury experiences when he returns to the hometown he despises and sees it as the place of "a majestic transformation," where "the flat of the roofs might at any moment turn into the mounting turrets of some exotic temple for a god he didn't know" (357). In "The Enduring Chill," Asbury looks to a godlike father figure to liberate him from a threatening tie to his mother, and encounters "a god he didn't know," a prophet figure who is the instrument of grace.

In essence, the father figure that Asbury imagines is like the symbolic father of Lacan's theory of identity development. According to Freud and Lacan, the father initiates an autonomous male identity by an act of exclusion. The mother is the first to be excluded and her alienation distinguishes male difference and superiority in a male-female binary opposition.[13] In "The Enduring Chill," O'Connor seems almost to parody this paradigm of male identity formation. Throughout the fiction, not only does Asbury fail to secure male autonomy through female exclusion, but, more than this, his efforts to extricate himself from his mother's closeness only tie him more closely to her. Like Tarwater in *The Violent Bear It Away*, Asbury finds that exclusions don't exclude; that every act intended to alienate becomes another reunion with his mother. For example, seeking to rebel against his mother's rules, Asbury drinks the cows' fresh milk, an act that "she don't 'low" (370), and encourages the dairy farm workers, Randall and Morgan, to join him. As he drinks the milk, which the farmhands refuse, he declares his independence from his mother: "Take the milk. It's not going to hurt my mother to lose two or three glasses of milk a day. We've got to think free if we want to live free!" (369). The gesture is intended to sever his bond with his mother, but, by drinking the milk of his mother's cows, Asbury drinks milk that belongs to his mother; that is, he drinks his mother's milk, and thereby elides the boundary between himself and her.

Asbury smokes with the black workers and offers to drink the fresh milk with them because, he says, he seeks a "moment of communion when the difference between black and white is absorbed into nothing" (368). Clearly, however, he wants no such breakdown of racial difference, since, when the farm workers, Morgan and Randall, visit him in his sickroom, he looks "wildly" to his mother to "get rid of them for him" (380). Like Julian in "Everything That Rises Must Converge" (1961), Asbury pays lip service to racial equality only to oppose his mother. Nevertheless, repeatedly throughout the story, his words prove prophetic as "moment[s] of communion" take place, and the difference between binaries like black and white, mother and father, or Asbury and his mother "is absorbed into nothing." The most striking example of this blurring of dualisms is the story's final disclosure, when Dr. Block, the country physician whom Asbury disdains, reveals that Asbury contracted a cow's disease by drinking unpasteurized milk. Ironically, the illness that Asbury proudly thought was "way beyond Block" (367) and that set him apart from his mother and her talk of cows is a cow's disease that signals his alignment with his mother and her world of cows.

The story moves inexorably toward a dramatic conclusion, Asbury's encounter with "a god he didn't know." While Asbury is anticipating an alliance with a transcendent father figure, "a man of the world" (360), the two father figures who appear in the story, Dr. Block and Father Finn, are wholly unlike the superior, "worldly," and "cynical" (371) figure Asbury expects. Block, the rural physician who makes jokes and funny faces to please children, is, Asbury says, an "idiot" (367). As for Father Finn, he is an old, red-faced man, deaf in one ear and blind in one eye, who brushes aside attempts at intellectual conversation "as if he were bothered by gnats" (375). Nonetheless, these homely men, with "literal mind[s]" (364) like Asbury's mother's, are prophet figures and the agents of grace. It is Dr. Block who delivers the "shattering" (381) revelation that Asbury's body is home to a cow's disease, and Father Finn who puts into words the fate that awaits Asbury when he "roars": "How can the Holy Ghost fill your soul when it's full of trash? . . . The Holy Ghost will not come until you see yourself as you are—a lazy ignorant conceited youth!" (377). Asbury hopes in death to be liberated from a maternal/material attachment; instead, Father Finn's words suggest what is coming: a violent obliteration of his illusions of independence and superiority and a new understanding of his "communion" with others.[14]

At the end of "The Enduring Chill," Asbury, "shocked clean" by the irony that the illness that was to emancipate him is a cow's disease, is "prepared for some awful vision about to come down on him" (382). This vision is pictured in the final paragraph of the story when a ceiling image of a fierce bird with an icicle in its beak, etched by water stains, seems to descend to pierce him. O'Connor describes the descent of the ceiling image bird with its threatening icicle as "the Holy Ghost, emblazoned in ice instead of fire, . . . implacable" (382), and this divine visitation is not the removal from the world of others Asbury expected, but rather an intrusion on his person from the outside, like the incursions that Asbury has sought futilely to escape throughout the story. To apprehend the significance of this final image, we need to note that this shattering penetration by the Holy Spirit has repeatedly been prefigured in the story. Like the fierce bird with the icicle poised in its beak, his mother, Father Finn, and Dr. Block are also invasive figures. Asbury accuses his mother of "pinion[ing]" his imagination; under the gaze of Father Finn, Asbury flails about "helplessly as if he were pinned to the bed by the terrible eye" (377); Dr. Block "press[es]" needles into Asbury's veins and "invad[es) the privacy of his blood" (367); and Dr. Block's diagnosis that Asbury has a cow's disease seems "to reach down like a steel pin"(381) and kill something in Asbury. These prefigurations of the descent of the Holy Spirit by Mrs. Fox, Dr. Block, and Father Finn suggest that these incursions of the outside on the inside are the precondition for the advent of grace.[15]

Flannery O'Connor always insisted that the "action of mercy" is an "intrusion" (112) and a moment of "contact" (111) with the divine, and she explains that, mysteriously, violence often enables this contact. Her words suggest that human access to the divine requires a violent disruption of self-protective borders that keep the other out and keep us feeling autonomous and intact. In story after story, her characters achieve their moment grace as they are stunned, shattered, pierced, lost, and helpless. In Kristeva's terms, they experience their moment of grace when they become abject.[16]

For O'Connor, like Kristeva, a third party mediates this shattering of the I so that transformation can take place. In O'Connor's fiction, the paradigm of a third party or father figure intervening in an overly close mother-child relationship is repeatedly staged. In "The Life You Save May Be Your Own," Tom T. Shiftlet separates the mother Lucyknell Crater from the daughter Lucyknell Crater; in "Good Country People," Manley Pointer appears to offer to Joy/Hulga an escape from a smothering relationship with her mother. In these early stories, these male figures fail to play the role of mediating go-between whose presence enables an equal relationship between self and other. Instead, like Lacan's symbolic or absent father, they introduce only alienation and loss. Shiftlet abandons Lucyknell in a diner far from her mother, and Pointer takes Joy/Hulga's prosthetic leg and leaves her stranded and helpless in a barn loft.

In Kristeva's terms, they fail to perform the role of the third party; in O'Connor's terms, they refuse the role of prophet.

Kristeva's third party, whom she calls "a blessing" and "a god-send" (*Tales* 41), is comparable to the figure that O'Connor calls a prophet. O'Connor's fiction is filled with characters who are called to be prophets and fail. Tarwater, for instance, resists the call to be a prophet until the end of *The Violent Bear It Away;* and in *Mystery and Manners,* O'Connor refers to the Misfit in "A Good Man is Hard to Find" as "a prophet gone wrong" (110). Other failed prophets in her fiction, I propose, include Manley Pointer and Tom T. Shiftlet. If, as I suggest, the prophet is called to a role like Kristeva's third party, her theory may help to explain why Christ imagery seemingly inexplicably attends these deeply flawed figures and why a good prophet is hard to find in O'Connor's fiction. According to Kristeva, the third party's role is to be the intermediary who enables solidarity with others without the colonization of the one by the other. To enable this balance, the third party has to share an identity with both the one and the other. This doubleness, which blurs culture's binaries, is precisely what Tarwater resists futilely throughout *The Violent Bear It Away.* It is this role as go-between that the Misfit, Tom T. Shiftlet, and Manley Pointer are also called to and refuse. Joy/Hulga alludes to the role of the third party or prophet when she senses that through the Bible salesman she could "los[e] her own life and f[ind] it again, miraculously, in his" (289). Her words refer both to Christ and to the mystery of a border, a place where identities are unmade, shared, and then remade through sharing. When Joy/Hulga surrenders her prosthetic leg to Manley, she compares it to her soul, and looks to him to be the substitute for loss, as he promises to do when he says, "Leave [the leg] off for a while. You got me instead" (289). But instead he leaves and takes her leg. In Kristeva's terms, Manley and characters like him lack "the courage to call [them] selves disintegrated" (*Strangers* 191–92). At the end of *The Violent Bear It Away,* Tarwater accepts disintegration; he throws himself to the ground, presses "his face against the dirt of [his great uncle's] grave" (242), and joins the ranks of Elijah and Moses. In other fiction, figures like the artificial Negro, the Greenleaf twins, Dr. Block, and Father Finn also accept the role of prophet or intermediary. Dr. Block and Father Finn are repeatedly described as invasive, intrusive figures, and, in the fiction of Flannery O'Connor, the advent of grace is always an "intrusion" (*Mystery* 112).

4   "Nobody Could Make It Alone"

Fathers and Boundaries in Toni Morrison's *Beloved*

Without someone on this threshold . . . then every speaker
would be led to conceive its Being in relation to some void.

JULIA KRISTEVA, *Desire in Language*

Toni Morrison's *Beloved* exposes the societally sanctioned, institutionalized terror tactics used by white slave owners to rob black women
and men of subjectivity and agency. As the novel begins, the ex-slave Sethe
and her daughter, Denver, are still experiencing the psychological wreck-
age inflicted by slavery some years after slavery has been abolished. Sethe
and Denver are living isolated from the community in a house haunted
by what appears to be the ghost of the baby daughter whom Sethe killed
eighteen years earlier. Mother and daughter seem to be on the edge of
madness. In the words of Barbara Schapiro, they are experiencing "psychic death, the denial of one's being as a human subject" (156). The work
of the novel is to chart the process by which Sethe, Denver, and other
African Americans recover from the effects of slavery and "claim ownership of [a] freed self" (95).[1]

To become an autonomous self, Sethe, Denver, and others who experience the after-effects of slavery must make their way back into the community because, as Teresa de Lauretis explains, identity is socially constructed through "a process whereby a social representation is accepted
and absorbed by an individual as her (or his) own representation" (12).
The need for relationships with others for the development of a social self
is the dilemma that the ex-slaves face. How do these ex-slaves dare risk
engagement in a white-dominant social order that systemically worked to
appropriate them? For that matter, Morrison's fiction points out that the
problem of domination is not even escaped by excluding whites and form-

ing an all-black community. Within the African American communities in *Song of Solomon, Paradise, Love,* and other Morrison novels, blacks often reproduce the marginalizing power structures of white culture.

The large body of scholarship on community in Morrison's texts reflects the contemporary debate about the need for and risks of identification within a community.[2] For example, while most Morrison scholars agree that "assuming identity . . . is a communal gesture" (Smith 283) and that her novels "reimagine community within an increasingly multicultural and multi-racial America" (Michael 2), others, such as Roberta Rubenstein and Barbara Christian, counter that we must not overlook the sometimes destructive effects of community on the individual. Elizabeth Abel even cautions that white feminist interpretations that find alliances between white and black women in Morrison's fiction have the potential to reproduce "the structures of dominance" that the feminist critic "wants to subvert" (837).[3] To resolve this seeming double bind, scholars such as Magali Cornier Michael, Jean Wyatt, Kevin Everod Quashie, and Barbara Schapiro have sought out a theory of identity that allows for relationships without colonizing another.[4]

My contribution to this discussion is to point to the critical role of the father in *Beloved* in helping to form boundaries that both distinguish an autonomous subject and allow for alliances with others. Two feminist thinkers who focus on the paternal function are Jessica Benjamin and Julia Kristeva, and, for both theorists, a father figure or third party—not necessarily the biological father or even a male, but someone different from the mother—introduces defining boundaries not by severing relatedness but by transforming it so as to introduce a new and different relationship, which is a double for an original mother-child unity.[5]

How does this model of fatherhood serve to introduce to a child a recognition of a gendered or raced identity? Raced and gendered identities are defined by a balance of likeness and difference. In *Beloved,* the father figure models precisely this balance of difference within relationship to induct a child into a world of socially defined identities. For example, when Paul D "put[s] his story next to [Sethe's]" (273), he risks his male difference and, when Amy Denver crosses racial boundaries to help deliver Sethe's child, she risks her white difference; and by blurring alterity, Paul D and Amy Denver model a mix of difference within sameness that is the key to becoming an individuated self within a racially heterogeneous community of male and female others. In both cases, they bring new life out of near-death. Amy Denver's willingness to triangulate the

Sethe-Denver mother/child dyad introduces Denver to a world of black and white others. Similarly, at the novel's end, when Paul D straddles the maternal and paternal roles, he enables Sethe to turn away from death and to begin the process of constructing an "I" in the social order.

Because the father is usually the first to model difference within a relationship, this socialization process is called the paternal function. But in *Beloved* this process of inducting a child into social relations with others is not only performed by the biological father or even by a male. Sometimes the biological father cannot perform this role. Under slavery, for example, slave fathers were separated from their children. As Morrison shows, in the absence of the biological father (as, for example, the absence of Halle, Denver's biological father), someone else must intervene between mother and child and serve as the hyphen that enables self-other relations. In *Beloved*, the "paternal function" is an ongoing socializing process that can be and should be performed by both men and women and by people of all races and ethnic groups as different relationships with others develop new and different social identities.[6] In this way Morrison intervenes in a theoretical debate about paternal authority and counters a white Western, phallocentric, exclusionary model of identity formation.[7]

As *Beloved* opens, the racist culture of the slave-holding South has blocked the transformational process necessary for acculturation, and, as a result, Sethe and Denver are living together isolated from the community in a house haunted by what appears to be the ghost of the daughter she killed eighteen years earlier. In my reading, the ghost literalizes both a particular instance of an undifferentiated, black mother-child dyadic relationship, the Sethe-Denver relationship, and, more generally, the condition of all the enslaved Africans, whose enslavement left them, in the words of Hortense Spillers, "culturally 'unmade'" (72). In Morrison's novel, to become interpellated into culture, the original undifferentiated mother-child relation, personified in Beloved, must be transformed by a father figure. As Kristeva explains, the intervention of a third term into the mother-child dyad is necessary for differential meanings in culture. "If no paternal 'legitimization' comes along to dam up the inexhaustible non-symbolized impulse," a woman will collapse "into psychosis and suicide" (*About Chinese Women* 41). As the novel begins, Denver and Sethe seem near psychosis or suicide, and the work of the novel is to explore the critical role of a third-party father figure in mediating the passage into a social order.

To help define the role of a father in the socializing process, Morrison's novel foregrounds a black man and a white man, Hi Man and school-teacher, who model, respectively, the father's transformative function and a white, slaveholding culture's perversion of the third party's inter-vention in the mother-child identificatory relation. Schoolteacher repre-sents a class of white slaveholders who refused to recognize black fathers and claimed to own all rights to black children as their property. In this way they erase the father/child relationship and substitute the master/slave relationship, an appropriation of the other. Set against school-teacher is Hi Man, a father figure who models social identity as a balance of similitude and difference.

It is because schoolteacher represents a monstrous cultural perver-sion of the paternal role that, as the novel begins in the time present, Sethe lives outside of the cultural order. When schoolteacher arrived at 124 eighteen years earlier, he came to intervene in the unbroken mother-child circuit and usher the child into a socially differentiated order. But because this slave-holding culture is intent on the immolation of people of color, Sethe thwarts this moment of appropriation by seeking to kill her children and herself. As she "face[s]" schoolteacher, she holds in her arms her dead daughter, and "that stopped him in his tracks" (193). When she stops schoolteacher's "tracks," she refuses to allow the white man to introduce her children to what Lacan calls the symbolic order, the order of language and culture, and she assumes the aspect of the phallic mother in Greek myth, the Medusa, a female creature whose hair is a mass of phallic snakes. The little hummingbird needle beaks she seems to feel "st[icking] . . . right through her headcloth into her hair" (192) are a phal-lic image, analogous to the Medusa's snaky hair. The Medusa, a female creature with phallic, snaky hair, aptly figures an obliteration of differ-ence in a totalizing identification. In the words of Jane Gallop, the phallic mother is "the whole" (22).

Sethe thwarts the moment of acculturation because the dominant white culture seeks to refigure a moment of transformation as a moment of black male and female devaluation. The white world's perversion of the black slave child's induction into culture is graphically represented when one of schoolteacher's nephews holds Sethe helpless, while another sucks the milk from her breasts. To understand how the scene of the child's introduction to culture has been refigured as a scene of the black moth-er's and father's degradation, it is useful to read the witnessed taking of Sethe's milk as a primal scene. The primal scene is a recurring fantasy image that depicts parental intercourse, witnessed by a child. The primal fantasy is widely interpreted to be a representation of the origin of self and social awareness, since the child is observing, in a sense, his/her own conception; and Freud argues that the scene images the domination (according to Freud, the child thinks the father is hurting the mother—even castrating her) that introduces boundaries. While I agree that the primal scene pictures boundary making, I would argue that the origin image formulates the introduction of cultural boundaries as a balance of inclusion and exclusion. It is an image of self-other union because the parents are united in sexual intercourse. It is also an image of exclusion because the child is excluded from this union.

The horrific scene of Sethe's mammary rape illustrates how a white racist phallogocentric culture attempts to reconfigure a scene of parental lovemaking as an image of black devaluation and domination.[8] The mammary rape conforms to the outline of a primal scene in that it is a witnessed sexual act committed on a mother figure, the pregnant, lactating Sethe. However, three deviations from the traditional scene stand out: the sexual act is not performed by the black biological father or a father figure, but by two white son figures, the nephews; the act itself is deviant—they suck milk from Sethe's breasts; and the witnesses are not children, but schoolteacher and Halle, the father of Sethe's children, who hides in the loft. These deviations point to this white slave-holding culture's attempts to disempower both the black mother and the black father. This forced sexual act dehumanizes Sethe because the nephews milk her like an animal. In addition, given the life-sustaining power of maternal milk, when the white boys suck the milk from her breasts, symbolically they divest the black mother of her power and ingest it. As for Halle, the black father is also symbolically castrated. Forced to watch helplessly, he is positioned in the role of the child witness, and he is prohibited from performing the father's authorizing role in the scene, which is to triangulate the mother-child relationship by joining it.

But even in this grotesque reenactment, when the origin scene is literally written by schoolteacher so as to divest the black mother and father of agency, still the father's mediating role emerges. When one of the white boys sucks the milk from Sethe's breast, he assumes the position of her own children, and becomes a double for Sethe's black children, even as he is joined with Sethe by incorporating her milk into his body. Because a father is father by virtue of an intervening relationship with a mother and child and because even binary categories of identity depend on a relationship, no matter how monstrously it is culturally distorted, the scene of the child's introduction to social identity always entails a blurring of identities. The inescapability of identification in the origin scene explains, I think, why schoolteacher elects to observe and inscribe the scene, instead of assuming the paternal role himself. Schoolteacher rejects the black-white, male-female merging, the boundary overrunning that is always a part of boundary making. He chooses for himself the Lacanian role of the disembodied symbolic father who represents alienation. By writing the events in his book, he seeks to align himself with the word-symbol, which he imagines is independent and autonomous. However, signification depends on relationships with others and with the material world. The ink schoolteacher writes with, we are reminded, was made by Sethe.

Whereas the mammary rape of Sethe seeks to figure the black child's induction into a white-ascendant patriarchal culture as a function of dominating tactics, the Hi Man–led escape from the underground cells in Alfred, Georgia, allegorizes the slave-prisoners' entry into cultural existence as a negotiation of a self-other relation. Morrison's narrative of the slave-prisoners' escape from the camp surely is meant to represent the acculturation of slaves whose enslavement has left them culturally unformed. In her telling, this entrance into social existence is analogous to the seed's sprouting in the earth and to the fetus's passage through the birth canal, and she stresses that social existence arises from a deathlike state. In the prison camp, Paul D and his fellow-prisoners are, in effect, dead to existence in culture. The black men are buried in the ground in a "grave calling itself quarters"; and they work to make themselves dead to all feeling so that they will be "safe" (128). In Morrison's allegory, this fearful, unformed, or dormant state is not the end; rather, it is part of a cycle and the necessary prelude to a new life, and this meaning is articulated in the text when Sethe tells Denver that "nothing ever dies" (44); when Stamp Paid acknowledges that nothing buried "stay[s] in the ground" (221); and, of course, when Sethe's dead daughter seems to return from the dead as Beloved.

In *Beloved*, when negotiated with a loving father figure, an original undifferentiated state is a death from which we arise anew. The nine days of relentless rain, which cause "all Georgia [to seem] to be sliding, melting away" (130–31), metaphorically represent a fearful loss of difference. The rain is turning the earth above the prisoners' underground cells into a primal soup that threatens to crush them, and, when Paul D hears someone screaming, he doesn't know if it is himself or someone else. Paradoxically, however, this formlessness and fluidity enable them to swim through the mud to the surface to be reborn. And the chain that joins them in unbroken unity, seemingly an analogue for the umbilicus, also enables the black prisoners to ascend: "For one lost, all lost. The chain that held them would save all or none, and Hi Man was the Delivery. They talked through that chain like Sam Morse, and Great God, they all came up. Like the unshriven dead, zombies on the loose, holding the chains in their hands, they trusted to rain and the dark, yes, but mostly Hi Man and each other" (130).

Beloved's narration of the slave-prisoners' move from a culturally un-formed condition to existence in culture seems both to rewrite Freud's death drive and to evoke Kristeva's theory of abjection. In *Beyond the Pleasure Principle,* Freud finds that all existence is driven by a desire "for the reinstatement of an earlier situation" (74) and that the "goal of life is an ancient starting point," a "return to the inorganic" (47). Freud calls this desire the death drive, and for him this drive represents the ultimate triumph of death over life. Morrison, on the other hand, teaches us to see that the desire to return to a precultural condition, which is also a desire for incorporation, plays a role in the boundary-making process, that is, that inmixing is a stage on the way to a new mixing or new social identity.[9] This same notion underlies abjection. For Kristeva, abjection is the death of the ego in the other that is part of a transformative process. Abjection "shatters the wall of repression. . . . It takes the ego back to its source . . . from which, in order to be, the ego has broken away—it assigns it a source in the non-ego, drive and death. Abjection is a resurrection that has gone through death (of the ego). It is an alchemy that transforms death drive into the start of life, of new significance" (*Powers of Horror* 15). The prison camp experience in *Beloved* almost seems to dramatize the concept of abjection. The prisoners, who seem to be dissolving into the earth, experience this "source in the non-ego, drive and death"; and they also materialize a "resurrection," as they erupt through the earth like "zombies." But how is this "alchemy" accomplished?

For both Morrison and Kristeva, the alchemy is performed by a father figure or third party. As Oliver explains, Kristeva rewrites Freud's stern Oedipal father as "an imaginary agent of love that allows the child to negotiate the passage between the maternal body and the Symbolic order" (*Reading* 69).[10] In Kristeva's theory, this passage involves "a combinatory moment" that requires a "dynamiting" of the self, "which is always pro-duced with reference to a moment of stasis, a boundary, a symbolic barrier" (*Revolution* 102). In Morrison's prison camp episode, we see both this terrible destructuring of the "I" and the resistance to it. When Hi Man tugs on the chain, signaling to the men to rise together, he becomes the "symbolic barrier" to dissolution, as the men struggle up through the enveloping mud: "blind, groping . . . [they] pushed out, fighting up, reaching for air" (130).

The move into social existence is always a move from the mother to the father, from an undifferentiated unity to a bordered relationship, and the father's mediation marks the border. Hi Man models the critical paternal role of boundary marker by being both similar and different. He shares an identity with the other convicts: he is bound to them by the chain that connects them all and is buried with them in the dissolving ground. But Hi Man is also different: his position as "the lead chain" (127) distinguishes him from them as "Hi Man." This combination, the same but different, is the formula for symbolization—that is, a word-symbol shares an identity with the signified but is not identical with it—and Hi Man is figured in the text as the entryway into signification. He introduces language's structuring practice both when he signals to the men by tugging on the chain, who then can "talk through that chain" (130), and when, each day in the prison camp, he "give[s] the signal that let the prisoners rise up off their knees" (127). In Morrison's identity narrative, entry into a world of diverse cultural meanings is mediated by a third party, and this is the role Hi Man plays. He "assume[s]" "the responsibility . . . because he alone knew what was enough, what was too much, when things were over, when the time had come" (127–28). Whereas, as Baby Suggs says, white people "don't know when to stop" (122–23)—that is, whites ceaselessly degrade blacks to produce white authority in a racial binary—Hi Man understands that social identity is a balance, a give-and-take between culture's categories.

Like Hi Man, who leads the bound convicts out of the devouring mud—symbol of a fearful indeterminacy—to existence in a structured, social order, Paul D would play this same role for Sethe and Denver. When Paul D arrives at 124, he finds Sethe and Denver in a state analogous to the figuratively dead convicts before their "delivery." Like the convicts drowning in the melting earth, Sethe and Denver seem to be losing themselves in the ghost that haunts them. They seem to be outside of the social order and fixed at the moment of origin, when Sethe stopped time by refusing to deliver her children to a slave-holding culture. For their successful entry into culture, mother and daughter need a mediating presence.

To materialize this socializing process, Morrison elects to personify the unmodified mother-child bond in the baby ghost, which, when banished, returns in the form of Beloved.

This reading explains the battle between Paul D and the baby ghost and the subsequent battle between him and Beloved. When Paul D arrives, he offers himself as a sustaining substitute for a precultural maternal bond: "He had become the kind of man who could walk into a house and make the women cry. Because with him, in his presence, they could. There was something blessed in his manner. . . . Strong women and wise saw him and told him things they only told each other" (20). Although he is different from them, they can share with him as they share with one another, and this "blessed" combination enables symbolization, which is the representation of what is absent in word-signs. In Morrison's narrative, just as the word-sign is not what it signifies, but substitutes for it, so also the father is the replacement for the lost mother-child relation. We can read Paul D as referring to this replacement for loss when he says to the baby ghost, "She got enough without you" (22). His "presence" is "enough" to compensate for the loss of a presymbolic unity that the ghost figures. This meaning emerges again when he takes Sethe and Denver to the carnival and three shadows holding hands follow them: "They were not holding hands, but their shadows were" (56). This linked threesome symbolizes that, as a triad, both joined and distinguished by an intervening presence, Sethe and Denver can form identities in culture.

Paul D senses that his gendered male difference depends on a relationship with Sethe. When his white owner calls him a man, Paul D feels profoundly the hollowness and arbitrariness of a symbolic designation: "Garner called and announced [the slaves at Sweet Home] men," but "did a whiteman saying it make it so? Suppose Garner . . . changed his mind? Took the word away?" (260). Paul D states clearly the dilemma of Lacan's theory, which posits a free-floating, assigned male identity.[11] As Lacan puts it, "Man speaks but it is because the symbol has made him man" (65). For Lacan, the foundation of opposing identities in culture is absence, and the phallus, the symbol of an always male authorizing power, stands for the empty space that holds apart oppositions like male and female or black and white. Morrison rewrites this traditional psychoanalytic thinking. In her revision, male and female identities depend on both a difference from and a relationship to the opposing gender. In *Beloved*, we see this conceptualization of gender identity at work when Paul D feels unmanned by Beloved, who is driving him out of 124. Recognizing that his manhood needs to "take root" (261), he asks Sethe to have a child with him. Whereas without Sethe he feels that his manhood "struck nothing solid a man could hold on to," by "getting in [Sethe's life] and letting it get in him" (261) he can "document his manhood and break out of the girl's spell—all in one" (151). For Morrison, it is a balance of male-female separation and attachment that enables different gender identities.[12]

At a symbolic level, Paul D's sexual intercourse with Beloved represents yet another image for the father figure's role as intermediary. If we interpret Beloved as the personification of the Sethe-Denver unmodified mother-child attachment, we can read the sexual intercourse as his intervention in this undifferentiated relation. Certainly, Paul D's sex with Beloved seems to differentiate: it seems both to stir new life in Beloved, who appears to become pregnant, and to be consciousness-quickening for Denver. Their lovemaking "woke" (138) Denver, who overhears them, and this waking symbolizes a first step in initiating her into a social world of relational difference. Another sign of Paul D's disruption of the mother-child unity that Beloved embodies appears the next day in the cold house: when Denver stands among the potato sacks where Paul D made love to Beloved, Beloved briefly vanishes from Denver's view.

This sexual commingling of Paul D and Beloved "w[akes]" not only Denver but also "Paul D himself" (138). To understand this waking effect on Paul D, we need to recall his experiences in Alfred, Georgia. When Paul D arrives at 124, he remembers well the chains of the prison camp—but not their life-sustaining role—and he shuns any relationship as a chain that will enslave him. This alienated state is metaphorically represented in the novel as a "tobacco tin buried in his chest where a red heart used to be" (85). To open the rusted-shut lid of the tobacco tin and set the red heart beating, he must become fluid and unbounded. In the words of Kristeva, he must have "the courage to call [himself] disintegrated"; that is, he must overcome his fear of a loving surrender of the self to another in the knowledge that the self is "a strange land of borders and othernesses ceaselessly constructed and deconstructed" (*Strangers* 192, 191). Because Beloved is the incarnation of an original undifferentiated mother-child relation, sex with her is a recognition of "the connection between them" (137) and literalizes a return to a precultural, fused existence. Like the dissolving mud that threatened Hi Man and the convicts but also enabled their ascent, Paul D's sex with Beloved figures a return "to some ocean-deep place he once belonged to" (311) that opens onto new life, as symbolized by Beloved's pregnancy.

Unlike the Paul D–Beloved coupling, which is transformative, the Sethe-Beloved identification contains no alteration, no passage forward into the new. It represents a narcissistic regression to a former unmarked unity. When Paul D learns that eighteen years earlier Sethe killed her infant daughter, he leaves 124. Without Paul D, Sethe decides that "there is no world outside my door" (217) and shuts herself up in 124 with Beloved and Denver. At this point, because there is no intervention in the mother-child unity, there is no difference. Before Denver's eyes, her mother appears to dissolve into Beloved. Beloved appears to get bigger as Sethe, who is starving, shrinks. After a time, "it was difficult for Denver to tell who was who" (283), and it seems to Denver "as though her mother had lost her mind" (282). In this way Morrison dramatizes the breakdown of subjectivity that occurs when what Freud names the death drive, a desire to return to a totalizing identification, is not checked. For there to be conscious existence in the world of social exchange, there must be a transformation of the sealed mother-child circuit, which now has "no crack or crevice available" (222).

As Wyatt writes in her ground-breaking essay, "It is Denver . . . who initiates the breakup of this self-consuming mother-child circle." In my reading, it must be Denver who makes this move because Beloved is Morrison's personification of the identificatory relation between Sethe and Denver that threatens them both. Wyatt's essay charts Denver's induction into the social order as "follow[ing] the Lacanian schema, in which taking the position of speaking subject requires a repudiation of continuity with the mother's body. . . . But Morrison . . . soften[s] this opposition between bodily communion and the abstractions of verbal exchange" ("Giving Body" 482, 484). My project builds on Wyatt's astute insight, as I explore the critical role of the third party in mediating the transition from an original, undifferentiated existence to a separate position as an "I" both apart from and related to others.

"Nobody could make it alone. . . . You could be lost forever, if there wasn't nobody to show you the way" (159). Baby Suggs's words refer to escaping slavery, and Morrison's novel charts the way into the world for former slaves who have been denied the loving mother-father ensemble that constitutes access to a culture defined by relational difference. To negotiate the borderland between body in the world and language-user in culture, Denver is guided by a series of father figures, Baby Suggs, Lady Jones, and the women who offer her gifts of food. In Morrison's allegory of socialization, the father, irrespective of gender or race, is whoever plays the paternal role, which is to straddle the threshold between an original inmixed existence identified with a mother-child fusion and a cultural order governed by a system of signs that assign different identities. This straddling is accomplished by becoming the mother's uncanny double, that is, by being like the mother, but not her; and this combination of relatedness and difference ushers the child into the social order where others share commonalities with the child and are also different.[13]

When Denver separates from her mother, Baby Suggs is the first to function as the middle ground between maternal intimacy and an outside world of others. As Denver "leaves the yard," she "steps off the edge of the world" (286) in the sense that she opens a space between herself and the maternal body that has been her world. To support this crossing from maternal body to a community of black and white others, Baby Suggs blurs the roles of mother and father. As Denver's grandmother, a nurturing, loving mother figure, she is a second mother; at the same time, she takes the place of her dead son, Denver's father, when she calls her granddaughter to separate from her mother and to "be swallowed up in the world beyond the edge of the porch" (286). Denver's fear of the outside world is a fear of whites that she learned largely from Grandma Baby, who told her "about Carolina," "about [her] daddy," and "about [her] mother's feet, not to speak of her back" (287). It was Grandma Baby who told her that "even when [whites] thought they were behaving, it was a far cry from what real humans did" and that against them "there was no defense" (287–88). Yet as Denver stands on the porch full of fear of whites, it is Grandma Baby's voice she hears summoning her to put herself at risk and join a community of blacks and whites. Denver hears Baby Suggs laugh and issue the call to know the dangers of the world outside her door, and "go on out the yard. Go on" (288).

Similarly, Lady Jones is another who straddles the roles between mother and father. When Denver comes to her and asks her for food, Lady Jones says, "Oh, baby," and "it was the word 'baby,' said softly and with such kindness, that inaugurated her life in the world as a woman" (292). As Wyatt observes, we see here a merging of the maternal and the verbal. Lady Jones is a substitute for the lost mother, but she also provides access to a world of symbolic meanings by teaching Denver to read. But doesn't this merging, to use Wyatt's word, "confound" (483) the two orders, the maternal presymbolic and the paternal symbolic? I argue that culture's differences not only survive this confounding but are also introduced by this overlap because boundaries are dual sites, both the one and the other.

As a compound border figure, Lady Jones introduces boundaries, which are sites of transformation; and, Morrison argues, the cultural order works by transformation of the maternal and material into symbols, and not, as a white, Western, exclusionary identity narrative posits, by eviscerating the one to distinguish the other.

The subsequent appearance of dishes of food with names marked on attached slips of paper allegorizes this transformational process. In the weeks that follow her visit to Lady Jones, Denver finds "lying on the tree stump at the edge of the yard" dishes of food, and "names appeared near or in gifts of food" (292–93). The tree stump is a material sign for the withholding that allows us to single out one meaning from all others so as to make order and identity in culture. However, this exclusion, which is analogous to the alienation of another to create our own different raced, gendered, or ethnic identity, is only one part of the signifying process. The process of signification is a balance between loss (or repression) and a transformed return. The names on a slip of paper, symbols for identities in culture, arise, not out of loss, but out of transformation: the food replaces the mother's nurturing body. A shared identity with the mother (the first to be made other) has not been entirely erased; it has been made into something different by culture.

Because Beloved is the fleshly incarnation of an original, unmodified mother-child relation, Morrison's fable of acculturation ends with Beloved's transformation. Morrison narrates this transformation, which is a move from the precultural to the cultural, as a move from the mother to the father, who is the way into a heterogeneous community. When the white Bodwin drives a cart to 124 to carry Denver to his home, where she is to stay the night, he acts the role of the father who introduces the child to the world outside the sealed mother-child relation, a world of culturally formed differences. In turn, because schoolteacher played a perverted version of this role some eighteen years before when he came to claim Sethe's children as his own, Bodwin also refigures schoolteacher. As Morrison revisits this critical moment in a black child's entry into a racially mixed, white-dominant American culture, she highlights the meaning that a border figure is needed to help negotiate the boundary zone between culture's categories, like black and white.

The scene of Denver's induction into the social order begins at the beginning, in a return to a precultural mother-child intimacy. For example, when the thirty women come to 124 to exorcise Beloved, they are rejoined with their former selves and their lost mothers: they "s[ee] . . . themselves.

Younger, stronger, even as little girls." "Mothers, dead now, moved their shoulders to mouth harps" (304). Likewise, the white Bodwin is riding toward "the house he was born in," where "women died . . . his mother, grandmother, an aunt and an older sister" (305). A return is also signi-fied by repetitions, as words and phrases from the former encounter with schoolteacher are repeated: "The sky was blue and clear. Not one touch of death in the definite green of the leaves" (162, 308). And when Sethe sees the white man coming for her child, she once again assumes the aspect of the pre-Oedipal or phallic mother: "Little hummingbirds stick needle beaks right through her headcloth into her hair and beat their wings" (192, 308–9). But in this repetition/return there is a critical, signifying difference. This time, the black community, which eighteen years ear-lier had "step[ped] back and "h[e]ld itself at a distance" (209), now joins her. When Sethe, hand-in-hand with Beloved, looks out her door, she sees "loving faces before her" even as "she sees him" (308).

The group of singing women who come to 124 to exorcise Beloved are doubles—the same and different—for both the black mother and a white father figure (or third party), and this duality is the key that ushers Den-ver into a world of black-white relations. On the one hand, they are black mothers, like Sethe, and as Sethe hears them sing, it seems "as though the Clearing had come to her . . . , where the voices of women searched for the right combination, the key, the code, the sound that broke the back of words" (308). Breaking "the back of words," they seem to be exponents of meanings and a power that exist prior to the advent of language, what Kristeva calls the *chora*, that is, a remnant of a pre-Oedipal unity that subsists within the symbolic order as the possibility of disruption (*Revo-lution* 26). On the other hand, these thirty black women are also stand-ins for a white man, who comes to intervene in the mother-child bond. In fact, in this reenactment of a black child's induction into a white-dominant, racially heterogeneous America, it is the black neighbor women and Den-ver who figure maternal displacement when they overpower, wrestle to the ground, and disarm Sethe as she tries to attack the white man. As in the Freudian/Lacanian identity narrative, the unbounded mother-child unity is disrupted, but in Morrison's revision the boundary makers are hyphenated mother-father, black-white figures, whose presence enables the transformation of a maternal undifferentiated relation into dynamic relationships with others, with whom the child shares commonalities and culturally made differences, such as Bodwin's white difference.

The penultimate scene of the novel drives home once again the critical importance of relatedness in the formation of social identities. After Beloved has been banished, Sethe is heartsick with grief. Arriving at 124, Paul D finds Sethe lying in the same bed where Baby Suggs died when her heartstrings were broken by whites. By separating from her mother, Denver "demarcates a space out of which signs arise" (*Powers* 10), and Sethe is the abject mother, "the radically excluded" "jettisoned object" "at the border of [her] condition as a living being" (*Powers* 2,3). Like Baby Suggs before her, Sethe is outside of culture, in the place of the abject, the edge of madness and death. To rescue Sethe from "the place where meaning collapses," someone from the outside, a father figure, must become a substitute both for a lost maternal intimacy that she reproduced with Denver and for the father she never knew.

Paul D, a black father figure, "serve[s] as go-between" between "the maternal entity" and "the symbolic realm," and this doubling, like healed, scarred tissue over a wound, paves the way so that Sethe can "become autonomous and authentic in [her] turn" (*Powers* 13). As Paul D enters 124, he finds "absence": "Something is missing from 124." What is missing, he comes to see, is himself: "It seems to him a place he is not" (319). A series of repetitions follow; and, in the first, Paul D's return reenacts his original entry. As she did when he first arrived, Sethe says, "You looking good," and Paul D repeats his former reply: "Devil's confusion" (8, 320). This replication is a doubling that prepares us for others. When Paul D asks permission to bathe Sethe and to "rub [her] feet" (321), he becomes the replacement for Baby Suggs and Amy Denver, two sustaining maternal figures, whose ministrations in the past had brought Sethe back from the dead. And when he says to Sethe, "What, baby?" (321), he becomes the double of another mother substitute, Lady Jones, whose word "Baby" had ushered Denver into a social order of culturally defined differences. By calling her "baby," in effect, he is saying that she is his baby, and that, like Lady Jones, Baby Suggs, and Amy Denver, he will "mother" her. Paul D is not Lady Jones, Baby Jones, or Amy Denver, but he is like them. He is related but not identical, the formula for meaning in the social order. An original, undifferentiated unity is gone, but, in the social order, other relationships that double for it can and must sustain us. And the "father" is the crucial boundary marker who ushers us into the social order by mediating between the one and the other.

In *Beloved*, the father inducts a subject into a world where seeming opposites—white and black, male and female, mother and father—are contiguous with one another without being identical. And the father performs this induction by finding common ground with another. The white girl Amy Denver becomes this grounding border figure when she crosses racial lines and, by acting as midwife to Denver, shares alliances with the black mother and child. A number of critics, including Abel, Moglen, Moreland, Fultz, and Michael, have astutely analyzed the unlikely and "blessed" Sethe-Amy alliance, which saves Sethe's life and gives Denver life. The shared view of these critics is ably expressed by Moglen, who points to Amy Denver, along with Baby Suggs and Lady Jones, as examples of those who, "by extending the boundaries of community, refute implicitly the view that relations of otherness are necessarily oppositional" (215). In analyzing this remarkable scene between Sethe and Amy, all these critics take note of Amy's culturally inbred racism. But, as Moreland thoughtfully observes, when Amy begins to tell Sethe her story, she "might well recognize by a kind of transference with Sethe's present condition a version of Amy's own story" (45). I would add to Moreland's important observation that this alignment blurs black and white identities. Whereas, when the scene opens, Sethe sees Amy as a "whitegirl" (and, at first, a "whiteboy" [38] and an enemy), and Amy Denver refers to Sethe with the racial slur "nigger" (38), as they interact with one another, these oppositional, culturally formed racial and racist designations fall away. The two are referred to as "they," a collective identity. They are "the two women" and "the wet sticky women" (99). Even a white racist pateroller, who would identify them by race, would, nevertheless, equate them as "two throw-away people, two lawless outlaws—a slave and a barefoot whitewoman with unpinned hair" (100). This elision of race difference is accompanied by an overlap of maternal and paternal roles. Like a mother, Amy nurtures and sustains Sethe and her child; like a father, she cuts the umbilicus, and her patronymic is bestowed on Sethe's child (Abel 837). This pairing of the mother's integrative role and the father's differentiating role models a balance of inclusion and exclusion, which is the key to enabling an individual culturally defined subjectivity within a community of others.

Similarly, Stamp Paid is another father figure who models a way to negotiate between the mother-child static relation and language's either-or categories. As Susan Mayberry notes, Stamp "incorporates [a] feminine masculinity" (177). He is the father who intervenes between mother and child when he snatches Denver from Sethe's grasp as she is about to kill her child, and he is also a nurturing, substitute mother figure when he gives Sethe food and water, wraps the newborn in a warm coat, and feeds the infant blackberries that "tast[ed] . . . like being in church" (160). He represents the outside world, the community, which is different, but is not wholly different from the sustaining relationship she shares with her mother. Both different and alike, he models the balance of inclusion and exclusion that enables social relations with others. At the novel's end, when Sethe turns away from the outside world and retreats into 124 with Beloved and Denver, Stamp Paid, I argue, would be the saving mediating figure for Sethe and Denver, but fails. More specifically, when Sethe seems to surrender herself to a precultural bond personified in Beloved, Stamp Paid comes to 124 with the intention of entering the house, and his presence in their midst would modify the sealed mother-child relation; but, hearing the roaring inside and unwilling to knock on the door, he turns away.

Others who model the father's role as mediator are Mr. Bodwin and his sister, the white abolitionists who offer Baby Suggs a safe house and, later, give Denver a job. As critics have pointed out, the Bodwins do not rise above racial prejudice: for example, among their household possessions is a coin jar in the form of a grotesque caricature of a kneeling black boy, and, as Mayberry observes, their "patronage" is "patronizing" (175). However, while a part of a racist white culture, they nonetheless risk white identity by offering inclusion to people of color, and the text denotes this risk by stressing their mixed coloring. Miss Bodwin, "the whitewoman who loved [Baby Suggs]" (56) and who teaches Denver "book stuff" (314), is a study in black and white, a mix of snow-white hair and "black thick eyebrows" (171). This same combination of black and white characterizes her brother, who is the most "visible and memorable person at every gathering" because of "his white hair and his big black mustache" (306). Mayberry notes this interplay of black and white in Bodwin and suggests it "implies . . . the ambiguity of his patronage" (175). In my reading, this crossing of black and white suggests racial ambiguity. This black and white imagery represents the borderline site which is not one thing or the other, but a balance of both. Because they cross a racial line and align themselves with people of color, the Bodwins are "blackened," and the whites who fear this interplay of black and white as a threat to white identity seek to expel them from the white community. When whites call Bodwin a "bleached nigger" (306) and shoe-black his white face and white hair, they externalize their fear that the recognition of black and white commonalities will erase a white identity. And when Bodwin helps to usher fugitive slaves and former slaves into a racially mixed America, he plays the role of mediating figure, who assumes the risk of indeterminacy by modeling a middle ground between white and black.

While many different people in the novel play the role of the father who enables a passage into a community of diverse but related cultural identities, unquestionably, among these hyphenated father-mother figures, men and women of color outnumber whites by a wide margin. Among whites, we count one white girl, Amy Denver, the runaway indentured servant, and perhaps Miss Bodwin, who takes it on herself to educate Denver even as Sethe seems "lost" (314) to Denver. But of course Miss Bodwin is only briefly alluded to in the novel, and the text pointedly acknowledges that Denver's alliance with the white woman is fraught with the danger of domination: when Denver tells Paul D that Miss Bodwin is "experimenting" (314) on her, Paul D is reminded of schoolteacher. And glaringly missing from the list of mediating doubles are white men, unless, as I have tried to do, we make a case for Mr. Bodwin, who helps Denver make the passage into a racially heterogeneous community.

This predominance of black mediating border figures seems to corroborate Hortense Spillers's contention in "Mama's Baby, Papa's Maybe" that Africans in America experienced a "different cultural text" and consequently became "a different social subject." More specifically, Spillers writes that "legal enslavement removed the African-American male . . . from *mimetic* view as a partner in the prevailing social fiction of the Father's name, the Father's law" and "handed" the African American male to the mother "in ways that the white American male is allowed to temporize by a fatherly reprieve." As a result, Spillers asserts that "the black American male embodies the *only* American community of males which has had the specific occasion to learn *who* the female is within itself" (80). In *Beloved*, the number of African American men who are able to straddle the border between mother and father seems to illustrate Spillers's assertion. However, despite the scarcity of whites who are willing to risk the boundary overrunning that is one part of boundary making, Morrison, who, in the words of Mayberry, "intones Other as integral to self identity" as her "mantra" (1), does not, I think, propose that only black men can play the mediating role of cultural father. Rather, the novel issues a call to people of every culturally defined race, ethnicity, and gender configuration to assume the father figure's socializing role by balancing attachment to others with separation from them.

5 Cross-Racial Identification in Blackface Minstrelsy and *Black Like Me*

> I think that the hard work of a nonracist sensibility is the boundary crossing, from safe circle into wilderness;. . . . It is the willingness to spoil a good party and break an encompassing circle. . . . The transgression is dizzyingly intense, a reminder of what it is to be alive. It is a sinful pleasure, this willing transgression of a line, which takes one into new awareness, a secret, lonely and tabooed world—to survive the transgression is terrifying and addictive.
>
> PATRICIA WILLIAMS, *The Alchemy of Race and Rights*

In the preceding chapters, I explored *literary* representations of the father figure's role in setting boundaries; in this last chapter, I propose to look closely at two *cultural* examples of fatherly mediation in setting a boundary between white and black racial identities in America. My objective is to distinguish between an authentic blurring of cultural differences that enables a multicultural community and border crossings that solidify societal hierarchies of dominance and subjection. Because, as Hortense Spillers, Dana Nelson, Patricia Williams, and numerous other theorists have contended, black and white are interdependent racial identities, the production of racial identities requires a self-other relation.[1] As Kristeva explains, this process is ongoing in culture: the deviser of boundaries "never stops demarcating his universe whose fluid confines . . . constantly question his solidity and impel him to start afresh" (*Powers* 8). The fluid middle always threatens difference and always has to be demarcated in a gesture that endlessly crosses and recrosses the color line, but there is a right way and a wrong way to negotiate the in-between.[2] A father figure's willingness to mediate between culture's polarized identities is the right way. The other way, a way that secures not racial heterogeneity but white racial dominance, is through a figure who mediates between whites and a degraded, white-invented signifier for the racial other.

To distinguish between these two modes of engagement, I turn to two cultural examples of transracial union: the figure of the nineteenth-century blackface minstrel—white entertainers who blackened their skin to impersonate men and women of color; and John Howard Griffin—a white man who chemically darkened his skin and lived as a black man among people of color for a little over a month in 1959. I focus specifically on these two cultural phenomena because, as interpreted by the eminent cultural critic Eric Lott, both of these two racial impersonations seem to perform the father's mediating function; that is, both are experiences at the racially indeterminate border that create racial boundaries and foster cross-cultural exchange.[3] On the other hand, scholars of white-to-black passing, including Susan Gubar, Gayle Wald, and Baz Dreisinger, fault white-passing-for-black as a white appropriation of black culture.[4] In this chapter, I contrast two instances of cross-racial identification. In my reading, blackface minstrelsy represents a perverse, polarizing formulation of the father figure's acculturating role. As for John Howard Griffin's assumption of a black identity, I argue that Griffin's performance of blackness as documented in *Black Like Me* exemplifies *both* a white racist appropriation of blackness *and* a productive sharing of racial identities. I intend to show that, when Griffin begins his quest to find out what it feels like "to experience discrimination based on skin color" (2), he, like the blackface minstrel, personifies a white stereotype of blackness. Later, however, as a result of his engagements with African Americans, he cross-identifies with a people rather than with a caricature.

The Blackface Minstrel as Cultural Mediator

As Eric Lott explains, prior to his critical intervention, the nineteenth-century theatrical practice of white men performing in blackface for white audiences had been interpreted as "a fairly pat instance of financial and cultural manipulation." In his landmark study *Love and Theft: Blackface Minstrelsy and the American Working Class*, Lott challenges this interpretation and argues that the minstrel show tradition represents "a more complex dynamic" ("White" 477). The title of Lott's immensely influential work, *Love and Theft*, sums up the "complex dynamic." Stated simply, Lott's impressively historicized study argues that blackface impersonation expressed a desire for transracial union even as it appropriated black culture. While Lott acknowledges that blackface promulgated a white racist stereotype of black culture, he nonetheless takes the position that these blackface performances represent "the first public acknowledgement by whites of black culture" (4), and he credits these racist impersonations as making possible an endless list of artistic achievements, from *Uncle Tom's Cabin* (1852) and *Huckleberry Finn* (1884) to Elvis Presley and rock 'n roll (*Love* 5; "White Like Me" 483–91). He maintains that blackface "began and continues to occur when the lines of 'race' appear both intractable and obstructive, when there emerges a collective desire (conscious or not) to bridge a gulf that is, however, perceived to separate the races absolutely" ("White Like Me" 475–76); he asserts that blackface functioned to bridge the racial gulf: "Minstrel shows worked for over a hundred years to facilitate safely an exchange of energies between two otherwise rigidly bounded and policed cultures"; and he concludes that minstrelsy "withered away" because of its "success in introducing the cultures to each other" (*Love* 6).

The overarching similarity between blackface theatrics and the father figure's mediation is that both are experiences at the border where culture's different identities are put at risk and distinguished. In the case of a blackface minstrel, the white minstrel who mockingly impersonates a black man shares an identity with both black and white, and this racial blurring, as Lott astutely points out, serves as "cultural marker or visible sign of cultural interaction," or boundary, between white and black identities (*Love* 6). But, while the blackface minstrel served as the point of contact between white and black necessary for a racial boundary, blackface structures the father's cross-cultural identification so as to enable the white audience to dismiss it. Blackface minstrelsy was so popular with white audiences because it met white needs to feel in control of a threatening white-black interdependency.

At this point in my narrative, a fuller account of blackface minstrelsy is in order. A blackface minstrel is a culturally defined white man who physically embodies a white caricature of the black man. These white men would apply greasepaint or burnt cork to their faces and skin; exaggerate their lips; and wear wild, woolly wigs and ragged, filthy, or oversized clothes. In this garb, they lampooned people of color for the entertainment of a white audience. Their performances would imitate what they imagined was black dialect and culture, and included a variety of elements: folklore, dance, jokes, songs, instrumental tunes, skits, mock oratory, satire, and racial and gender cross-dressing or impersonation. White minstrel comedy traded in black stereotypes, chief among them "the slow-witted but irrepressible 'plantation darky' and the 'foppish northern dandy Negro,' known as Zip Coon"; and the entertainments "pretend[ed] that slavery was amusing, right, and natural" (*Love* 15, 3). Lott's perceptive analysis finds that the largely white male audience's response to these white impersonations of people of color was conflicted: "The pleasure they derived from their investment in blackness always carried a threat of castration" (*Love* 9). The theatrical practice began as early as the 1820s and was widely popular both in the United States and in Britain in the nineteenth century. Minstrelsy achieved its greatest popularity in 1846–54, years characterized by political strife over slavery and the white immigrant working class. This strange white practice of blacking up to perform a black identity has had both its detractors and its fans. Lott notes that figures such as Mark Twain and Walt Whitman were aficionados of the blackface performance (*Love* 4). On the other hand, Frederick Douglass denounced blackface imitators as "the filthy scum of white society, who have stolen from us a complexion denied to them by nature, in which to make money, and pander to the corrupt taste of their white fellow citizens" (October 27, 1848). More recently, James Baldwin condemns "Negro posers" as those who "malign the sorely menaced sexuality of Negroes in order to justify the white man's own sexual panic" (230–31).

This brief overview already suggests points of contact with and differences from the father's boundary-setting role as it has been identified in the texts of Faulkner, Wright, O'Connor, and Morrison. Before turning to differences, I want to address the similarities, because it is these characteristics, the characteristics of a border crossing, that Lott cites to support his claim that the white man in blackface makeup is a "cultural mediator" who enabled "an almost full absorption of a black tradition into white culture" (*Love* 37, 7).

Blackface minstrelsy and the father figure's mediation between culture's racial identities are similar in that both set racial boundaries in an always contested site of inclusion and exclusion. In making his case for the productive cultural value of the minstrel show, Lott stresses that this white mimicry of black people and culture coupled "cross-racial desire" with "self-protective derision" (*Love* 6). Lott astutely traces the source of this "cross-racial desire" to a need to use blackness so as to construct

American whiteness: "[White American manhood]," he writes, "simply could not exist without a racial other against which it defines itself and which to a very great extent it takes up into itself as one of its own constituent elements" ("White Like Me" 476). Here Lott appears to define racial and gendered identities as they have been theorized in the previous chapters, as what Hortense Spillers calls our confounded identities. This view of race is summed up by Omi and Winant, who write that racial designations are "an unstable and 'decentered' complex of social meanings constantly being transformed by political struggle" (68).[5]

Another similarity between blackface and the father's mediating role is that, like the father figure, who blurs different identities within one person, the minstrel in blackface also condensed two into one. Because the blackface performer is both white and black, he, like the father figure, experiences an in-between state that threatens the loss of a defining racial difference. Lott writes that early audiences of minstrel shows often thought "that they were being entertained by actual Negroes" and that the white performers of blackface often resorted to advertising their whiteness by circulating sheet music that featured pictures of them with and without their blackface masks and costumes (*Love* 20). In his analysis of blackface performances, Ralph Ellison points out that precisely this terror of racial indistinguishability is at the heart of the minstrel show: "When the white man steps behind the mask of the trickster his freedom is circumscribed by the fear that . . . he will become in fact that which he intends only to symbolize; that he will . . . lose that freedom, which . . . he would recognize as the white man's alone" (53).

If we agree with Lott's reading of the positive impact of the blackface mask, another seeming similarity is that blackface worked to make a white identity more inclusive in much the same way that the father figure's mediation enables cross-cultural relationships. As previously noted, according to Lott, the blackface act was responsible for channeling black culture into white society and helped to create new cultural forms. Also, Lott points out that, prior to the Civil War, performing in blackface on minstrel stages enabled the Irish to be accepted as "white" (*Love* 94–96); and Michael Rogin shows that, in the 1920s, Jewish performances in blackface makeup, like Al Jolson's, helped Jews to be assimilated into "white" America (73–119).

Like the father's mediating role, blackface minstrelsy negotiates a need for common ground, but the blackface minstrel show staged a moment of transracial union in a way that enabled white domination of the border. As I propose to show, even as Lott seeks to support his thesis that in blackface acts there was a "dialectical flickering" (*Love* 18) toward the "love" of his title, he casts as love what he more accurately terms elsewhere a "fascination" (6), "a racial envy" (18), an "attraction" (20), or an "obsession" (25) consistent with an urgent need for a black reference point to define a white identity. Ultimately, what distinguishes a blackface border crossing from the father figure's facilitation of cross-racial exchange is the absence of love from blackface minstrel humor.

Whereas the father figure forges an even-handed relationship between the one and the other that fosters a cross-cultural alliance, blackface minstrel comedy is white male–dominated. In the meeting of white and black in the minstrel show rendition, the blackface mask was "highly responsive to the emotional demands of its audience" (*Love* 6). This audience was largely white male (*Love* 9)—women were "usually not even on the sidelines" (Roediger 121)—and people of color were represented on stage by white men who played the roles of not only black men but also black women, even though at this time women commonly performed on stage (*Love* 26). The signature characteristic of minstrelsy was white control; and Lott admits from the outset that whites used the blackface mask to "divest black people of control over elements of their culture and over their own cultural representation generally" (*Love* 18).

While the father's role is to enable a common ground between culture's polarized identities, blackface is designed by whites to focus on precisely that necessary common ground so as to mock and deny their own feared need of it. Blackface comedy developed out of clowning (*Love* 24–25), and, as Freud shows in his analysis of jokes, clowns embody our fears and enable us to laugh at them. Lott's careful documentation of minstrel show lyrics, sheet music, jokes, dialogues, skits, dialect, and so on concludes that the minstrel performance "offered [whites] a way to play with collective fears of a degraded and threatening—and male—Other while at the same time maintaining some symbolic control over them" (25). Lott's stress on the words "and male" suggests that white men feared a common maleness. This fear explains the central theme of the minstrel show. Lott writes that "white men's investment in the black penis appears to have defined the minstrel show" (121) and "in a real sense the minstrel man *was* the penis, that organ returning in a variety of contexts, at time ludicrous, at others rather less so" (25–26). To suggest "white men's obsession with a rampageous black penis" (25), he quotes a popular minstrel show song, "Long Tail Blue" (1827), which I include here.

Some Niggers they have but one coat,
 But you see I've got two;
I wears a jacket all the week,
 And Sunday my long tail blue.

Jim Crow is courting a white gall,
 And yaller folks call her Sue;
I guess she back'd a nigger out,
 And swung my long tail blue.

As I was going up Fulton Street,
 I hollered arter Sue,
The watchman came and took me up,
 And spoilte my long tail blue.

. . . .

If you want to win the Ladies hearts,
 I'll tell you what to do;
Go to a tip top Tailor's shop,
 And buy a long tail blue. (*Love* 120, 25)

Because the penis is a point of contact between white men and black men and a potential point of contact between white and black through miscegenation, minstrel show lyrics put on display this threat of racial mixing ("Jim Crow is courting a white gall" with his "long tail blue") so as to make a joke of it and to stage a symbolic castration: the white "watchman" "spoilte my long tail blue," and it now can be appropriated by the white man at the tailor's shop. As Lott notes, such songs were not "simple indulgence"; rather they speak "of a culture trying to contain . . . [that] which could more historically be called intermixture and insurrection" (25). This interpretation would explain what Lott calls "the sheer overkill" typical of the minstrel show songs in which "black men are roasted, fished for, smoked like tobacco, peeled like potatoes, planted in the soil, or dried and hung up as advertisements" (150).

This same obsession with white male mastery of a racial boundary characterizes the blackface minstrel show's portrayal of black women. First of all, recall that white male performers played the black female roles, so the minstrel show staged a confusion of male and female bodies: the "'female' bodies," Lott writes, "were 'also' male" (27). This gender confusion sought to make a joke of the real threat to white male identity posed by the white man's desire for the black female body: the threat of a miscegenous union. This desire for mastery of the black female body, I propose, is the impetus behind the motif of black female castration that Lott finds frequently recurring in blackface performances (152–53). I include here the lyrics of "Gal from the South," which Lott states "is fairly typical of the representation of women on the minstrel stage" (26).

> Ole massa bought a colored gal,
>   He bought her at the south;
> Her hair it curled so very tight
>   She could not shut her mouth.
> Her eyes they were so bery small,
>   They both ran into one.
> And when a fly light in her eye,
>   Like a June bug in the sun.
>
> Her nose it was so berry long,
>   It turned up like a squash,
> And when she got her dander up
>   She made me laugh, by gosh;
> Old massa had no hooks or nails,
>   Or nothin' else like that,
> So on this darkie's nose he used
>   To hang his coat and hat.
>
> One morning massa goin' away,
>   He went to git his coat,
> But neither hat nor coat was there,
>   For she had swallowed both;
> He took her to a tailor shop,
>   To have her mouth made small,
> The lady took in one long breath,
>   And swallowed tailor and all. (26)

Lott observes that this image of the "black wench" was often presented on stage both as a narrative and as an act: "the narrative detailing the jokey blazon, the oblivious 'wench' ridiculed in person on another part of the stage" (*Love* 26). He glosses this "representative" example of minstrelsy's many "wench" characterizations by saying that these portraits "offer one of the most revealing discourses on male sexuality in America at mid-century" (26). But what exactly does this miming of the black "wench" reveal about (white) male sexuality at mid-century? The black woman's mouth, a ravening maw that threatens the white man with engulfment, is a scarcely veiled vaginal reference, and the ditty makes a joke of the white man's fear of envelopment. The narrative describes the woman of color in terms that suggest gender ambiguity. Her nose, "so bery long" and "turned up like a squash," is a phallic image, and the words "got her dander up" suggest an erection, while the mouth is unmistakably vaginal. This mouth is the "hole" that threatens the white man with "wholeness," a merging of black and white and male and female. To cancel the threat, the narrative references twice the word "bought," signaling white ownership, and indicates that the devouring hole-like mouth is to be "made small" by the tailor. While, in the end, the black woman "swallow[s] tailor and all"—a reminder that her body threatens incorporation—the language of the ditty works relentlessly to objectify her. She is compared to a "squash" and to "hooks and nails," on which the master hangs his coat and hat. The reference to eyes "so bery small, they both ran into one," stresses her difference, an inhuman freakishness. Noting these "grotesque trans-mutations" of black women, Lott attributes them to "white men's fear of female power" (27). I would add that white men fear their own desire to cross a racial and gender boundary.

That the blackface minstrel show ritually performs intermixture is the insight of no less an acute observer than Charles Dickens. During a visit to the United States, Dickens made his way to the lower East Side of Manhattan to be entertained by the minstrel performer "Juba," William Henry Lane. In *American Notes* (1842), he records being dazzled by the blackface minstrel's dancing:

> Suddenly the lively hero dashes in to the rescue. Instantly the fiddler grins, and goes at it tooth and nail; there is new energy in the tambourine; new laughter in the dancers; new smiles in the landlady; new confidence in the landlord; new brightness in the very candles. Single shuffle, double shuffle, cut and cross-cut; snapping his fingers, rolling his eyes, turning in his knees, presenting the backs of his legs in front, spinning about on his toes and heels like nothing but the man's fingers on the tambourine; dancing with two left legs, two right legs, two wooden legs, two wire legs, two spring legs—all sorts of legs and no legs—what is this to him? (139)

What is striking about Dickens's description of Juba's dancing is the over-whelming sense of the possibilities of unstable identities, that is, of one thing not being only what it is but something else as well. The "front" and "backs of his legs" become interchangeable. His toes and heels some-how become "fingers on the tambourine." Every part of his body seems to be sliding into something else. His right leg becomes his left; his legs become wooden legs, then wire legs, then spring legs, then no legs. Citing Dickens's review of Juba's performance, Lott says that Dickens "ends up producing an account that lacks an immanent purpose" (116). But Lott, I think, fails to apprehend Dickens's "immanent purpose." If Dickens's response seems to Lott unfocused, it is because Dickens is trying to cap-ture in words the sense of inchoate fluidity and transformative possibili-ties that is the power of the performance—a power that whites needed to feel they controlled.

While Lott maintains that blackface minstrelsy represents something of an aberration from typical American racism because it is driven by a "dialectical flickering" between "racial envy" and "racial insult" (*Love* 18), I find that the blackface mask stages as a comic entertainment the way whites typically tried to dominate racial relations. This desire for control of the racial in-between explains why minstrel shows were so popular at a time when, according to the contemporary observer Thomas Low Nichols (Walt Whitman's editor in the 1840s), "there was not an audi-ence in America that would not have resented, in a very energetic fashion, the insult of being asked to look at the dancing of a real negro" (*Love* 112).[6] This need for mastery of an interracial space also explains why an authentic African American entertainer who could out-dance any white imitator could only take the white stage if he pretended to be a white man pretending to be a person of color. This was the case of "Juba," the "blacked-up" performer who dazzled Dickens. "Juba" was William Henry Lane, the most famous and "nearly the only" black performer to appear in white theaters in the mid-1840s (*Love* 113). The story of how Lane became the first person of color to don blackface is told by Nichols in a memoir. When an Irish blackface dancer abruptly quit P. T. Barnum's minstrel show, Barnum found a far superior African American dancer, William Henry Lane. Nichols writes that Lane's race would be an "insuperable obstacle" to any but Barnum, who "blacked up" Lane and presented him on stage as a counterfeit "Negro" (*Love* 112–13). But it was only by wearing blackface—that is, by acquiescing to play his race as scripted by whites—that Lane could perform before the white audience.

The appearance on the minstrel stage of actual black "blackface" performers would seem to suggest a real breakthrough in the color barrier and the possibility of an authentic grafting of black and white cultures that Lott postulates. The question of the racial authenticity of performances by African American blackface minstrels has been widely debated, but most historians of the blackface tradition find that black performers were largely forced to perform the caricatures of blackness that white minstrels had initiated (Roediger 116; Strausbaugh 70). Robert Toll points out that, prior to the Civil War, blacks could not perform without blackface makeup, regardless of how dark-skinned they were, and that while the black "blackface" performers did not include some of the most racist and self-demeaning minstrel show skits and songs, their material focused on a sentimental, white fantasy of "carefree plantation life" (179, 198, 234). While scholars have argued persuasively that the appearance of real African Americans before a white audience enabled people of color to display their authentic musical talent and provided an escape from poor-paying, menial labor, some of the indignities that these black performers suffered might seem to outweigh such advantages. In the worst-case scenarios, Toll writes, white managers of minstrel troops composed of "genuine sons of Africa" "put them on exhibit—like animals in a zoo" (205–6). Even more detrimental to the argument that blacks in blackface advanced the cause of racial equality is Toll's contention that the stage performances of African American minstrels only helped to strengthen white racism in that these "real" black minstrels "added credibility to the [racist] image by making it seem that Negroes actually behaved like minstrelsy's 'black caricatures'" (196).

My position on African American "minstrels" in blackface makeup largely aligns with that of Michael Rogin, the author of a study of minstrelsy in the motion picture industry, who notes that "whether or not literally under burnt cork," African Americans "perform against themselves for white eyes" (18). People of color could easily take the stage to perform blackface because, as Toll soberly observes, "acting the 'nigger' was precisely what whites expected blacks to do" (202). Ralph Ellison, who has focused on the issue of blackface minstrelsy in "Change the Joke and Slip the Yoke," writes that the blackface mask "was once required of anyone who would act the role" (47) and that "its function was to veil the humanity of Negroes thus reduced to a sign" (49). Because every interaction between white and black is an experience at the border where racial designations are both produced and put at risk, in these exchanges just as on the minstrel stage, typically, whites demanded that blacks act the role of inferior.

Certainly, my examination of fictional representations of black-white relations in the preceding chapters has suggested that, in most inter-changes with whites, African Americans were constrained to wear a black-face mask. In *Native Son,* Bigger Thomas knows well the subordinate role he is supposed to play in the presence of whites. When he visits a rich white man, Mr. Dalton, he stands "with his knees slightly bent, his lips partly open, his shoulders stooped, and his eyes held a look that went only to the surface of things. There was an organic conviction in him that this was the way white folks wanted him to be when in their presence" (54); and Bigger is shocked when Mary and Jan do not expect this pose. In *Intruder in the Dust,* white men are outraged by the dignity and manli-ness of Lucas Beauchamp, and they insist that he "act like a nigger" (48). In *Beloved,* when the abolitionist Mr. Bodwin crosses racial lines, he is "blacked up" by whites in a gesture that seeks to turn him into the black-face minstrel. To cite a real-life example, when John Griffin, the author of *Black Like Me,* darkens his skin and sets out to experience life as an Afri-can American man, he begins with the intention of "still [being] the same man" (5), and he quickly discovers that, in blackface, white men and women demand that he behave like an inferior. The degrading, white-scripted blackface role is perhaps most strikingly embodied in the mock-ing figures of African Americans with which white Americans, particu-larly in the South, decorated their homes in a cultural practice that seems to represent the continuing need into the twentieth century for the role of the nineteenth-century blackface minstrel. In her story "The Artificial Nigger," O'Connor powerfully points out that, like the blackface enter-tainer, this racist statuary figures an encounter between whites and a white-constructed signifier for blackness that sets a racial boundary in accordance with white racist ideology.

In a work of Southern literature not examined in my study, *To Kill a Mockingbird,* Harper Lee provides an instructive example of how South-ern culture insists that the figure who straddles the racial middle play the role of the minstrel in blackface. In Lee's novel, Dolphus Raymond is an upper-class white Southerner who loves a woman of color, lives with her, and makes a family with her. His actions make him a cultural mediator, a borderland father. But, unlike Lucas Beauchamp in *Intruder* who will not play the blackface role, Dolphus knuckles under to a white racist culture. Like the blackface minstrel, who plays the part of a laughable, inferior figure, Dolphus pretends he is a depraved drunkard. This play-acted role, like the blackface minstrel's, allows a white racist culture to countenance a racial crossing by ridiculing it.

By staging an encounter between whiteness and a white-constructed disparaging image of blackness, blackface minstrelsy served to polarize white and black racial identities at a time in American history when the artificiality and arbitrariness of the racial binary was becoming apparent. As Lott, Roediger, and others have pointed out, blackface arose during a period of "anti-immigrant hysteria," when immigrants were pouring into America, and these working-class immigrants and African Americans were holding the same menial jobs and living in the same teeming slum neighborhoods in American cities (Roediger 117). Roediger notes that in the years before the Civil War, contemporary accounts often equated African Americans and the Catholic Irish "race" (133–34), and Lott writes that the working-class immigrants "feared they were becoming blacker" (*Love* 71). Roediger argues that the popularity of the minstrel show at this time was not a coincidence; nor was it coincidental that poor Irish immigrants often "blacked up" and enriched themselves by doing so. Because blackface radically exaggerated racial difference, juxtaposed with the "Coons" and "plantation darkies" of the minstrel show, the new Irish immigrants came to seem "white" (Roediger 117–18). Even as they wore blackface, the Irish minstrels engaged in practices that contrasted their authentic, "respectable" "whiteness" with the "unruly" blackness they counterfeited on stage: they circulated playbills that featured paired pictures of the performers in blackface "As Plantation Darkies" and, without makeup, "As Citizens"; and minstrels changed back and forth from black to white on stage (Roediger 117). Roediger states that these Irish blackface minstrels were the "first self-consciously *white* entertainers in the world. The simple physical disguise—and elaborate cultural disguise—of blacking up served to emphasize that those on stage were really white and that whiteness really mattered" (117).[7] As Lott rightly points out, the blackface mask enabled working-class immigrants to be identified as "white" Americans, but it performed this work by grotesquely racializing people of color as "other." As Alan W. C. Green's study of minstrelsy finds, the blackface mask "moved [the Negro] into a solo spot center stage, providing a relationship model in contrast to which masses of Americans could establish a positive and superior sense of identity" (Roediger 118). While not alluding specifically to minstrelsy, Toni Morrison makes much the same point about the production of American "whiteness." She writes that Americans "wrested" a white identity "through a self-reflexive contemplation of a fabricated, mythological Africanism ... [which] must be ... decidedly not American, decidedly other" (*Playing* 47–48). Unlike the father figure's relationship model, which acknowledges a kinship with the racial or gendered other and risks self-identity, the blackface minstrel's performance uses the racial middle to strengthen white hegemony.

Cross-Racial Identification in *Black Like Me*

I began this study with this question: When does a cross-cultural identification violate the agency of another and reify positions of dominance and subjection? I have analyzed at length blackface minstrelsy, a widely debated cultural phenomenon, because it seems to represent a textbook example of a border crossing that co-opts the racial other and perpetuates racial hegemony. I propose to end this study with an example of a nonfictional cross-racial identification that eventually becomes a border negotiation that opens up avenues of cultural exchange. In what follows, I examine *Black Like Me*, John Howard Griffin's autobiographical account of his experience as a white man passing for black for a little over a month in 1959.[8] My objective is to show that when Griffin begins his racial impersonation, he, like the blackface minstrel, masquerades as a black man. That is, when he first assumes a black identity, his own unacknowledged, deep implication in white America's sense that white identity is essential and superior causes him to see a black identity—including the one he inhabits—as a racial caricature utterly alien to himself. But Griffin's experiences living as a black man among people of color transform him. By the end of his monthlong cross-racial experience, he is no longer a racial impostor; rather, like Lucas Beauchamp, he is "not black nor white either" (13), but a liminal, two-in-one figure who bridges a racial divide and can serve as an interpreter between white and black America.

My position that Griffin ultimately risks racial indeterminacy counters the prevailing critical view that his act of passing for black is a white appropriation of blackness. According to Eric Lott, Griffin's project is continuous with the blackface minstrel's in that "he enters blackness according to the dictates of white desire" ("White" 486) and "goes on to uncover the contours of blackness for whites" (485). Gayle Wald and Baz Dreisinger largely agree that Griffin is another white man in blackface. Wald holds Griffin guilty of "critical voyeurism" and compares him to white ethnographers who make the other "merely objects of the (white) gaze" (155). For Wald, because Griffin appropriates the black experience "without compromising white entitlement to speak for this experience" (180), he "solidifies hierarchies of subject/object" (155). Taking a similar position, Dreisinger finds that Griffin's whiteness is never in danger because white and black are always essential identities for him (62). Dreisinger modifies this position somewhat, however, by arguing that he does become a "better white through his excursion into blackness" (11).

While I agree with these scholars that, in the early phase of his experiment with racial crossing, Griffin sees people of color, including himself in his identity as a black man, through the racializing gaze of the dominant white culture, I take issue with their claim that Griffin never compromises his white subject position. In my reading, Griffin comes to "see" differently. He goes undercover as a black man essentially to "see" people of color as they "really" are. Ultimately, what he sees is that "the Negro is the same human as the white man" (96). In other words, Griffin comes to see common ground. More than this, Griffin, who states early on that people of color have "a view of the white man that the white man can never understand" (48), eventually comes to share the black view of the white man. In her study of Griffin's passing for black, Wald focuses on looking and frequently cites Du Bois's theory of double consciousness. According to Du Bois, the person of color develops a double consciousness, an awareness of a racialized identity bestowed on her by the controlling gaze of the dominant white culture. Throughout Griffin's autobiographical account of his time as a black man, he focuses intensively on the way white people look at him. He, like people of color, feels trapped in this controlling, devalorizing gaze. He sees as well the detrimental effects of this gaze on the white lookers, and he becomes aware of his own implication in this gaze as a white man. He develops the double consciousness of a person of color, and he sees both as a white man and as a black man.

As Black Like Me opens and Griffin explains his project and his motivations, he seems to be either disingenuous or lacking in self-knowledge. For example, he writes that he had long been "haunted" by the idea of "becoming a Negro" (1) and that he embarks on this racial "experiment" (179) as the only way to "learn the truth" (1) because "the Southern Negro will not tell the white man the truth" (2). As Griffin makes this statement, the year is 1959, and, as Michael Awkward observes, "voluminous black-authored fictive, poetic, sociological, and historical texts . . . existed in the late 1950s" that tried to convey to whites " 'the truth' of blackness" in America (13). When one surveys the list of black authors and leaders who had been speaking out about race from the earliest days of slavery to 1959, the reader can only surmise that, if Griffin is, as he states, "a specialist in race issues [who] really knew nothing of the Negro's real problem" (2), it is not because people of color won't "tell the white man the truth"; it is because whites—Griffin included—cannot or will not hear them.

I propose that Griffin's statement of purpose in the first journal entry—a desire "to learn the truth"—is a tactful evasion that masks his real objective, which emerges in subsequent entries. When Griffin writes that he is looking for the truth, he means that he seeks to know which of two contrary narratives about "the Negro" is true—the white one or the black one. Bluntly put, he wants to know who is telling the truth and who is lying. Later in his narrative, Griffin's real purpose is suggested both when he writes that he will go undercover as black as "the best way to find out if we had second-class citizens" (3) and again, in the epilogue, when he writes that his "experiment was undertaken to discover if America was involved in the practice of racism against black Americans" (179). The word "if" speaks volumes. Contrary to Griffin's assertion that people of color won't speak to a white man, he is well acquainted with black charges that they are treated unjustly, but Griffin is not persuaded by their claims because there is also a white counter-narrative of black life, one in which he is deeply indoctrinated. The Southern whites Griffin knows, he repeatedly states, are "kind and wise," and these men tell him that, in "the natural order of things" (106–7), people of color are unequal to whites. Seen this way, Griffin's project is to assess the cause of the glaring social inequities between blacks and whites—inequities in standard of living, education, achievements, and so on. Specifically, are these inequities produced by social injustice, as people of color claim? Or do they come about as a result of "racial default" (121), as Southern whites claim? If we understand Griffin's objective in this way, we can read more into the question he asks as he sets out: "Do you suppose they'll treat me as John Howard Griffin, regardless of my color—or will they treat me as some nameless Negro, even though I am the same man?" (5). His question, which seems naive, in fact suggests his belief in the decency of Southern whites and his attendant belief that people of color are treated by whites according to their merits—or lack of them. As he initiates his "experiment," he is putting to the test the theory that a black man of intellect and dignity—like the black version of John Griffin—would be treated with respect by Southern whites and would prosper, regardless of color. It does not take long for the test results to come back.

Griffin's narrative is organized around a series of mirror scenes, each of which charts a stage in his racial transformation.[9] By definition, a mirror image is a double because the mirror image reflects the self but is not the self. In Griffin's case, each of these mirror scenes represents an encounter between Griffin's white self and his uncanny black double. In the course of his episodic journey, Griffin's mirror image changes, and the change reflects a change in the way he "sees" his own identity. These mirror-image doubles are not limited to reflections in a glass; rather, they also include a series of white and black men whom he meets along the way.

The first of these mirror scenes registers Griffin's initial reaction to his appearance after he has applied dye to his skin. Paradoxically, this initial response reveals that this white man who wants to "become a Negro" (1) conceives of people of color as irreconcilably "other." As Griffin works to "disguise himself" (11) by shaving his head and dyeing his skin, pointedly, he does not look in a mirror. Then, when the transformation is complete, he confronts his mirror image, and the man he sees there, he insists, is not himself. He writes that "a stranger—a fierce, bald, very dark Negro— glared at me from the glass. He in no way resembled me" (11). Griffin's response suggests the extent to which his sense of self-identity is bound up with whiteness. A dark skin estranges him from himself. When he looks in the mirror, he sees a racial caricature dictated by white ideology. The language he uses to describe the man in the mirror, "fierce" and "glared," denotes a fearful figure. Of course Griffin knows that the man imaged in the mirror is himself, but, nonetheless, a dark-skinned man betokens a threat even—or perhaps especially—when the man is himself. As Griffin describes his altered appearance, he seems unable to stress enough that the man in the mirror is radically other to himself. The black man in the mirror is "an utter stranger, an unsympathetic one with whom I felt no kinship. All traces of the John Griffin I had been were wiped from existence" (11). His protestations that there are no signs of commonalities between himself and his mirror image seem absurd. Clearly there is continuity between white John Griffin and Griffin in blackface makeup, and it seems that he denies the similarity so vehemently to refuse any common ground between black and white. His emphatic denial seems to support Baz Dreisinger's compelling argument that whites reject proximity with people of color because they fear it will reduce their whiteness. Here Griffin seems to refuse proximity with his own adoptive black guise so as to protect his own threatened whiteness. For an answer to the question that he posed at the outset, "Do you suppose they'll treat me as John Howard

Griffin, regardless of my color—or will they treat me as some nameless Negro, even though I am still the same man?" (5), Griffin need look no further than to himself. Not only do others not treat the black and white John Griffin as the same man, even Griffin himself refuses to accept his own dark-skinned self as the same man.

As *Black Like Me* opens, the challenge for Griffin is to change himself. While he thinks that the application of dye to his skin has created "a change so profound it filled me with distress" (11), essentially he is unchanged. He is still the same white man with the same white racial ideology as before, except that now he feels radically other not only to people of color but also to his own contrived black identity. As Wald notes, he is now two people inhabiting one body: he is the white John Griffin, the subject, who, like an ethnographer, observes, and the black Griffin, who is the object of the white gaze. To become the "bridge" between whites and blacks that he claims he wants to be, he will have to change more than his appearance. He will have to bridge the distance between his white self and his black mirror-image double.

As Griffin sets out on his cross-racial experience, he distances himself from his own assumed blackness by being the white observer of himself in blackface. He states explicitly that his goal is to be "objective in [his] observations" (122) and he undertakes his racial experiment "in the spirit of scientific detachment" (122). As he records in his journal his daily experience as a black man in black territory, he seems to bear a resemblance to schoolteacher in *Beloved*, who also fancies he is writing a scientific treatise about black difference. Like schoolteacher, Griffin too seems to assert his mastery of people of color by representing them. This same white desire to control black people by controlling their representation was also the compelling motivation behind blackface minstrelsy. In *Black Like Me*, Griffin seems to play both the role of the white man in blackface *and* the white audience as he performs in blackface before his own observing white gaze.

Griffin's experience on his first night as a black man suggests that, at this early stage in his racechange, he is the double of both the nineteenth-century white audience who relished blackface sexual comedy and of the contemporary white men he meets who display an obsessive interest in black male sexuality. As Eric Lott repeatedly stresses, the "defin[ing]" element of the blackface minstrel show was "white men's investment in the black penis" (*Love* 121). This obsession with the black man's penis, Griffin finds, continues in his day. When Griffin in blackface hitchhikes, the white men who give him rides want him to entertain them with stories about "the depths of depravity" (91). These white men continually prod Griffin to expose himself both literally—at least one white man asks to see his "oversized genitals" (91)—and psychologically; that is, they want the racial other to act out their own forbidden sexual fantasies. Like the white, largely male audience of blackface, these white men would appropriate the black body for the purpose of gratifying and disowning their own sexually perverse appetites.

When Griffin meets these men on the road, he is sickened, but, unknown to himself, Griffin's project may be driven by a similar desire to have black men expose themselves to him. As both Wald and Dreisinger point out, he *is* a white undercover agent who trains a detached, racializing gaze on people of color. Griffin once even lets drop that he fears he will be taken as "a spy for whites" (69). In particular, Griffin may be the double of one young man who gives him a ride. The young man speaks with "an educated flair" and pretends to be questioning Griffin "with the elevation of a scholar seeking information" (93), but his questions reveal that he is obsessed with black male sexuality. Like this young white man, Griffin too is an educated man, who professes a scholarly, elevated purpose, but who also seems to be something of a racial voyeur. Eric Lott goes so far as to argue that Griffin acts the part of a sexual voyeur. Lott makes this claim on the basis of an experience that occurs on the first night of Griffin's racial passing. Unable to sleep in a windowless hotel "cubicle" (15), Griffin walks down the corridor to the men's room and finds there two black men, one in the shower and the other, naked, sitting on the floor waiting to take a shower. Griffin lingers in the bathroom; offers the naked man on the floor a cigarette; and engages him in conversation until the man in the shower finishes and steps out. At one point, Griffin leans into the shower to wash his hands because the sink doesn't work, and reports that "in the shower's obscurity, all I could see was a black shadow and gleaming white teeth" (17). Clearly Griffin is straining to see the naked black man. For Lott, the scene and Griffin's "mapping" of it enable Griffin to indulge a "voyeuristic urge to expose the black man's body" ("White" 487). Lott argues that, like the audience of the blackface minstrel show, Griffin's observation of the scene allows him both "proximity" to and "distance" from "the walking black penis that forms the object of white male desire" ("White" 487).

Another early mirror scene reiterates that, as he sets out to "become a Negro," Griffin is like a white minstrel in blackface in that he feels like an intensely white man wearing to the world's eyes an utterly alien black disguise. The mirror scene occurs on the second night of his racial "experiment" (179) in a room he has rented in a private home. As he is writing in his journal, his landlady enters to light his fire. He looks up from his writing and sees a scene in a facing mirror from which he feels that he is absent: "Light gleamed from the elderly Negro's head as he looked up to talk to the Negro woman. The sense of shock returned; it was as though I were invisible in the room, observing a scene in which I had no part" (35). Griffin's interpretation of his own mirror image suggests that this man who is "experimenting" with blackness refuses any link between his white self and a black-appearing man. Because he identifies himself as white and because the mirror images a black man and woman, Griffin sees the scene as a disembodied white presence.

When Griffin sets out on his "research project" (143), he writes that he will "merely change [his] pigmentation" and that he will "not change . . . [his] identity" (5). But his identity does change as a result of a "mere change" in pigmentation. In subsequent days, Griffin finds that because he now appears not-white, he is not welcome in the white world. He discovers that white people now turn to him "a different face" (107). His journal entries become a catalog of humiliations. A white bully follows him and threatens to beat him up; a white bus driver won't allow him to get off the bus at his stop; whites train on him "the hate stare" (51) and drive him out of public parks and public waiting rooms; whites expect him to lower his eyes when he speaks to them and forbid him from looking at a white woman; whites refuse to allow him to use bathrooms they use; whites won't hire him for any but the "most menial work" (41). Whites, he writes in his journal, demand that all people of color, including the now black-appearing Griffin, act in accordance with "the garbage of their stereotyped view of us" (180). In a move that reflects a shift in Griffin's point of view, gradually he begins using the inclusive first-person plural "we" to refer to himself and people of color (as in the quotation in the preceding sentence). Eventually, Griffin comes to see that "the Negro sees and reacts differently not because he is Negro, but because he is suppressed" (107), and now Griffin himself experiences this white suppression of people of color. Early in his experience as a black man, Griffin had reflected that what separated white and black America was "far more than miles. . . . It was an area of unknowing" (39). Griffin is a case in point: before his racechange, Griffin acknowledges that he, "a specialist in race issues," knows "nothing of the Negro's real problem" (2). But, after living as a black man, he now knows black people; he knows how it feels to be treated as an inferior by whites; and he begins to feel estranged, not from the black double in the mirror but from his identity as a white man.

Signs of this developing estrangement from his white self surface in another mirror scene, which takes place in a shack in Hattiesburg, Mississippi. Following a white Mississippi jury's refusal to indict whites in the case of the lynching of Mack Parker, Griffin travels to racially torn Hattiesburg because he wants to "see if [he] can understand" (51) these white Mississippians.[10] Whereas Griffin originally assumed a racial disguise to satisfy a desire to know about the mysterious racial other, now the object of his inquiry becomes whites. He has come to understand that black identity is bound up with white identity and with a white desire to maintain racial dominance. As soon as he walks down a street in the Negro quarter of Hattiesburg, a carful of white men and boys speed past and yell obscenities as they hurl trash at him. He finds himself surrounded by "an immense terror" (68), "an infernal circus" (69), and he seeks refuge in the shack. There, he looks at his reflection in a shard of mirror nailed to the wall: "The bald Negro stared back at me from its mottled sheen. I knew I was in hell. Hell could be no more agonizingly estranged from the world of order and harmony" (70). Looking in the mirror, Griffin sees himself imprisoned in flesh, which, because of its "mere pigmentation" is "estranged" from a white world "of order and harmony." In this mirror scene, as in previous ones, Griffin is two men, a white and a black, but he is no longer the detached white who loftily observes "an utter stranger . . . with whom I felt no kinship" (11). Instead, Griffin seems to inhabit both the white self and the black self:

> I heard my voice, as though it belonged to someone else, hollow in the empty room, detached, say: "Nigger, what you standing up there crying for?"
> I saw tears slick on his cheeks in the yellow light.
> Then I heard myself say what I have heard them say so many times. "It's not right. It's just not right." (70)

The voice of Griffin belongs to two men, the white Griffin observer and the black Griffin participant. As before, Griffin speaks as the "detached" white observer; but he speaks also as the uncanny black double, the crying black man in the mirror. At this point in his racial crossing, he begins to identify with his dark-skinned alter ego, as he speaks the words he "had heard them say so many times." Before when Griffin heard people of color speak what was self-evident to them—the "hell" to which whites consigned them—their words carried no meaning for white Griffin. Now as he utters these words himself, he begins to understand how it feels to be black in white-dominant America.

Driven by a profound need to "escape" (71) this budding sense that he inhabits this black identity, Griffin turns to writing. First, he takes out his notebook and tries to write his way back to whiteness. Writing his journal entries has been the way he asserts white control over black experience. Like the blackface minstrel, who assumes a black identity so as to master it by representing it, Griffin's intent, from the first, was to be the white man who offers a white symbolization of blackness. For example, he frankly admits that writing his journal entries provides him with a sense of "intimate contentment." His choice of words is revealing. I would suggest that, because writing positions him as the white observer, writing makes him feel once again "intimate" with his own white identity, which is threatened by his racial disguise, and that he derives "contentment" from writing because it makes him feel in control of his racial experiment. But on this night in Mississippi, "the intimate contentment would not come" (71). When his notebooks fail him, Griffin tries to write to his wife. In writing to her, his purpose is clearly to position himself as the white man who is married to a white woman and the father of white children. This desire explains his profoundly felt "need" (71) to write her, but he finds that he

> could tell her nothing. No words would come. She had nothing to do with this life, nothing to do with the room in Hattiesburg or with its Negro inhabitant. It was maddening. All my instincts struggled against this estrangement. . . . My conditioning as a Negro, and the immense sexual implications with which the racists in our culture bombard us, cut me off, even in my most intimate self, from any connection with my wife. . . . The observing self saw the Negro, surrounded by the sounds and smells of the ghetto, write "Darling" to a white woman. The chains of my blackness would not allow me to go on. . . . I could not break through. (70–71)

Griffin thinks he understands what is happening. He thinks that, having pretended to be a person of color so long, he has been "conditioned" to respond "as a Negro" who may not address a white woman. In his reading of the situation, "learned behavior patterns so deeply engrained" (71) are clouding "the reality" that he is a white man. Perhaps Griffin's analysis is correct. But his repeated emphasis on the words "estrangement" and "cut off" suggests that he can't find his way back to his white self. Griffin, much against his will—"all my instincts struggled against this estrangement"—feels "cut off" from a white identity. He is no longer playacting, like the white minstrel in blackface. Instead, his white self seems alien, and his black identity no longer feels feigned.

I propose that his "blackness" is no longer feigned; that is, as a result of inhabiting a black identity, Griffin is beginning to become a border-figure who shares an identity with both blacks and whites. On this night in Mississippi, he demonstrates that he now sees with a double vision. He sees both what whites see and what people of color see. Unable to bear the squalor and confinement of the room, he goes outside. There, "the night, the hoots and shouts surrounded me." Listening to the beat of the music, which "consumed in its blatant rhythm all other rhythms, even that of the heartbeat" (73), he knows that "whites in their homes" would view this spectacle and say: "'The niggers are whooping it up over on Mobile Street tonight. . . . They're happy.'" And then he imagines how "all of this would look" to the eyes of "a scholar," a man like his former white self, and he knows that the scholar would say: "Despite their lowly status, they are capable of living jubilantly." But Griffin now also sees what these whites would not see: "Would they see the immense melancholy that hung over the quarter, so oppressive that men had to dull their sensibilities in noise or wine or sex or gluttony in order to escape it? The laughter had to be gross or it would turn to sobs, and to sob would be to realize, and to realize would be to despair. So the noise poured forth like a jazzed-up fugue, louder and louder to cover the whisper in every man's soul, 'You are black. You are condemned'" (73).

Ultimately, it is Griffin's position as a father that enables him to risk his whiteness and become an intermediary between black and white. This turning point arrives in a shack in the backwoods of Alabama. Griffin is walking the roads outside of Mobile when a young African American man offers him a ride. It is late; Griffin has no place to spend the night; and the young man, who lives with his wife and six small children in a two-room shack in a swamp, shares all he has with Griffin—a meal of beans cooked in water and a feed sack on which to sleep on the floor. After dinner, Griffin offers some candy bars to the children and they are overcome with joy: "In the framework of nothing, slices of Milky Way become a great gift" (115). For the children, this is a party, and, when Griffin tells them that this day is his daughter's birthday, they ask: will she have a party with candy like they had tonight? At this point, Griffin begins to compare his own children with these children. He "fights back glimpses of [his] daughter's birthday party in its cruel contrasts with our party here tonight" (118) and he finds unbearable the juxtaposition: his children in their clean beds in a warm house with these children who sleep on sacks on the floor of an unheated shack in a swamp. The moment comes when the children ask to kiss Mr. Griffin good night; he holds out his arms to them as one by one they embrace and kiss him, and Griffin writes, "It was too much" (121). "Overwhelmed," he goes out into the night and weeps. There, he feels again "Negro children's lips soft against [his] so like the feel of my own children's good night kisses," and he sees that "these children resembled [his] in all ways except the superficial one of skin color, as indeed they resembled all children of all humans" (120). Griffin no longer sees this family in culture's narrow, mutually exclusive black and white terms but in more inclusive "human" terms: "I saw it not as a white man and not as a Negro, but as a human parent" (120). These children, who "resemble" his "in all ways except the superficial one of skin color," he now sees are the doubles of his own children, "so like" them and also different; and, as a parent, Griffin will not deny this over-lap. His identity as a parent takes precedence over any culturally defined racial designation. Griffin knows well his responsibility as a father, and, as a "human parent," he has a responsibility to these children, as to his own. He sees that if some group in the human family can be "marked for inferior status," then all in the family are at risk: "It became fully terrify-ing when I realized that if my skin were permanently black, they would unhesitatingly consign my own children to this bean future" (120). It is as a father that he finds the courage to risk his white identity. To save Afri-can American children from a future of poverty and misery, he will be the double of their caring black father, and will help them to be "at home" in a multiracial America. From this time on, he acknowledges a kinship with people of color that positions him as a white man who can interface between white and black cultural identities.

Griffin is not the only person in *Black Like Me* who assumes the man-tle of the father figure who mediates between culture's polarized identi-ties. At least two other men whom Griffin meets during his journey fear-lessly make cross-racial identifications. One such border figure is a white young man who offers Griffin a ride. Because other white men who had picked him up on the road had tormented him with questions about black sexuality, Griffin is wary when "a heavy-set, round-faced, tough-looking young man" in an old model car stops beside him. But, to his amazement, this young man is "color blind": "he appeared totally unaware that I was Negro" (99). For an hour the two men "delight" in talk of their children; and when it is time to eat, because no restaurant in the area will serve Griffin, the young man purchases food for them both, and the two men eat together in the car. Griffin is filled with wonder that this man, unlike other whites he has met, seems to make no distinction between black and white, and he asks himself what sets this young man apart: "How had he escaped the habit of guarded fencing that goes on constantly between whites and Negroes in the South wherever they meet?" (100). He questions the young man and finds that he is, in all ways, unexceptional, except for his powerful love for his son; and Griffin draws the conclusion that the young man makes no division because his "overwhelming love for his child [is] so profound it spilled over to all humanity. I knew that he was totally unaware of its ability to cure men; of the blessing it could be to someone like me after having been exhausted and scraped raw in my heart by others this rainy Alabama night" (100–101).

While Griffin does not recognize it, the young man is Griffin's double. Like this man, because he is a loving father, Griffin can now cross-identify with the people of color without dominating them, as he had when he began his racial "project" (2). Love, I have said, is what is absent from the blackface minstrel's cross-racial identification, and, without love, an identification is a takeover that serves only the dominant culture's needs. Love opposes self-interest; it is a self-less drive toward the other and toward inclusivity.[11] Of course, love, starting with the infant's identificatory love for the mother, poses the risk of losing the self in the other, and Griffin and this young white man risk becoming less white when they align themselves with people of color. But their love for their children, who need a father's mediating presence, helps them to see others as the doubles of their children, and to court this risk. In the passage above, Griffin observes that love "cures" men; by this, he means that love moderates an egocentric impulse to alienate in the name of self-identity, and when Griffin describes the young white man's ability to reach out to him as "a blessing," he echoes a line in Morrison's *Beloved*. Speaking of Paul D, the narrator notes that "there was something blessed in his manner. . . . Strong women and wise saw him and told him things they only told each other" (20). What is "blessed" and healing in Paul D's manner is a willingness to find the common ground with someone who is culturally defined as different, and this blessedness, or what Griffin calls "caritas" (101), also characterizes both the young man in the old model car and John Howard Griffin.

Griffin finds the young white father singular and writes that "he was the first man I met of either color who did not confuse the popular image of the thing with the thing itself" (100), but I suggest that Griffin overlooks one other who, like this young man, reaches across the color line. The man is Sterling Williams, whom Griffin identifies as his "contact for [his] entry into the Negro community" (9). Williams is introduced in the first pages of Griffin's narrative as "the shine boy" in the French Quarter whose shoe stand Griffin visits each day as he prepares to make his racechange. It is a measure of the extent to which Griffin is steeped in white racist ideology at this time that he could ever use the term "boy" in reference to Sterling Williams, an elderly man who lost his leg while fighting for his country in World War I. Williams, whom Griffin describes as "keenly intelligent and a good talker" (9), bears comparison to Lucas Beauchamp in Faulkner's *Intruder in the Dust*. Like Lucas, Williams "showed none of the obsequiousness of the Southern Negro" (9); and, like Lucas, who is mentor/father-figure to Chick Mallison, Williams is Griffin's mentor, who tutors him in black culture. Arguably, without Williams's guidance, Griffin would never have been able to pass successfully into the African American community.

Williams assumes the role of father figure to Griffin both when he thinks Griffin is an authentic African American and, later, when Griffin divulges that he is a white man masquerading as black. At first, when Williams thinks that Griffin is a man of color, he welcomes this black newcomer to New Orleans, and he offers the younger man fatherly advice about how a black man should behave: "Show some dignity," he says, and don't "bow or scrape" (24). When Griffin reveals to Williams that he is a white man in blackface, the older man is the same to him: he becomes Griffin's "enthusiastic coach" (24) and, like a father, he is even protective of him, worrying that he will be found out and helping him to perfect his disguise. While Griffin quickly passes over the role Williams plays, Williams's warm, welcoming response to this white man passing for black is remarkable. Williams has reason not to trust a white man "playing black." A wounded veteran of the Great War, who, on his return to his country, can only find work as a "shine boy," he might well think that Griffin, like the blackface minstrel, has "blacked-up" so as to exploit people of color for his own profit. Moreover, a recurring theme in Griffin's narrative is that African Americans are closed off from whites. But if, as

Griffin states, a black distrust of whites is the rule, Williams is a striking counter-example. From first to last, Williams demonstrates a willingness to cross over to this white man. He is "delighted" (24) when Griffin confides his project to him and immediately becomes a co-conspirator. Knowing that Griffin is a privileged white, he gives him work as a fellow "shineboy"; offers him what little food he has; and introduces this racial passer to a black racial identity. While Griffin, at this early stage in his cross-racial experience, sees himself as a white man merely disguised as a black man, Williams believes in Griffin's "Negro-ness." As Griffin records in his journal, "something odd happened": Williams "seemed to forget that I was once white" and "began to use the 'we' form and discuss 'our situation.'" More amazing still, Williams's acceptance of Griffin as black becomes a self-fulfilling prophecy. That is, Williams's willingness to include this white man in a black community has a transformative effect on Griffin: "The illusion of my 'Negro-ness' took over so completely that I fell into the same pattern of talking and thinking. It was my first intimate glimpse. We were Negroes and our concern was the white man and how to get along with him" (26).

How completely Williams bonds with Griffin is demonstrated at their parting. One day when Griffin arrives at the shoe stand, a distraught Williams greets him with the news that sends Griffin to Mississippi: the Mississippi Grand Jury's refusal to indict in the Mack Parker kidnap-lynching case. In effect, the jury's failure to indict gives approval to white terrorism of blacks. Williams, overcome with anger at this lack of any kind of white accountability for crimes against blacks, rails against whites: "This is what we can expect from the white man's justice" (50). Curiously, even in this moment when whites refuse to offer people of African ethnicity protection under the law, Williams does not reject Griffin and continues to include the racial passer when he speaks of blacks. For example, when Griffin announces his plan to travel to Mississippi, Williams and his partner, Joe, try to dissuade him from making the proposed trip, as if Griffin were an authentic African American: "That's no place for a colored man," Joe says; and Williams warns him, "They're going to treat any Negro like a dog. You sure better not go" (50). Both men make no distinction between Griffin, whom they know is a white passing for black, and a person of color. For them, Griffin's gesture toward blackness is enough; and they cross-identify with him. When Griffin writes that Williams is his black "contact," the word perfectly describes Williams's role as a border figure: Williams, who has reason to turn away from whites, selflessly makes "contact" with this culturally defined white man, and his mediation makes it possible for Griffin to pass for black in the black community.

When Griffin puts an end to his racial disguise and attempts to resume his life as a white man, he is changed more than he knows. More specifically, as a result of his temporary "racechange," he is now not a black man, but he is not the same white man he was before. As subsequent events suggest, he now no longer fits into culture's polarized racial identities. For example, when Griffin first begins to pass back into white society, he elects to "zigzag" back and forth between white and black; that is, he alternates between two identities, "the Negro Griffin" and the white Griffin. He writes that "I was the same man, whether white or black" (133) and all that changes is how others, white and black, treat him depending on his skin color that day. This ability to "zigzag" between black and white suggests that Griffin has double membership in white and black communities. Duality characterizes him both when he passes for black and later when he resumes his white identity for good. Whereas Griffin starts off as a white man posing as black, when he ends his racial disguise and returns to being white, he himself both feels like and others—both black and white—take him for a man who is passing for white. For instance, when he stops applying dye to his skin with the intention of being assimilated back into white society, Griffin feels "strangely sad to leave the world of the Negro after having shared it so long—almost as though I were fleeing my share of his pain and heartache" (155). Griffin's feelings of guilt here as he "passes back into white society" (130) are characteristic of the person passing for white, who, according to Wald's study of racial passing, feels guilty of "racial disloyalty" (16).

Certainly, when Griffin resumes his life as a white and publicly acknowledges that he has lived as a man of color, he is treated by whites like a person who is invisibly black, and whose blackness is all the more threatening because it is undetectable. Griffin is shocked when an anonymous woman who calls his mother says that he has "turn[ed] against [his] own race" and "thrown the door wide open for those niggers, and after we've *all* worked so hard to keep them out" (160); but, in a sense, the woman has summed up the effect of Griffin's racial "project." It may not have been his original objective, but his cross-racial experience—that is, that he, a white, could live as a black—exposes as a lie that whites and blacks are polar opposites with no common ground. Like the person who passes for white, he has duped whites; in his case, whites have treated a white man as if he were a black man, and this mis-seeing refutes the idea of racial difference as infallible "natural law." Often, during his sojourn as an African American, when Griffin was treated with contempt by whites, he would wonder to himself, what would this person think if she knew I were white? When he returns to white society, he has the answer to his question: because they mistook him for black, whites refuse to acknowledge that he is "really" white. Like a white-appearing person who, when found out to be of African descent, is cast by whites as black, so also now Griffin, who has passed for black, is designated as black by whites because they refuse to recognize racial ambiguity. They adjust his race to suit their oppositional racial logic. He must be either white or black, and, having crossed the color line, he must now be black. Like Mr. Bodwin, the white abolitionist in *Beloved,* whom whites blacken with shoe black to externalize an invisible blackness, whites now work to paint Griffin black. Specifically, they drive him out of their white communities; they hang him in effigy; and they threaten to castrate him. Castration, as Eric Lott's study documents, is the obsessive theme of the blackface minstrel show, and meets a white need to deny the black man's equality with the white man.[12]

Griffin takes the final step toward becoming "the bridge" between black and white in the years following the publication of *Black Like Me,* when, as a civil rights activist, he relinquishes the subject position of the "I" who controls racial representation. As Wald justly charges, throughout *Black Like Me* Griffin controls the symbolization of people of color through writing. As we have seen, there comes a time when he is so unmoored that even writing fails him, but writing is the way he seeks to master black experience. It is only later as a civil rights activist, as he writes the epilogue to his narrative, that Griffin condemns this white monopoly of racial representation. In the years following the nearly six weeks he lived as a black man, Griffin finds himself summoned by white community leaders to help settle racial disputes, and he is appalled by the way these "well-disposed white men tended to be turned off and affronted if black men told them truths that offended their prejudices" (190). He writes that there was always the same "pattern" to these visits. He would be taken into the black community, where he would be briefed by black leaders and then he would be asked to "report" back to "a room full of white men" (193). Whites would listen to his representation of black exploitation, but "the things that needed saying . . . would be rejected if black men said them" (191). Blacks who speak of social inequality, he writes, are seen by whites as "lack[ing] . . . graciousness and courtesy"

(192). At this time, Griffin unmasks this white practice: What whites object to as a lack of "courtesy" is, in fact, a lack of black subordination to a white script. Whites want to engage only with a white representation of black experience out of a fear of forfeiting white control of the relation between black and white. In the epilogue, Griffin repeatedly stresses that as long as whites engage only with their own white representations of people of color, there can be no "communication" between the two ethnicities. At this time Griffin insists that the white leaders talk directly with black leaders and not through him. In other words, they must engage directly with blacks as equals and risk the transformative intersubjective space between black and white. His final act as intermediary is to be silent and relinquish agency to people of color. In the last pages of the epilogue, he writes that in the 1960s he served solely as "an observer": "I hardly ever opened my mouth" (196).

Conclusion

Bridging Difference

I and the Father are One.
John 10:30

We think of a boundary as a place that distinguishes identities by shutting out. But this is a popular misconception. A boundary is the middle, a mysterious, dangerous, two-in-one place that differentiates between the one and the other precisely because it is both the one and the other. It is not exclusion but doubleness that forms a boundary; and when we draw a boundary, we always occupy a threatening, liminal, in-between space; and we always experience a cross-identification with the other.

The idea that doubleness distinguishes cultural identities seems paradoxical. Doubleness seems to be tantamount to indeterminacy. The double is both the one thing and the other, and we define an identity as being the one thing and not the other. But this very "not the other" implies a relationship; it implies that the term is defined *in relation* to another term. Meanings in culture are devised by a difference within a relationship—a sign is both the same as and different from the thing it signifies—and doubleness both threatens identity and is the support of what Lacan calls the symbolic order, a shared system of culturally assigned meanings.

Every interaction with others is a boundary-setting moment, and boundaries are contested sites of relationship where both sides struggle for control of the sign, the power of representation. We tend to think of two alternatives: either dominate the other or be dominated by the other. But there is a third alternative. The alternative to either the one thing or the other is both the one and the other, the double, the place that is related to both but is identical with neither. On the face of it, this alternative seems to be no alternative. Because we define the one in terms of the other, to be both the one and the other risks meaninglessness, or what

Julia Kristeva calls the abject: "the in-between, the ambiguous, the composite" (*Powers* 4).

Whatever our culturally defined identity, the in-between middle terrifies us, and we eschew it. Kristeva states plainly the real terrors of the abject borderline. As the place where culture's oppositions merge, it is the embodiment of the inchoate. It is the site where oppositions like me and not-me or life and death flow into one another. At the same time that the abject borderline "pulverizes" (*Powers* 5) cultural formations, however, it is also "the safeguard" and "the primer of my culture" (2). Indeed, as Kristeva explains, it is because the borderline unmakes identity that it can remake identity. The borderline, the place where life meets death, is both death and new life. The borderline shatters us, and out of this disintegration arises the new "I," like Hi Man and the convicts, the living dead, who rise from the ground where they have been buried. Kristeva is clear: "If I acknowledge [the abject middle] it annihilates me," but this acknowledgment, which is an acknowledgment that I "am homologous to another" (2), creates a new hybrid cultural form. The "in-between," as Kristeva and these four Southern writers show us, is a grafting of one identity onto another that creates new possibilities. It is a leap forward into the new.

Of course, the transformation of the "I" is terrifying. Transformation is an incursion from the outside on the inside, a violation of our boundaries. We do not want to be transformed; we want to preserve our culturally and historically shaped racial and gendered identities. We want to be static and autonomous. But, as Michael Awkward reminds us, "there is no racial or gendered purity, no space to which we can go to locate an untainted state of being, no irreducible difference" (15). As long as we are alive, identity is never stable or independent. Our identities, which we like to think of as ours alone, are, in fact, upheld by others; the boundaries that we think of as solely excluding are two-sided and shared with another. We try to deny the doubleness of the middle; indeed, the Freudian/Lacanian psychoanalytic narrative, which erases the supporting doubleness at the middle and insists that absence alone is the foundation of identity, is a lengthy exercise in denial. Denial is useless, however, as an interface is necessary to support culture's identities. As blackface minstrelsy shows, we turn to doubleness to reinforce identities at times when cultural signifiers, like the meaning of "whiteness," are at risk. We have to have a self-other relation to designate boundaries; the only question is, how will we negotiate the self-other relation? Will we, like John Howard Griffin when he first confronts his black mirror-image double, see this doubleness as a threat and deny a relation where there is a relation? Or will we, like Lucas Beauchamp who is "not black nor white either" (13), fearlessly accept our own in-betweenness and its transformative possibilities?

Acknowledgment of the interdependence of self and other will not put an end to the possibility of the one dominating the other. Lucas's acknowledged in-betweenness incites whites to attempt to lynch him. Similarly, because Griffin's assumption of a black identity confuses racial categories, he is the target of death and castration threats. In both cases, communities are responding to doubleness the same way the Freudian/ Lacanian identity narrative does, as a threat to identity that must be eradicated. But, as John Howard Griffin's real-life experience also shows, as more people on both sides of culture's binaries acknowledge that each one of us is the double of the other—both the same *and* different—step by step, together, we move closer toward a more equitable society.

Notes

Introduction

1. Fuss 1–3, and Abel, "Black Writing" 107–18.

2. For feminist challenges to the traditional psychoanalytic role of the father in gender development, see Yaeger and Kowaleski-Wallace.

3. O'Connor calls the Misfit a "prophet gone wrong" and writes that the grandmother's encounter with the Misfit is oddly beneficial to her, because by forcing her to "fac[e] death" (*Mystery* 110), he helps to prepare her for a moment of grace—her recognition that "she is responsible for the man before her and joined to him by ties of kinship which have their roots deep in the mystery she has been prattling about so far" (111–12). See 109–14.

1. Beyond Oedipus

1. My suggestion that Faulkner's fiction represents a return to a childhood memory is also supported by correspondences between his 1948 novel and his reminiscence "Mississippi" (1954). For example, in both, the narrator refers to himself with the third-person pronoun "he." In the essay we find the real-life source for *Intruder's* notorious Beat Four in Sullivan's Hollow (33); Aleck Sander seems like a fictional incarnation of a black boy Faulkner evokes in the autobiographical piece (17); and Lucas Beauchamp seems to be modeled after "Uncle" Ned Barnett, an elderly black man and longtime servant of the Faulkner family, who is virtually elegized in the piece.

2. Williamson suggests that prominent white people in the town may have had reason to want to see Patton, who was a bootlegger, eliminated. See 159–61.

3. Cullen observes that the lynching of Nelse Patton is "more widely known than anything else of this kind that ever happened in Lafayette County" and that Faulkner "must have heard numerous stories about the Patton case" (92). Blotner points out that Hal Cullen, brother of John, was a good friend and fifth-grade classmate of Faulkner's and that talk in the schoolyard was all about the lynching (114).

4. In his landmark study of doubling in Faulkner, John T. Irwin notes that the double is the formulation of repressed material: "Rejected instincts and desires are

cast out of the self, repressed internally only to return externally personified in the double" (33).

5. In "The Dissolution of the Oedipus Complex," Freud theorizes that because of "a threat . . . that this part of him which he values so highly will be taken from him," the child represses Oedipal desire and performs a symbolic self-castration: he "preserve[s] the genital organ" by "paralyz[ing] it—remov[ing] its function"; and, "if [the repression] is ideally carried out," it accomplishes "the abolition of the Oedipal complex." Freud admits, however, that all may not be well with an ego born of such a process, and he sounds this cautionary note: "If the ego has in fact not achieved much more than a repression of the complex, the latter [the Oedipal complex] persists in an unconscious state in the id and will later manifest its pathogenic effect" (*Standard Edition* [hereafter *SE*] 19: 177). In other words, the hoped-for "dissolution" may merely be the repression of a desire that, if only repressed, will endlessly resurface in reconfigured forms, such as the double. The Lacanian commentator James Mellard explains that "castration is the symbolic function within the Oedipus complex that establishes the 'position' of the father in the psychic structure" (*Using Lacan* 29).

6. Moreland argues insightfully that, with Lucas Beauchamp, Faulkner is trying to identify a model of manhood that does not exclude women and blacks, but that the author writes about this manhood "without ever quite understanding . . . how Lucas manages somehow to maintain this kind of dignity even when he is seen as black by everyone around him and therefore unentitled to this kind of self-possession" ("Faulkner's Continuing Education" 65). Gwin contends that "Lucas speaks out of a sense of himself . . . that . . . is as bisexual as it is biracial" and that, from Lucas, Chick learns to develop "a masculine identity which comes to accept its own feminine elements" (93). For Towner, Lucas represents Faulkner's attempt "to imagine the scope of effort it would take for a 'black' man in the late 1940s to create an audience of 'white' believers who will act upon his 'word'" (53). Several critics maintain that Lucas fails to represent a viable alternative to a fatherhood constituted by an Oedipal threat. Weinstein states that both father figures in the novel, Lucas and Gavin Stevens, are "impotent," and that the Oedipal legacy is "bypassed, not dismantled, not even attacked" (125). The Morrises read *Intruder* as a failed quest for "a difference that did not mythologize itself in exclusive/inclusive oppositions." They find that "Lucas is virtually silenced in the novel" and that "the novel does not really seem to eliminate the word difference from the vocabulary of racism, classism, and sexism" (235). Schmitz observes that Faulkner is able to show "the majesty of . . . Lucas's patriarchal authority" but that ultimately the presentation of him fails because "Lucas's defiance of white racism, always prompt, is itself racist" (259).

7. Kristeva observes that a master/slave dialectic "provokes regressive and protectionist rage . . . : must we not stick together, remain among ourselves, expel the intruder, or at least, keep him in 'his' place?" (*Strangers* 20).

8. Similarly imagined scenes of psychic identification appear in *Absalom, Absalom!* and *The Unvanquished*. See Irwin 58–59; and my *Faulkner: The Return of the Repressed*, 121–27. My interpretation owes a debt to Irwin's seminal, psychoanalytic study of repression and doubling. My approach differs from his, however, in that

whereas Irwin applies Freudian and/or Lacanian formulas to Faulkner's fiction, my essay attempts to show that these imaginative texts revise the master narrative of identity.

9. Kristeva discusses this Freudian identification of woman and death. See *Strangers* 183–85. See also Lydenberg 1076–79.

10. "Fright," Kristeva writes, "anchor[s]" and "locate[s] uncanny strangeness "outside." She explains that "the builder of the *other* and, in the final analysis, the strange is indeed repression and its perviousness" (*Strangers* 183, 184).

11. In a review in the *New Yorker*, Edmund Wilson wrote that "the author's ideas on this subject are apparently conveyed, in their explicit form, by the intellectual uncle, who . . . gives vent to long disquisitions . . . so 'editorial' in character that . . . the series may be pieced together as something in the nature of a public message delivered by the author himself'" (476). Taylor states that *Intruder*'s plot works to "justify Gavin's polemics" (163); according to Sundquist, *Intruder* is a "ludicrous novel and a depressing social document" (149); and Snead finds "narrative complicity" in Stevens's "restrictive and stereotyping tone" and concludes that "in the end the fear of chaos conquered Faulkner" (221–22). Other commentators have argued that a dialogic tension exists in the novel. The Morrises note that Chick's objection to Stevens's argument "provides an important moment of dialogic disruption in Stevens' overpowering monologue" and that "the plot of the novel . . . reinforces Chick's objection to Stevens' racist, 'go slow' rationalizations" (233). According to Polk, Stevens's views are undermined by the references to the smoke that he blows (135). Dussere writes that Stevens's authority is undercut by appearances in Faulkner's other novels where he "is the very image of the obtuse liberal" (52).

12. Faulkner's denial is problematic; he disowns Stevens, but he does not denounce him. Faulkner told Malcolm Cowley that "Gavin Stevens was not speaking for the author but for the best type of liberal Southerner, that is how they feel about the Negro" (*Faulkner-Cowley File* 110–11).

13. Peavy argues that the "go slow" tactics of Southern moderates, advocated by Faulkner, were an attempt to deny by forever delaying social equality to people of color. Towner contends that Faulkner's segregationist stance is the product of his "belie[f], at base, only in individual reality" (127). Dussere makes the case that the Southern approach to desegregation is informed by a notion of Southern honor (52).

14. This regional loyalty argument also appears in Faulkner's interviews. See Meriwether and Millgate 262. In an essay that provides a useful counterpoint to mine, Kartiganer offers a more sympathetic reading of Stevens and maintains that, as used by Stevens, the term "homogeneity" includes Lucas in a regional identity.

15. The notion that omnipotence can be achieved by exclusion is also suggested in the Lacanian script, which is obsessed with the phallus as the figure of difference that authorizes meaning and identity. Even while Lacan acknowledges that the phallus is only a signifier, still, given its role in the securing of (never secure) subjectivity, he calls it "the transcendental signifier" (Eagleton 168) and seems to hold out the hope of transcendence through repression.

16. Lucas Beauchamp makes his first appearance in *Go Down, Moses,* where he engages in a number of power struggles, but ultimately rejects the dominant role in a

binary so as to preserve a loving relationship with his wife, Mollie. See my *Faulkner: The Return of the Repressed*, 163–64, and Davis 136–40.

2. Crossing a Racial Border

1. Jonathan Elmer makes the case that the novel's scenes of violence are "forever infected by ambiguity" because, like every scene of racial trauma, "Wright's text can never be entirely free of the suspicion that its representations are repetitions rather than revisions, contributions to racial impasse and the violence of stereotype rather than exposés of them" (772).

2. Scholars have proposed interpretations of Bigger's sense of self-validation through violence. In his biography of Wright, Michel Fabre attributes the affirmation of violence in the novel to Wright's "fierce determination to deny the heritage of Uncle Tom" (529–30). Jerry Bryant suggests that Bigger feels truly alive when he kills because, by saving himself, he is prioritizing himself over another in a way that is denied to him by a white racist culture. Joseph T. Skerrett Jr. theorizes that Bigger feels empowered by the violence against women because Wright himself desired "to strike out against the women who limited, repressed, censored, and punished his rebellious initiatives" (137). Alan France explains that Bigger feels empowered when he kills because he has internalized a phallocentric ethic that reduces women to "objects of male status conflict" (414). Sondra Guttman suggests that Wright means to show that there can be no unification of the classes and the races as long as there is violence against women. Petar Ramadanovic interprets Bigger Thomas as an Oedipal figure (as revised by Lacan) who achieves self-realization and self-ownership by determining his own fate and the significance of his death.

3. Scholars who have argued that Wright's portrayal of women characters is sexist include Sylvia Keady and Nagueyalti Warren. Trudier Harris takes the view that in Wright's fiction black women are "portrayed as being in league with the oppressors of black men" because they preach subservience (63). Citing Robin Wiegman's work on the imbrications of race and gender formations in America, Abdul R. JanMohamed reasons that Bigger's misogyny stems from an urgent need to resist "racial feminization"; that is, it is a by-product of his rebellion against a white culture that would deny patriarchal privileges to black men (*Death-Bound-Subject* 81–83). See also JanMohamed's "Sexuality on/of the Racial Border," 99–105. Other scholars have countered the charge of misogyny. Joyce Anne Joyce takes issue with this position as being "biased and extreme" (378). Looking at the character of Sarah in "Long Black Song," she finds that Wright presents Sarah as "wiser" and "morally superior to" (385) her husband and the white salesman. William Maxwell takes up the issue of Wright's well-known critical review of Zora Neale Hurston's *Their Eyes Were Watching God* and challenges the view that Wright's critique represents black male dominance over a black female voice. In an essay arguing that Wright's philosophical modernism played a leading role in spreading the black diaspora, Paul Gilroy astutely points out that scholars have not yet assessed Wright's contribution to gender studies and his "inauguration of a critical discourse on the construction of black masculinity" or the "proto-feminist statements" in his works (176). My study builds on the groundwork

laid by Gilroy, as I try to explore specifically how Wright's masterwork, *Native Son*, anticipates feminist positions about masculinity. Finally, Cheryl Higashida argues that Wright's most pro-Communist work contains a nuanced critique of patriarchy that feminist indictments of Wright have overlooked. Higashida's study also aligns with my project, since she maintains that Wright's desire for community was in conflict with a masculinist ethic.

4. France takes the position that, in the cases of both women, Bigger's self-defense argument is not credible. France maintains that Bigger's ability to move about Mary's room undetected by Mrs. Dalton undermines his assertion that he had no opportunity to escape. Similarly, France finds unpersuasive Bigger's contention that he had to kill Bessie because she would have revealed his hiding place. As France correctly observes, Bigger does not know himself where he is going and could reveal nothing to her that would aid his capture.

5. Hazel Rowley notes that Wright "was an avid reader of Freud and psychoanalysis" (278), and she argues that his novel *Savage Holiday* "reads like a case study" (410). In 1941 Wright read *Dark Legend*, a Freudian analysis of matricide. The book so interested Wright that he became friends with its author, the Freudian psychotherapist Frederic Wertham. Subsequently, he underwent therapy with Wertham and helped the psychoanalyst establish a free clinic in Harlem to make Freudian therapy available to black youth (Fabre 236, 272, 292). At the time of his death in 1960, Wright's personal library contained eight books written by Freud including *Basic Writings, The Future of an Illusion, Interpretation of Dreams*, and *The Questions of Lay Analysis* (Ward and Butler 142).

6. In this regard, it is interesting to note that in *Black Boy* Wright states that Ella's pain and paralysis "grew into a symbol in my mind [for] all the poverty, the ignorance, the helplessness; the painful, baffling hunger-ridden days and hours; . . . the futile seeking, the uncertainty, the fear, the dread; the meaningless pain and the endless suffering" (117); in short, everything Wright would like to stamp out. Wright also notes that when his mother confided in him that she wished to die he "ceased to react to [her]; [his] feelings were frozen" (117).

7. In a deeply probing and sensitive study of American crime novels (among them, Faulkner's *Sanctuary*), Greg Forter also examines women as a threat to the bounded male self, and frequently refers to abjection. Observing that "this dissolution is associated with the mother through the accident of her role in parturition," he writes that men "repudiate . . . this state in the name of autonomy" and "later experience boundary confusion" (214). Forter's thoughtful analysis of male boundary confusion is congruent with my own objectives, but, unlike my project, Forter focuses on psychic dissolution and does not attempt "to trace the reconstitution of masculinity among less toxic lines" (215), as he candidly acknowledges in his afterword.

8. The Indian maiden can also be read in terms of Gloria Anzaldúa's theory of a new *mestiza* (an Aztec word meaning "torn between two ways") or borderlands consciousness, which strikingly correlates with Kristevan abjection. Like abjection, the work of the *mestiza* "is to break down the subject-object duality" (102).

9. A focus on how racialization affects what Freud calls the death drive is the subject of Abdul R. JanMohamed's book *The Death-Bound-Subject: Richard Wright's*

Archaeology of Death. The telling difference between my reading and JanMohamed's is his uncritical use of a Freudian/Lacanian methodology. He argues that, as a racialized subject, Bigger's subjectivity has been produced by hate and fear, and is therefore "death-bound." As a result, "within the dialectical structure created by social-death," only the embrace of actual death "can have value" (103–4), and when he kills Mary and Bessie, he is acting out an acceptance of his own death. JanMohamed writes that "Mary's murder [is] an inchoate but profoundly significant act of creation for someone in Bigger's position" (126). Elmer's interpretation of the sexualized, deadly scene in Mary's bedroom complements mine in that he argues that the trauma of this central scene is in its "in-between[ness]": "It is not the fantasy of rape that traumatizes; and it is not the accidental murder of Mary that traumatizes. It is in the 'in-between' that the traumatic event resides" (785). The traumatic in-betweenness that Elmer points to in the scene is the defining characteristic of abjection; abjection, Kristeva writes, is "the in-between, the ambiguous, the composite" (*Powers* 4). In other words, it is the threat of a breakdown of alterity that terrifies Bigger in this scene.

10. Laplanche and Pontalis explain that "repression occurs when to satisfy an instinct—though likely to be pleasurable in itself—would incur the risk of provoking unpleasure because of other requirements" (390).

11. See *Black Boy* 16–18; 38–41.

12. A foundation for meaning and identity is precisely what the traditional psychoanalytic identity narrative lacks, as this narrative insists that the alienation of another constitutes a raced or gendered identity. As Juliet Mitchell explains, according to Lacanian theory, "To be human is to be subjected to a law which decentres and divides" (26). Many feminists have derided the Freudian/Lacanian narrative of identity formation, which valorizes a phallic difference that is nothing more than a symbol of lack.

13. As Fabre records, Wright asked to be schooled in the philosophical thinking of Nietzsche, Kierkegaard, and Heidegger. See 67, 299, 366. For Wright's familiarity with Nietzsche, see also Rowley 46, 120, 322.

3. Flannery O'Connor's Prophets

1. Scholars have struggled to understand why "bodily injury signals the penetration of the divine" (Brinkmeyer, "Jesus, Stab Me" 83). For example, Crawford finds that these violent encounters seem "closer to dissociative moments of panic than glimpses of the divine" (12). Havird describes these aggressive penetrations as "saving rapes," and writes that, while union with the Holy Spirit makes Asbury in "The Enduring Chill" "at least a sometimes potent male" (17), in "Greenleaf," the bull's violent penetration of Mrs. May is meant to teach her submissiveness. Ciuba interprets the pervasive violence in O'Connor's fiction in terms of Girard's theory that "a compelling sense of unfulfillment at the center of the subject" leads to violence against another "who seems to possess the fullness of being for which the subject yearns" (7). Discounting O'Connor's insistence that the aggression in her fiction is compatible with Christian tenets, Prown proposes that O'Connor "claims that her writing served the needs of God" to "justify even its most shocking elements—particularly the

unrelenting violence—within a context of Christianity and in so doing justify as well the needs of her artistic self" (20–21). Similarly, Yeager "refuse[s] O'Connor's Catholicism as the pivotal focus of her work," and suggests that the mayhem in the fiction is "a painful reenactment of a sadistic world whose sanity is hopelessly compromised by its race and class politics" (187).

2. Important earlier studies helped me to form my interpretation. Brinkmeyer argues that O'Connor "shatter[s] the characters' Cartesian worship of consciousness" so as to "return the characters violently to their bodies into which the divine has somehow penetrated" ("Jesus, Stab Me" 84). John Duvall's astute study of race and white identity in O'Connor's fiction dovetails with my project. Duvall finds a pervasive "figurative blurring of racial binaries in O'Connor's fiction" (64) and argues that this blurring shows "how precarious [social] hierarchy is, threatened as it is by more fluid, transgressive possibilities and becomings" (65). In a seminal essay, Asals perceptively notes the almost obsessive recurrence of doubling in O'Connor's fiction, and observes that inherent in the double is "a dualistic conception of the self" (51). While the double, in my reading, has a positive valence and models a communal identity, Asals follows a Freudian reading of the double as a threatening "unwanted kinship" (49). Crawford's thesis that "'the action of grace' in O'Connor's fiction [is] intelligible from a cultural perspective" (22) parallels my own, but his analysis ultimately concludes that a "religious solution is invoked in order to leapfrog unpleasant social realities and personal failures" (9).

3. Sally Fitzgerald has addressed O'Connor's title in a letter to the editor of *The Flannery O'Connor Bulletin*. John Crowe Ransom's letter to O'Connor, dated 12 January 1955, O'Connor's reply, and Fitzgerald's commentary are published in *Flannery O'Connor Bulletin* 23 (1994–95): 175–82.

4. For Freud, the boundary on which the social order rests is the incest prohibition, which is enforced by the father. Derrida directs us to see that a boundary is "a pure, fictive and unstable, ungraspable limit. One crosses it in attaining it . . . before the prohibition it is not incest; forbidden, it cannot become incest except through the recognition of the prohibition" (267).

5. If we apply Lacanian terms, the upper level is what Lacan calls the symbolic order, the order of language and culture. The lower level represents Lacan's Imaginary or presymbolic. It is characterized by completeness and interrelatedness, and is associated with the close or dyadic relationship of a mother and an infant.

6. See O'Connor's letter to Ben Griffith, dated May 4, 1955 (*Habit* 78). For an analysis of the story's exposure of the cultural production of race and gender difference, see my essay "Deconstructing Racial Difference: O'Connor's 'The Artificial Nigger.'" Perreault argues that O'Connor attributes "body" to the African American woman in the story and, in so doing, "subverts her own deeply held belief in the necessity of unifying body and spirit for true spiritual integrity" (389–90).

7. Prown writes that the statuary represents "the signifier against which white identity is defined" (73). See also Paulson 81.

8. See Duvall 78; Asals 192; and Burkman and Meloy 230–47. A number of other critics have noted resemblances between the yard statue and Mr. Head and Nelson. Kahane observes that the "complicated network of psychological involvement and

mutual dependency between black and white . . . is one of the more ignored themes of [O'Connor's] fiction" (187). Brinkmeyer maintains that the racist image reveals to the grandfather and grandson that "they share with blacks and with all people a common identity as a fallen people" (*Art and Vision* 80). MacKethan finds correspondences between Mr. Head, Nelson, and the plaster figure of the African American (31). Nesbitt suggests that the grandfather and grandson "perhaps have come to recognize their own essential and shared 'blackness'" (168).

9. Scholars often have discussed the racist yard ornament as a figure of the archetypal scapegoat, whose suffering is redemptive. See, for example, Giannone, Okeke-Ezigbo, Cheatham, Strickland, Burkman and Meloy, and Wood.

10. As Duvall astutely observes, Mr. Head and Nelson go home "physically," but "in a figurate sense, that home is no longer there" because of the newly "compromised sense of white identity that the day has given them" (79).

11. For many scholars, Mrs. May's violent death by penetration signifies that "true male power ultimately wins out" (P. Smith 45). See also Westling, *Sacred Groves* 166; Prown 50; and Havird 17–20. Katz finds a pattern of male domination throughout O'Connor's fiction. She writes that fathers in the fiction "are usually sadistic figures, their aggressiveness associated with the sexual role of the male as penetrator" (63). Similarly, in "Mothers and Daughters," Westling observes that O'Connor writes about a "male-dominated culture" (513) "where women are "tricked, taken advantage of, jilted, and misused" (518). In my interpretation, paternal penetrations, while destructive, also work to elide and refigure. Accordingly, my reading of the deaths of Mrs. May and the bull as an image for male-female convergence stands in direction opposition to Smith's contention that in "Greenleaf" "any attempt to mix male and female roles is destined to fail" (47).

12. As a figure of elision, the Greenleaf bull can also be read as an avatar of the force toward integration that is analyzed by Teilhard de Chardin, a French theologian, whose work O'Connor greatly admired and whose central tenet she made the title of her collection, *Everything That Rises Must Converge*. For de Chardin, the whole created universe is related and ultimately returns to the Omega point, the creator. Critics have offered various interpretations of the bull. Schiff argues that the Greenleaf bull is a totem animal, that is, a substitute for the dead father, a father-deity. According to Schiff, when Mr. Greenleaf sacrifices the bull, he becomes the "agent of grace" because he "rejects his primitive religion" (60). Shields discusses the bull as a mythic figure. For Walker, who relates O'Connor's illness to Christian doctrines, the bull represents both Christ, to whom we must surrender ourselves completely, and the lupus that was devouring O'Connor.

13. According to Lacan, domination produces gender difference: "For the [male] soul to come into being, she, the woman, is differentiated from it . . . called woman and defamed" (*Écrits* 156).

14. Focusing on "Greenleaf" and "The Enduring Chill," Bleikasten finds that, for O'Connor, grace is the recognition of one's own nothingness and guilt; he then maintains that such a definition is irreconcilable with orthodox Christianity.

15. Thus I disagree with Schleifer, who contrasts "The Artificial Nigger" with "The Enduring Chill" and argues that, in the latter story, none of the fiction's plot develop-

ments prepares the reader for the supernatural intervention at the story's climactic conclusion.

16. In her discussion of "The Enduring Chill," Walker alludes briefly to Kristeva's theory of abjection and proposes that O'Connor creates in Mrs. Fox an ironic version of Kristeva's death-bearing mother who leads her child to an encounter with death. Walker seems to interpret abjection as solely a destructive experience.

4. "Nobody Could Make It Alone"

1. In her delineation of the identity destruction wrought by slavery, Morrison's fictional account of slavery can be read profitably alongside Hortense Spillers's landmark scholarly examination of historical slave narratives, "Mama's Baby, Papa's Maybe: An American Grammar Book." Spillers's analysis of historical accounts reveals the "moves" by which "the dominant symbolic order, pledged to maintain the supremacy of race" (72), systematically attempted to prevent people of color from becoming social subjects. Writing of the Middle Passage, for example, Spillers observes that captured Africans, "suspended in the 'oceanic,'" "removed from their indigenous . . . culture and not-yet American," and "without names their captors would recognize," were "culturally unmade" (72). Like Morrison's novel, which was inspired by her study of historical records, Spillers's scholarly essay finds that white owners separated children from their mothers and fathers, from family structures, from relationships with others, and from the recognition and answering response that would have fostered a social self.

2. Ann duCille poses the dilemma of exclusivity versus a colonizing identification from the standpoint of a black woman writer. See 21–56.

3. My interpretation owes a debt to a number of important, earlier studies that have located a critique of oppositional difference in Morrison's fiction. Davis investigates the mythic pattern of African American community identity that Morrison sets against white America's racist, repressive ideology. In *Beloved* and novels by other African American authors, King identifies a tension between a monolithic racial identity and "a move away from it"; she writes that "racial unity may have always been in tension with differences of social level, class, caste, and regional heterogeneity among blacks" (211). Weinstein observes that "Morrison . . . seems to register the penetrability of identity as both burden and promise" (103). Moreland (*Learning*), Moglen, and Fultz analyze the Amy Denver-Sethe relationship as an example of coalition building. In the words of Fultz, this interracial friendship "exposes the tenuous lines that separate individuals and lays the groundwork for broader and more lasting cross-racial and cross-cultural friendships" (38). Romero's analysis of *Paradise* concludes that the novel encourages its readers to "reimagine more inclusive, accepting communities that disrupt the violent exclusions that characterize both mainstream American and traditional African-American concepts of race, history, and nation" (415). Joining Rubenstein and Christian, who have critiqued the scholarship on communal identity in Morrison's novels, is Demetrakopoulos, who finds that maternal bonding poses a threat to individuation.

4. Michael argues that the "notion of constructing a 'we,' does not negate the in-

dividual subject; however, it depends on a conception of the subject as involving a continuous interchange and interdependencies between the individual and various communities" (12). Wyatt attempts to reconcile identification with a separate cultural identity by turning to a partial identification that allows the subject to retain a vision of particular difference even in the moment of identification (*Risking Difference* 172–98). Quashie finds in the texts of contemporary black women writers a model of selfhood that locates identity in an "oscillating identificatory process between self and other" (1). In a similar move, Schapiro applies Jessica Benjamin's theory of inter-subjectivity to *Beloved* and argues that in the novel an identification with another is "a balance of two like but separate selves" (170).

5. My analysis of the father's role in identity construction in *Beloved* builds on the insights of a number of scholars who have addressed manhood and/or black manhood in Morrison's fiction. Chief among these scholars are Cummings, Sitter, Schapiro, and Mayberry. Sitter's seminal essay astutely notes that *Beloved* critiques a Western, phallic, "assertive" model of manhood and substitutes a conception that affirms commitment, compassion, and tenderness. Cummings shows that Paul D develops a new definition of manhood in the course of the novel. He begins as a flawed copy of his white master and eventually learns to emulate Sixo's model of manhood, a shift that culminates when he "mothers" Sethe at the end of the novel. Schapiro observes that Paul D counters a typical Western notion of masculinity and that his "power lies precisely in his maternal nurturing quality; he is that 'other' with the power to recognize and affirm the inner or essential self" (166). Similarly, Mayberry finds an interrelatedness of masculine and feminine qualities in Morrison's male and female characters, and characterizes Sixo, Stamp Paid, and Paul D as embodying "feminine masculinity" (178). While my essay owes a debt to this scholarship, my focus differs in that I argue that Morrison's fiction presents a new theoretical model of the father's role in helping to initiate social individuation and social relations. I should also note that the interpretations of Sitter, Cummings, Schapiro, and Mayberry are countered by other scholars who have argued that Morrison's portrayal of both black and white men does not challenge a traditional heterosexist model. For example, Keith Mitchell writes that in *Beloved* "we encounter the reification of ideas about (black) masculinity and (black) patriarchal heteronormativity predicated by the dominant society" (262). Another dissenting voice is Demetrakopoulos, who finds that the male figures in *Song of Solomon* are ungrounded in nature or the feminine.

6. In suggesting that the paternal role in the socialization process is not essentialized, Morrison's novel aligns with Benjamin's position that "the figures of mother and father are cultural ideals, but they need not be played by 'biological' mothers and fathers or even by women and men" (105) and that "both parents can be figures of separation *and* attachment for their children" (112). Julia Kristeva also insists that the father does not need to be the biological father or even a male. See interview in *Women Analyze Women* 136–39.

7. A number of critics have discerned a postmodern concept of the self in Morrison's fiction. McDowell writes that in *Sula* "the self is multiple, fluid, relational, and in a perpetual state of becoming" (153). See also Rigney and King.

8. According to Freud, the child who observes the primal scene imagines that the

father is castrating the mother, and the notion of female castration causes the child to separate from the mother so as to avoid being similarly castrated. See "From the History of an Infantile Neurosis" (*SE* 17: 7–122). Because Freud's interpretation has become the standard reading, feminists have denounced the primal scene as our culture's "dominant patriarchal fantasy." Maria Ramas writes that, in the primal scene, "ultimately and always, a woman is being degraded" (157).

9. Gallop suggests a similar paradigm: "It could be said that the symbolic can be encountered only as a tear in the fabric of the imaginary, a revealing interruption. The paths to the symbolic are thus *in* the imaginary" (60).

10. Oliver argues that Kristeva's notion of the Third Party or the imaginary father "undermines the maternal/paternal dualism" (*Reading* 69), but that this breakdown is not to be read as a return to an original mother-child dyadic unity.

11. For Lacan, words arbitrarily assign meanings to what was identical before the advent of the sign. See *Écrits: A Selection* 146–59.

12. Benjamin explains that "the core sense of belonging to one sex or the other is not compromised by cross-sex identifications" and that "individuals ideally should integrate and express both male and female aspects of selfhood (as culturally defined)." She points out that it is only a long history of "the derogation of the female side of the polarity" that has led to "a hardening of the opposition between male and female individuality as they are now constructed" (113).

13. See "The Uncanny" (*SE* 17: 217–56). This doubling of the mother and father is written both in myth and in the psychoanalytic identity narrative. Summing up the "monomyth," or single framework he finds uniting all myths, Campbell writes that "[male and female] are the same, each is both, and the dual form . . . is only an effect of illusion. . . . This is a supreme statement of the great paradox" (170). Freudian theory holds that in the Oedipal moment the child switches an identification from the mother to the father. See Ragland-Sullivan 278. Similarly, Lacan writes that at the moment of subjectivity formation, as the mother is made other, the father or phallus is the Other who is substituted for her and is the object of desire. The use of the same word, "other," changed only by the use of the upper- and lowercase first letter, calls attention to the substitution that takes place in the moment of dislocation. Freud, however, has little to say about paternal identification, and Lacan insists that the paternal replacement for the mother is an absence, the "always missing object of desire at the level of sexual division" (Juliet Mitchell 24).

5. Cross-Racial Identification in Blackface Minstrelsy and *Black Like Me*

1. See Spillers 65–81; Nelson; and Patricia Williams.

2. John Duvall's important study, *Race and White Identity in Southern Fiction: From Faulkner to Morrison*, locates a series of white figures in Southern literature who straddle the in-between and seem to become less white. Duvall does not investigate these characters as border figures; rather, he argues that race is constituted by performance and that when culturally defined whites digress from the script of white privilege, they "challenge the epistemology of the white-Negro cultural opposition"

(27); create "ruptures in culture's normative structures of identy" (xv); and expose racial categories as a social fiction.

3. See Lott, "White Like Me."

4. Both Wald and Dreisinger analyze examples of white-passing-for-black in an attempt to distinguish between cross-identifications that appropriate the other and cross-identifications that enable greater social and political inclusivity. However, ultimately, both Wald and Dreisinger find fault with every example of white-passing-for-black that they examine. In each instance, they find that whites who cross the color line fail to transcend white self-interest.

5. The notion of confounded identities raises the much debated issue of an "authentic" blackness. In a controversial move, Walter Benn Michaels takes the position that the insistence on a culturally defined racial identity promulgates racial distinctions and racial barriers, and he urges Americans to "give up the idea of race altogether." "Either race is an essence," he writes, "or there is no such thing as race" (125). Both Wald and Dreisinger take issue with Michaels's summons to abandon race as a category. Wald observes that such an argument "neglects the dialectics of identity" (10), and Dreisinger points to African American writers who "defend and/or define the 'black' in 'black culture'" (144). My approach to black subjectivity owes much to E. Patrick Johnson. He suggests that "the mutual constructing/deconstructing, avowing/disavowing, and expanding/delimiting dynamic that occurs in the production of blackness is the very thing that constitutes 'black' culture" (2). According to Johnson, blackness is a "complex and nuanced racial signifier" that is appropriated by various individuals or groups so as to "circumscribe its boundaries or to exclude other individuals or groups" (3). While Johnson is well aware that, as a cultural signifier, race has been and continues to be exploited and co-opted, he nonetheless warns against the "dangers" of proprietary ownership: "The key here is to be cognizant of the arbitrariness of authenticity, the ways in which it carries with it the dangers of foreclosing the possibilities of cultural exchange and understanding" (3). My goal in this book is to find the way to negotiate the border between cultural signifiers so as to make possible "cultural exchange" without dominating the other.

6. According to Dreisinger, even as late as the 1940s, there are instances where culturally defined whites still would accept black entertainment only when performed by whites pretending to be black. Dreisinger cites the example of the radio pioneer Vernon Winslow, a man of African descent, who coached whites in "jive" diction for a local radio show. When one day the host did not show up for work, Winslow took his place on air and delivered his own "jive" routine. When whites learned they had been entertained by an authentic African American, they protested and Winslow was fired. See Dreisinger 146.

7. Dreisinger notes that during three decades, the 1890s, 1920s, and 1990s, "a potentially vanishing white population abounded, fueling passing narratives of both black and white varieties" (8). In other words, at times when racial boundaries seemed to be shifting, writers and readers turned to fictions of the in-between to help define racial identities.

8. The journal entries that compose *Black Like Me* were originally published in monthly installments in *Sepia,* a now defunct black periodical. *Black Like Me* was

published in book form in 1961 and has been continuously in print since its publication. It has sold more than twelve million copies and has been translated into fourteen languages. Although, as Griffin records, the original publication prompted death and castration threats, his book sold well and reviews were positive. An African American reviewer, Louis E. Lomax, rejoiced in Griffin's biracial experience: "It was a joy to see a white man become black for a while and then re-enter his own world screaming in the tones of Richard Wright and James Baldwin" (53). A white reviewer, while praising Griffin's project, nevertheless expressed anxiety about transgressing racial boundaries: "It seems perverse to tamper with one's identity in this way, no matter what the motive" (Cook 129).

9. In a move relevant to my examination of mirror scenes in *Black Like Me*, Kimberly Benston analyzes face-to-face encounters in works by African American authors. In such an encounter, he writes that two "distanced parties" "no longer read each other: they are each other, and in this melting they pose a radical challenge to our own liminal stance as interpreters." The "topos of facing," he continues, is a recurring metaphor in African American literature and represents "a paradoxical drive toward a self-effacing self-fulfillment" (106, 107).

10. On April 25, 1959, Mack Parker, a twenty-three-year-old truck driver, was being held in a jail in Poplarville, Mississippi, when he was lynched by a white mob. The FBI investigated the lynching and compiled a 378-page report, including admissions of guilt. Nonetheless, a Mississippi jury composed of twenty whites and one African American found no basis for prosecution. See "Mack C. Parker."

11. In Lacanian terms, love is a drive toward identification with the other, while ego acquisition in the symbolic is a drive toward self-alienation.

12. Symbolic castration is the obsessive motif of the Freudian/Lacanian identity-narrative. See Mellard, *Using Lacan* 28–33.

Works Cited

Abel, Elizabeth. "Black Writing, White Reading: Race and the Politics of Feminist Interpretation." Rev. version. *Feminisms: An Anthology of Literary Theory and Criticism.* Edited by Robyn R. Warhol and Diane Price Herndl. Rev. ed. New Brunswick, NJ: Rutgers University Press, 2007. 827–52.

Abel, Elizabeth, Barbara Christian, and Helene Moglen, eds. *Female Subjects in Black and White: Race, Psychoanalysis, Feminism.* Berkeley: University of California Press, 1997.

Anzaldúa, Gloria. *Borderlands La Frontera: The New Mestiza.* 3rd ed. San Francisco: Aunt Lute Books, 2007.

Appiah, Anthony. "The Uncompleted Argument: Du Bois and the Illusion of Race." Gates 21–37.

Asals, Frederick. "The Double in Flannery O'Connor's Stories." *Flannery O'Connor Bulletin* 9 (1980): 49–86.

Awkward, Michael. *Negotiating Difference: Race, Gender, and the Politics of Positionality.* Chicago: University of Chicago Press, 1995.

Bakhtin, Mikhail. "Discourse in the Novel." *The Dialogic Imagination.* Translated by Caryl Emerson and Michael Holquist. Austin: University of Texas Press, 1981. 259–422.

Baldwin, James. *Nobody Knows My Name: More Notes of a Native Son.* New York: Dell, 1961.

Benjamin, Jessica. *The Bonds of Love: Psychoanalysis, Feminism, and the Problem of Domination.* New York: Routledge, 1992.

Benston, Kimberly W. "Facing Tradition: Revisionary Scenes in African American Literature." *PMLA* 105.1 (1990): 98–109.

Bhabha, Homi. *The Location of Culture.* London: Routledge, 1994.

Bleikasten, André. "The Heresy of Flannery O'Connor." *Les Americanistes: New French Criticism on Modern American Fiction.* Edited by Ira D. and Christiane Johnson. Port Washington, NY: Kennicat, 1978. 53–70.

Blotner, Joseph. *Faulkner: A Biography.* 2 vols. New York: Random House, 1974.

Brinkmeyer, Robert. *The Art and Vision of Flannery O'Connor.* Baton Rouge: Louisiana State University Press, 1989.

———. "'Jesus, Stab Me in the Heart': *Wise Blood,* Wounding, and Sacramental Aesthetics." *New Essays on Wise Blood*. Edited by Michael Kreyling. Cambridge: Cambridge University Press, 1995. 71–90.

Bryant, Jerry H. "The Violence of *Native Son*." *Southern Review* 17.1 (Spring 1981): 303–19.

Burkman, Katherine H., and J. Reid Meloy. "The Black Mirror: Joseph Conrad's 'The Nigger of the Narcissus' and Flannery O'Connor's 'The Artificial Nigger.'" *Midwest Quarterly* 8 (1987): 230–47.

Campbell, Joseph. *The Hero with a Thousand Faces*. Princeton, NJ: Princeton University Press, 1973.

Cheatham, George. "Jesus, O'Connor's Artificial Nigger." *Studies in Short Fiction* 22 (1985): 475–79.

Christian, Barbara. *Black Women Novelists: The Development of a Tradition, 1892–1976*. Westport, CT: Greenwood, 1980.

———. "The Race for Theory." *The Black Feminist Reader*. Edited by Joy James and T. Denean Sharpley-Whiting. Oxford: Blackwell, 2000. 11–23.

Ciuba, Gary. *Desire, Violence, and Divinity in Modern Southern Fiction*. Baton Rouge: Louisiana State University Press, 2007.

Cixous, Hélène. "Castration or Decapitation?" *Signs* 7 (1981): 41–55.

Cook, Bruce A. "What Is It Like to Be a Negro?" *Commonweal*, October 1961, 129.

Cowley, Malcolm. *The Faulkner-Cowley File: Letters and Memories, 1944–1962*. New York: Viking, 1966.

Crawford, Nicholas. "An Africanist Impasse: Race, Return, and Revelation in the Short Fiction of Flannery O'Connor." *South Atlantic Review* 68.2 (2003): 1–25.

Cullen, John B., and Floyd C. Watkins. *Old Times in the Faulkner Country*. Chapel Hill: University of North Carolina Press, 1961.

Cummings, Kate. "Reclaiming the Mother('s) Tongue: *Beloved, Ceremony, Mothers and Shadows*." *College English* 52.5 (1990): 552–69.

Davis, Cynthia. "Self, Society, and Myth in Toni Morrison's Fiction." *Contemporary Literature* 23 (1982): 323–42.

Davis, Thadious M. *Games of Property: Law, Race, and Gender in Faulkner's "Go Down, Moses."* Durham, NC: Duke University Press, 2003.

de Lauretis, Teresa. *Technologies of Gender: Essays on Theory, Film, and Fiction*. Bloomington: Indiana University Press, 1987.

Demetrakopoulos, Stephanie A. "Maternal Bonds as Devourers of Women's Individuation in Toni Morrison's *Beloved*." *African American Review* 26 (1992): 51–59.

Derrida, Jacques. *Of Grammatology*. Translated by Gayatari Chakravorty Spivak. Baltimore: Johns Hopkins University Press, 1974.

Dickens, Charles. *American Notes*. 1842. New York: Penguin, 1972.

Douglass, Frederick. *North Star*, October 27, 1848.

Doyle, Donald H. *Faulkner's County: The Historical Roots of Yoknapatawpha*. Chapel Hill: University of North Carolina Press, 2001.

Dreisinger, Baz. *Near Black: White-to-Black Passing in American Culture*. Amherst: University of Massachusetts Press, 2008.

duCille, Ann. "The Occult of True Black Womanhood: Critical Demeanor and Black Feminist Studies." Abel, Christian, and Moglen 21–56.

Dussere, Eric. "The Debts of History: Southern Honor, Affirmative Action, and Faulkner's *Intruder in the Dust.*" *Faulkner Journal* 17.1 (2001): 37–57.

Duvall, John N. *Race and White Identity in Southern Fiction: From Faulkner to Morrison.* New York: Palgrave Macmillan, 2008.

Eagleton, Terry. *Literary Theory: An Introduction.* Minneapolis: University of Minnesota Press, 1983.

Ellison, Ralph. *Shadow and Act.* 1953. New York: Vintage, 1972.

Elmer, Jonathan. "Spectacle and Event in *Native Son.*" *American Literature* 70 (December 1988): 767–98.

Fabre, Michel. *The Unfinished Quest of Richard Wright.* Translated by Isabel Barzun. New York: William Morrow, 1973.

Faulkner, William. *Faulkner in the University: Class Conferences at the University of Virginia.* Edited by Joseph Blotner. Charlottesville: University of Virginia Press, 1959.

——. *Intruder in the Dust.* 1948. New York: Vintage, 1991.

——. "Mississippi, 1954." *Essays, Speeches, and Public Letters.* Edited by James B. Meriwether. London: Chatto and Windus, 1967. 11–43.

——. *Selected Letters.* Edited by Joseph Blotner. New York: Random House, 1977.

Fitzgerald, Sally. Letter to the editor. *Flannery O'Connor Bulletin* 24 (1994–95): 175–82.

Forter, Greg. *Murdering Masculinities: Fantasies of Gender and Violence in the American Crime Novel.* New York: New York University Press, 2000.

Fowler, Doreen. "Deconstructing Racial Difference: O'Connor's 'The Artificial Nigger.'" *Flannery O'Connor Bulletin* 24 (1995–96): 22–32.

——. *Faulkner: The Return of the Repressed.* Charlottesville: University of Virginia Press, 1997.

Fowler, Doreen, and Ann J. Abadie, eds. *Faulkner and Race: Faulkner and Yoknapatawpha, 1986.* Jackson: University Press of Mississippi, 1987.

——, eds. *Faulkner and Women: Faulkner and Yoknapatawpha, 1985.* Jackson: University Press of Mississippi, 1986.

France, Alan W. "Misogyny and Appropriation in *Native Son.*" *Modern Fiction Studies* 34.3 (Autumn 1988): 413–23.

Freud, Sigmund. *Beyond the Pleasure Principle.* Translated by James Strachey. New York: Norton, 1961.

——. *Civilization and Its Discontents.* Translated by Joan Riviere. London: Hogarth, 1939.

——. *The Standard Edition of the Complete Psychological Works of Freud.* Edited and translated by James Strachey. 24 vols. London: Hogarth, 1961.

Fultz, Lucille P. *Toni Morrison: Playing with Difference.* Urbana: University of Illinois Press, 2003.

Fuss, Diana. *Identification Papers: Readings on Psychoanalysis, Sexuality, and Culture.* New York: Routledge, 1995.

Gallop, Jane. *Reading Lacan.* Ithaca, NY: Cornell University Press, 1985.

Gates, Henry Louis, Jr., ed. *"Race," Writing, and Difference.* Chicago: University of Chicago Press, 1986.

Giannone, Richard. *Flannery O'Connor, Hermit Novelist.* Chicago: University of Illinois Press, 2000.

Gilroy, Paul. *The Black Atlantic: Modernity and Double Consciousness.* Cambridge, MA: Harvard University Press, 1993.

Gooch, Brad. *Flannery: A Life of Flannery O'Connor.* New York: Little, Brown, 2009.

Green, Alan W. C. "'Jim Crow,' 'Zip Coon': The Northern Origins of Negro Minstrelsy." *Massachusetts Review* 11 (1970): 385–97.

Griffin, John Howard. *Black Like Me.* 1961. 2nd ed., with author's epilogue. Boston: Houghton Mifflin, 1977.

Gubar, Susan. *Racechanges: White Skin, Black Face in American Culture.* New York: Oxford University Press, 1997.

Guttman, Sondra. "What Bigger Killed for: Rereading Violence against Women in *Native Son.*" *Texas Studies in Literature and Language* 43.2 (2001): 168–93.

Gwin, Minrose C. *The Feminine and Faulkner: Reading (Beyond) Sexual Difference.* Knoxville: University of Tennessee Press, 1990.

Harris, Trudier. "Native Sons and Foreign Daughters." *New Essays on "Native Son."* Edited by Keneth Kinnamon. Cambridge: Cambridge University Press, 1990. 63–84.

Havird, David. "The Saving Rape: Flannery O'Connor and Patriarchal Religion." *Mississippi Quarterly* 47.1 (1993–94): 15–26.

Higashida, Cheryl. "Aunt Sue's Children: Re-viewing the Gender(ed) Politics of Richard Wright's Radicalism." *American Literature* 75.2 (June 2003): 395–427.

Irigaray, Luce. *Speculum of the Other Woman.* Translated by Gillian C. Gill. Ithaca, NY: Cornell University Press, 1985.

———. *This Sex Which Is Not One.* Translated by Catherine Porter with Carolyn Burke. Ithaca, NY: Cornell University Press, 1985.

Irwin, John T. *Doubling and Incest/Repetition and Revenge.* Baltimore: Johns Hopkins University Press, 1975.

JanMohamed, Abdul R. *The Death-Bound-Subject: Richard Wright's Archaeology of Death.* Durham, NC: Duke University Press, 2005.

———. "The Economy of Manichean Allegory: The Function of Racial Difference in Colonialist Literature." Gates 78–106.

———. "Sexuality on/of the Racial Border: Foucault, Wright, and the Articulation of 'Racialized Sexuality.'" *Discourses of Sexuality: From Aristotle to AIDS.* Edited by Domna C. Stanton. Ann Arbor: University of Michigan Press, 1992. 94–116.

Johnson, Barbara. "The Re(a)d and the Black." *Modern Critical Interpretations of Richard Wright's "Native Son."* Edited by Harold Bloom. New York: Chelsea House, 1988. 115–23.

Johnson, E. Patrick. *Appropriating Blackness: Performance and the Politics of Authenticity.* Durham, NC: Duke University Press, 2003.

Joyce, Joyce Anne. "Richard Wright's 'Long Black Song': A Moral Dilemma." *Mississippi Quarterly* 42.4 (Fall 1989): 370–86.

Kahane, Claire. "The Artificial Niggers." *Massachusetts Review* 19.1 (1978): 183–98.

Kartiganer, Donald M. "Faulkner's Comic Narrative of Community." *A Gathering of*

Evidence: Essays on William Faulkner's "Intruder in the Dust." Edited by Michel Gresset and Patrick Samway, S.J. Philadelphia: Saint Joseph's University Press and Fordham University Press, 2004. 131–49.

Katz, Claire. "Flannery O'Connor's Rage of Vision." *American Literature* 46.1 (1974): 54–67.

Keady, Sylvia. "Richard Wright's Women Characters and Inequality." *Black American Literature Forum* 10 (1976): 124–29.

King, Nicole. "'You Think Like You White': Questioning Race and Racial Community through the Lens of Middle-Class Desire(s)." *Novel: A Forum on Fiction* 35 (2002): 211–30.

Kinnamon, Keneth. *The Emergence of Richard Wright: A Study in Literature and Society.* Urbana: University of Illinois Press, 1972.

———. "*Native Son.*" *Major Literary Characters: Bigger Thomas.* Edited by Harold Bloom. New York: Chelsea House, 1990. 60–72.

Kristeva, Julia. *About Chinese Women.* Translated by Anita Barrows. London: M. Boyars, 1977.

———. *Desire in Language: A Semiotic Approach to Literature and Art.* Edited by Leon S. Roudiez. Translated by Thomas Gora, Alice Jardine, and Leon S. Roudiez. New York: Columbia University Press, 1980.

———. *In the Beginning Was Love.* Translated by A. Goldhammer. New York: Columbia University Press, 1988.

———. Interview, Paris, Summer 1980. *Women Analyze Women.* Edited by Elaine Hoffman Baruch and Lucienne J. Serrano. New York: New York University Press, 1988. 129–45.

———. *Powers of Horror: An Essay on Abjection.* Translated by Leon S. Roudiez. New York: Columbia University Press, 1982.

———. *Revolution in Poetic Language.* Translated by Margaret Waller. New York: Columbia University Press, 1984.

———. *Strangers to Ourselves.* Translated by Leon S. Roudiez. New York: Columbia University Press, 1991.

———. *Tales of Love.* Translated by Leon Roudiez. New York: Columbia University Press, 1987.

Lacan, Jacques. *Écrits.* Paris: Seuil, 1966.

———. *Écrits: A Selection.* Translated by Alan Sheridan. New York: Norton, 1977.

Laplanche, J., and J.-B. Pontalis. *The Language of Psycho-Analysis.* Translated by Donald Nicholson-Smith. New York: Norton, 1973.

Laub, Dori. *Testimony: Crises of Witnessing in Literature, Psychoanalysis, and History.* New York: Routledge, 1992.

Lomax, Louis E. "It's Like This." *Saturday Review,* December 1961, 53.

Lott, Eric. *Love and Theft: Blackface Minstrelsy and the American Working Class.* New York: Oxford University Press, 1993.

———. "White Like Me: Racial Cross-Dressing and the Construction of American Whiteness." *Cultures of United States Imperialism.* Edited by Amy Kaplan and Donald Pease. Durham, NC: Duke University Press, 1993. 474–95.

Lydenberg, Robin. "Freud's Uncanny Narratives." *PMLA* 112.5 (1997): 1072–86.

"Mack C. Parker of Lumberton, Miss., Kidnapped and Lynched: The Story behind the Lynching." *Jet*, May 14, 1959, 12–15.

MacKethan, Lucinda. "Redeeming Blackness: Urban Allegories of O'Connor, Percy, and Toole." *Studies in the Literary Imagination* 27.2 (1994): 29–39.

Maxwell, William. *New Negro, Old Left: African-American Writing and Communism between the Wars*. New York: Columbia University Press, 1999.

Mayberry, Susan Neal. *Can't I Love What I Criticize? The Masculine and Morrison*. Athens: University of Georgia Press, 2007.

McDowell, Deborah E. "'The Self and the Other': Reading Toni Morrison's *Sula* and the Black Female Text." *Critical Essays on Toni Morrison*. Edited by Nellie Y. McKay. Boston: Hall, 1988. 77–90. Rpt. in *Toni Morrison: Modern Critical Views*. Edited by Harold Bloom. New York: Chelsea House, 1990. 149–63.

Mellard, James. "Flannery O'Connor's *Others:* Freud, Lacan, and the Unconscious." *American Literature* 61 (1989): 625–43.

——. *Using Lacan, Reading Fiction*. Urbana: University of Illinois Press, 1991.

Meriwether, James B., and Michael Millgate, eds. *Lion in the Garden: Interviews with William Faulkner, 1926–1962*. New York: Random House, 1968.

Michael, Magali Cornier. *New Visions of Community in Contemporary American Fiction: Tan, Kingsolver, Castillo, Morrison*. Iowa City: University of Iowa Press, 2006.

Michaels, Walter Benn. "Autobiography of an Ex-White Man: Why Race Is Not a Social Construction." *Transition* 73 (1998): 122–43.

Millgate, Michael. *The Achievement of William Faulkner*. New York: Vintage, 1963.

Mitchell, Juliet. Introduction 1. *Feminine Sexuality: Jacques Lacan and the "École freudienne."* Edited by Juliet Mitchell and Jacqueline Rose. Translated by Jacqueline Rose. New York: Norton, 1982. 1–26.

Mitchell, Keith. "Femininity, Abjection, and (Black) Masculinity in James Baldwin's *Giovanni's Room* and Toni Morrison's *Beloved*." *James Baldwin and Toni Morrison: Comparative Critical and Theoretical Essays*. Edited by Lovalerie King and Lynn Orilla Scott. New York: Palgrave Macmillan, 2006. 261–86.

Moglen, Helene. "Redeeming History: Toni Morrison's *Beloved*." Abel, Christian, and Moglen 201–20.

Moi, Toril. Introduction. *The Kristeva Reader*. By Julia Kristeva. Edited by Toril Moi. New York: Columbia University Press, 1986.

——. *Sexual/Textual Politics: Feminist Literary Theory*. New York: Routledge, 1985.

Moreland, Richard C. "Faulkner's Continuing Education: From Self-Reflection to Embarrassment." *Faulkner at One Hundred: Retrospect and Prospect*. Edited by Donald M. Kartiganer and Ann J. Abadie. Jackson: University Press of Mississippi, 2000. 60–69.

——. *Learning from Difference: Teaching Morrison, Twain, Ellison, and Eliot*. Columbus: Ohio State University Press, 1999.

Morris, Wesley, and Barbara Alverson Morris. *Reading Faulkner*. Madison: University of Wisconsin Press, 1989.

Morrison, Toni. *Beloved*. 1987. New York: Vintage International, 2004.

———. "Faulkner and Women." Fowler and Abadie, *Faulkner and Women* 295–302.

———. Interview with Nellie McKay. *Conversations with Toni Morrison*. Edited by Danille Taylor-Guthrie. Jackson: University Press of Mississippi, 1994. 138–55.

———. *Jazz*. 1992. New York: Penguin (Plume), 1993.

———. *Playing in the Dark: Whiteness and the Literary Imagination*. New York: Vintage, 1993.

———. "Unspeakable Things Unspoken: The Afro-American Presence in American Literature." *Toni Morrison: Modern Critical Views*. Edited by Harold Bloom. New York: Chelsea House, 1990. 201–30. Rpt. of *Michigan Quarterly Review* 28 (1989): 1–34.

Napier, James J. "Flannery O'Connor's Last Three: 'The Sense of an Ending.'" *Southern Literary Journal* 14 (1982): 19–27.

Nelson, Dana D. *The Word in Black and White: Reading 'Race' in American Literature, 1638–1867*. New York: Oxford University Press, 1992.

Nesbitt, Laurel. "Reading Place in and around Flannery O'Connor's Texts." *Post Identity* 1.1 (1997): 145–97.

Nietzsche, Frederick. *On the Genealogy of Morality*. Edited by Keith Ansell-Pearson. Cambridge: Cambridge University Press, 1999.

O'Connor, Flannery. *The Complete Stories of Flannery O'Connor*. New York: Farrar, Straus, and Giroux, 1971.

———. *The Habit of Being*. New York: Farrar, Straus, and Giroux, 1979.

———. *Mystery and Manners: Occasional Prose*. Edited by Sally and Robert Fitzgerald. New York: Farrar, Straus, and Giroux, 1969.

———. *The Violent Bear It Away*. 1960. New York: Farrar, Straus, and Giroux, 2007.

Okeke-Ezigbo, Emeka. "Three Artificial Blacks: A Re-examination of Flannery O'Connor's 'The Artificial Nigger.'" *College English Association Journal* 27 (1984): 371–82.

Oliver, Kelly. *Reading Kristeva: Unraveling the Double-Bind*. Bloomington: Indiana University Press, 1993.

———. *Subjectivity without Subjects: From Abject Fathers to Desiring Mothers*. New York: Rowman and Littlefield, 1998.

Omi, Michael, and Howard Winant. *Racial Formation in the United States: From the 1960s to the 1980s*. London: Routledge, 1986.

Paulson, Suzanne Morrow. *Flannery O'Connor: A Study of the Short Fiction*. Boston: Twayne, 1988.

Peavy, Charles. *Go Slow, Now: Faulkner and the Race Question*. Eugene: University of Oregon Press, 1964.

Perreault, Jeanne. "The Body, the Critics, and 'The Artificial Nigger.'" *Mississippi Quarterly* 56.3 (2003): 389–410.

Polk, Noel. "Man in the Middle: Faulkner and the Southern White Moderate." Fowler and Abadie, *Faulkner and Race* 130–51.

Prown, Katherine Hemple. *Revising Flannery O'Connor: Southern Literary Culture and the Problem of Female Authorship*. Charlottesville: University of Virginia Press, 2001.

Quashie, Kevin Everod. *Black Women, Identity, and Cultural Theory: (Un)becoming the Subject.* New Brunswick, NJ: Rutgers University Press, 2004.

Ragland-Sullivan, Ellie. *Jacques Lacan and the Philosophy of Psychoanalysis.* Urbana: University of Illinois Press, 1986.

Ramadanovic, Petar. "*Native Son*'s Tragedy: Traversing the Death Drive with Bigger Thomas." *Arizona Quarterly* 59 (2003): 81–105.

Ramas, Maria. "Freud's Dora, Dora's Hysteria." *Dora's Case: Freud—Feminism—Hysteria.* Edited by Charles Bernheimer and Claire Kahane. New York: Columbia University Press, 1985. 149–80.

Rigney, Barbara. *The Voices of Toni Morrison.* Columbus: Ohio State University Press, 1991.

Roediger, David R. *The Wages of Whiteness: Race and the Making of the American Working Class.* 1991. Rev. ed. New York: Verso, 2007.

Rogin, Michael. *Blackface, White Noise: Jewish Immigrants in the Hollywood Melting Pot.* Berkeley: University of California Press, 1996.

Romero, Channette. "Creating the Beloved Community: Religion, Race and Nation in Toni Morrison's *Paradise.*" *African-American Review* 39.3 (2005): 415–30.

Rose, Jacqueline. Introduction 2. *Feminine Sexuality: Jacques Lacan and the "École freudienne."* Edited by Juliet Mitchell and Jacqueline Rose. Translated by Jacqueline Rose. New York: Norton, 1982. 27–57.

Rowley, Hazel. *Richard Wright: The Life and Times.* New York: Henry Holt, 2001.

Rubenstein, Roberta. *Boundaries of the Self: Gender, Culture, Fiction.* Urbana: University of Illinois Press, 1987.

Schapiro, Barbara. "The Bonds of Love and the Boundaries of the Self in Toni Morrison's *Beloved.*" *Contemporary Literature* 32.2 (1991): 194–210. Rpt. in *Understanding Toni Morrison's "Beloved" and "Sula": Selected Essays and Criticisms of the Works by the Nobel Prize-winning Author.* Edited by Solomon O. Iyasere and Marla W. Iyasere. Troy, NY: Whitston, 2000. 155–72.

Schiff, Jonathan. "'That's a Greenleaf Bull': Totemism and Exogamy in Flannery O'Connor's 'Greenleaf.'" *English Language Notes* 32 (1995): 69–76.

Schleifer, Ronald. "Rural Gothic: The Stories of Flannery O'Connor." *Modern Fiction Studies* 28 (1982): 475–85.

Schmitz, Neil. "Faulkner and the Post-Confederate." *Faulkner in Cultural Context.* Edited by Donald M. Kartiganer and Ann J. Abadie. Jackson: University Press of Mississippi, 1997. 241–62.

Shields, John C. "Flannery O'Connor's 'Greenleaf' and the Myth of Europa and the Bull." *Studies in Short Fiction* 18 (1981): 421–31.

Sitter, Deborah. "The Making of a Man: Dialogic Meaning in *Beloved.*" *African-American Review* 26.1 (1992): 17–30.

Skerrett, Joseph T., Jr. "Composing Bigger: Wright and the Making of *Native Son.*" *Modern Critical Interpretations of Richard Wright's "Native Son."* Edited by Harold Bloom. New York: Chelsea House, 1988. 125–42.

Smith, Peter. "Flannery O'Connor's Empowered Women." *Southern Literary Journal* 26.2 (1994): 35–47.

Smith, Valerie. *"Song of Solomon:* Continuities of Community." *Toni Morrison: Critical Perspectives Past and Present.* Edited by Henry Louis Gates Jr. and K. A. Appiah. New York: Amistad, 1993. 274–83. Rpt. of "'The Quest for and Discovery of Identity in Toni Morrison's *Song of Solomon.*" *Southern Review* 21 (1985): 721–32.

Snead, James A. *Figures of Division: William Faulkner's Major Novels.* New York: Methuen, 1986.

Spillers, Hortense J. "Mama's Baby, Papa's Maybe: An American Grammar Book." *diacritics* 17 (1987): 65–81.

Strausbaugh, John. *Black Like You: Blackface, Whiteface, Insult and Imitation in American Popular Culture.* New York: Penguin Books, 2006.

Strickland, Edward. "The Penitential Quest in 'The Artificial Nigger.'" *Studies in Short Fiction* 25 (1988): 453–59.

Sundquist, Eric J. *Faulkner: The House Divided.* Baltimore: Johns Hopkins University Press, 1983.

Taylor, Walter. *Faulkner's Search for a South.* Urbana: University of Illinois Press, 1983.

Theweleit, Klaus. *Male Fantasies.* Translated by Stephen Conway. Foreword by Barbara Ehrenreich. Theory and History of Literature Series. Minneapolis: University of Minnesota Press, 1987.

Toll, Robert C. *Blacking Up: The Minstrel Show in Nineteenth-Century America.* New York: Oxford University Press, 1974.

Towner, Theresa M. *Faulkner on the Color Line: The Later Novels.* Jackson: University Press of Mississippi, 2000.

Wald, Gayle. *Crossing the Line: Racial Passing in Twentieth-Century U.S. Literature and Culture.* Durham, NC: Duke University Press, 2000.

Walker, Margaret. *Richard Wright: Demonic Genius.* New York: Warner Books, 1988.

Walker, Sue. "The Being of Illness: The Language of Being Ill." *Flannery O'Connor Review* 25 (1996–97): 33–58.

Ward, Jerry W., Jr., and Robert J. Butler. *The Richard Wright Encyclopedia.* Westport, CT: Greenwood, 2008.

Warren, Nagueyalti. "Black Girls and Native Sons: Female Images in Selected Works by Richard Wright." *Richard Wright: Myths and Realities.* Edited by C. James Trotman. New York: Garland, 1988. 59–77.

Weinstein, Philip M. *What Else but Love? The Ordeal of Race in Faulkner and Morrison.* New York: Columbia University Press, 1996.

Westling, Louise. "Flannery O'Connor's Mothers and Daughters." *Twentieth Century Literature* 24 (1978): 510–22.

———. *Sacred Groves and Ravaged Gardens: The Fiction of Eudora Welty, Carson McCullers, and Flannery O'Connor.* Athens: University of Georgia Press, 1985.

Willett, Cynthia. "Masculinity and Existential Freedom: Wright, Ellison, Morrison, and Nietzsche." *Critical Affinities: Nietzsche and African American Thought.* Edited by Jacqueline Scott and A. Todd Franklin. Albany: State University of New York Press, 2006. 203–23.

Williams, Patricia J. *The Alchemy of Race and Rights: Diary of a Law Professor*. Cambridge, MA: Harvard University Press, 1991.

Williams, Sherley Anne. "Papa Dick and Sister-Woman: Reflections on Women in the Fiction of Richard Wright." *American Novelists Revisited: Essays in Feminist Criticism*. Edited by Fritz Fleischmann. Boston: G. K. Hall, 1982. 394–415.

Williamson, Joel. *William Faulkner and Southern History*. Oxford: Oxford University Press, 1993.

Wilson, Edmund. *Cannibals and Christians*. New York: Farrar, Strauss, 1958.

Wood, Ralph C. "Where Is the Voice Coming From? Flannery O'Connor on Race." *Flannery O'Connor Bulletin* 22 (1993–94): 90–118.

Wright, Richard. *Black Boy (American Hunger): A Record of Childhood and Youth*. 1945. The Restored Text Established by the Library of America. New York: Harper Perennial, 1991.

———. "How 'Bigger' Was Born." *Native Son*. The Restored Text Established by the Library of America. New York: Harper Perennial, 1993. 505–540.

———. "I Tried to Be a Communist." *The God That Failed*. Edited by Richard Crossman. New York: Harper, 1949. 115–62. Rpt. of *Atlantic Monthly* 159 (August 1944): 61–70.

———. *Native Son*. 1940. The Restored Text Established by the Library of America. New York: Harper Perennial, 1993.

Wyatt, Jean. "Giving Body to the Word: The Maternal Symbolic in Toni Morrison's *Beloved*." *PMLA* 108 (1993): 474–88.

———. *Risking Difference: Identification, Race, and Community in Contemporary Fiction and Feminism*. New York: State University of New York Press, 2004.

Yeager, Patricia. "Flannery O'Connor and the Aesthetics of Torture." *Flannery O'Connor: New Perspectives*. Edited by Sura P. Rath and Mary Neff Shaw. Athens: University of Georgia Press, 1996. 183–206.

Yaeger, Patricia, and Beth Kowaleski-Wallace, eds. *Refiguring the Father: New Feminist Readings of Patriarchy*. Carbondale: Southern Illinois University Press, 1980.

Index

Blotner, Joseph, 24, 46, 145n3
boundaries: and abjection, 142–43; and blackface minstrelsy, 114–24; defined, 6–7, 141–43; and doubleness, 141–42; in *Intruder in the Dust*, 32–36; in *Native Son*, 50–54, 61–65; and paternal function, 6–13; and transgression, 1–2
Brinkmeyer, Robert, 72–73, 150n1, 151n2, 152n8
Browning, Preston, 72
Bryant, Jerry, 148n2
Burkman, Katherine H., 80, 152n9
Butler, Robert J., 15

Campbell, Joseph, 155n13
Cheatham, George, 152n9
Christian, Barbara, 1, 94
Ciuba, Gary, 150n1
Cixous, Hélène, 2
Coindreau, Maurice, 14
community identification, problem of, 1–5, 63–67, 93–94
Cook, Bruce A., 157n8
Crawford, Nicholas, 151n2
cross-racial identification, 3–4; and blackface minstrelsy, 114–24; in *Native Son*, 65–67
Cullen, John B., and lynching of Nelse Patton, 23–24, 145n3
Cummings, Kate, 154n5

Davis, Cynthia, 153n3
Davis, Thadious M., 147–48n16
De Chardin, Teilhard, 152n12
De Lauretis, Teresa, 5, 93
Demetrakopoulos, Stephanie A., 153n3, 154n5
Derrida, Jacques, 151n4
Dickens, Charles, 119–20
doubling: in "Greenleaf," 83–87; in *Intruder in the Dust*, 25–27, 42–44; in *Native Son*, 56–57, 58
Douglass, Frederick, 114
Doyle, Don, 24

Dreisinger, Baz, 112, 124–25, 127, 129, 156nn4–7
Du Bois, W. E. B., 125
duCille, Ann, 3–4, 153n2
Dussere, Eric, 46, 147nn11–13
Duvall, John N., 72–73, 80, 151n2, 152n10, 155–56n2

Eagleton, Terry, 32
Ellison, Ralph, 5, 115, 121
Elmer, Jonathan, 148n1
"Enduring Chill, The" (O'Connor), 73–74, 87–91; abjection and grace, 87–88, 91–92; identification, threat of, 87; prophet figures in, 88–89, 90, 91–92

Fabre, Michel, 51, 52, 148n2, 150n13
father figures: and mother's double in *Intruder in the Dust*, 27–29, 30–36; in *Native Son*, 61–65; Oedipal father in *Intruder in the Dust*, 26–27; and prophets in O'Connor, 74, 145n3
Faulkner, William, 5, 12, 13–16, 21–48, 147n12; *Absalom, Absalom!*, 15–16; chapter synopsis, 15–16; "Dry September," 24; *Faulkner in the University*, 15–16; "On Fear," 41, 42; *Go Down, Moses*, 37, 47; interview, Russell Howe, 40, 41, 42; *Light in August*, 30–31; *Lion in the Garden*, 40, 41, 42; and lynching of Nelse Patton, 23–24; "Mississippi," 46, 145n1; *The Sound and the Fury*, 14. See also *Intruder in the Dust*
Fitzgerald, Sally, 75, 151n3
Forter, Greg, 149n7
Fowler, Doreen, *Faulkner: The Return of the Repressed*, 146n8, 147–48n16, 151n6
France, Alan, W., 148n2, 149n4
Freud, Sigmund, 116, 151n4; *Beyond the Pleasure Principle*, 51, 56; *Civilization and Its Discontents*, 69; death instinct, 51, 99, 107–9; "Dissolution

of the Oedipal Complex," 146n5; Oedipal model, in *Native Son*, 69–70; and primal scene, 96–98, 154–55n8; repression and return of the repressed, 22–23; and the uncanny, 155n13; and Wright, 51

Fultz, Lucille P., 108, 153n3

Fuss, Diana, 2, 4

Gallop, Jane, 32, 96, 155n9

Gates, Henry Louis, Jr., 4–5

Giannone, Richard, 152n9

Gilroy, Paul, 148–49n3

Gooch, Brad, 14

Green, Alan W. C., 123

"Greenleaf" (O'Connor), 73, 83–87; doubling and boundary-making in, 83–86; and redemptive violence, 83, 86–87

Griffin, John Howard, 19–20, 124–40, 142–43. See also *Black Like Me.*

Gubar, Susan, 79, 80, 112

Guttman, Sondra, 148n2

Gwin, Minrose C., 46, 146n6

Harris, Trudier, 148n3

Havird, David, 150n1, 152n11

Higashida, Cheryl, 149n3

identification: and love, in *Intruder in the Dust*, 28–29; masculine identification in *Native Son*, 67–71; problem of, in *Beloved*, 93–94; risks of in *Native Son*, 50–59, 65–67; totalizing tendency of, 103

identificatory father figures, 6–13; in *Beloved*, 98, 99–100, 100–101, 103–5, 106, 107, 108–10; in *Intruder in the Dust*, 27–29, 30–36; in *Native Son*, 61–65

Intruder in the Dust (Faulkner), 21–48, 143; Barnett, Ned, and Lucas Beauchamp, 46–48; chapter synopsis, 15–16; cross-identification in, 65–66; doubling in, 25–27; father figures,

identificatory, 27–29, 30–36; fathers, boundary-setting role in, 27–29, 32–36; and *jouissance*, 38; love and identification in, 28–29; and Oedipal father, 26–27; racial integration and Southern resistance to, 39–42; and racial lynching, 21–24; repression and return of the repressed, 22–23; the uncanny, 39

Irigaray, Luce, 59

Irwin, John T., 145–46n4, 146–47n8

JanMohamed, Abdul R., 4, 54–55, 148n3, 149–50n9

Johnson, Barbara 49, 51

Johnson, E. Patrick, 156n5

Jolson, Al, 115

Joyce, Joyce Anne, 148n3

Kahane, Claire, 151–52n8

Kartiganer, Donald M., 147n14

Katz, Claire, 17, 18, 72, 73, 152n11

Keady, Sylvia, 148n3

Kenyon Review, 74–75

King, Nicole, 153n3, 154n7

Kinnamon, Keneth, 49

Kowaleski-Wallace, Beth, 145n2

Kristeva, Julia, 1, 3, 7, 37, 146n7, 147nn9–10, 154n6; and abjection, 10–12, 50–51, 52, 58, 59, 142; and boundary-making, 111–12; *About Chinese Women*, 95; *chora*, 106; *Desire in Language*, 62, 93; and paternal function, 61–63, 96, 189; *Powers of Horror*, 50–51, 52, 59, 63, 67, 73, 74, 86, 99, 107, 142; *Revolution in Poetic Language*, 50, 59, 68, 71, 73, 81, 100; socialization, theory of, 9–12; *Strangers to Ourselves*, 71, 92, 102; *Tales of Love*, 63, 92

Lacan, Jacques, 147n1, 151n5, 152n13, 155n11, 157nn11–12; and boundaries, 142, 143; on language, 30–31; on the mirror stage, 31–32